MODERN
LONG DISTANCE SWIMMING

By the same Author

LONG DISTANCE SWIMMING

FIRST STROKES IN SWIMMING

MODERN LONG DISTANCE SWIMMING

by

GERALD FORSBERG
O.B.E., Master Mariner
Past President, Morecambe Cross Bay Association
Vice-President, Channel Swimming Association
Vice-President, Otter and Serpentine Swimming Clubs
Life Member, British Long Distance Swimming Association

with a Foreword by
F. W. HOGARTH

Routledge & Kegan Paul
LONDON

First published 1963
by Routledge & Kegan Paul Ltd
Broadway House, 68–74 *Carter Lane*
*London, E.C.*4

Printed in Great Britain
by Western Printing Services Ltd
Bristol

TO MY WIFE

Helpmeet, critic, grammarian,
spelling-checker, typist . . .
and long-suffering putter-up
with the swimming way of life.

Foreword

F. W. Hogarth, M.B., B.S.
Chairman, Morecambe Cross Bay Swimming Association

LONG ago, Mr. Isaak Walton wrote a book for fishermen which was so full of detail that it became a classic. He called it *The Compleat Angler*. Here is a book for swimmers which could equally deservedly be called *The Complete Long Distance Swimmer*.

In its twenty-eight chapters will be found the answer to almost every problem which might confront a swimmer who has reached the stage of feeling 'at home' in the water, and now wishes to try conclusions with other swimmers in increasingly long distance events.

Here will be found the secret of the amazing difference between the marathon swimmer and other stylists; that apart from their being more or less physically immune from the effects of cold and prolonged immersion, they have a rigorously graduated training which, in any other branch of athletics, would probably lead only to gloomy dismay.

Yet, they love it! And, for a fact, the author much prefers to swim five miles than to walk the same distance.

Certain basic standards seem to have developed fairly recently. Just as no young aspirant in the football world has today any chance unless he can call himself two-footed, so does competitive marathon swimming now call for a bilateral method of aquatic breathing.

It is interesting to note the gradual change through the years of what is deemed necessary in the matter of greasing, and of eats and drinks. When Morecambe Bay was first crossed by Professor Stearne in 1907, a positively gargantuan amount of food and drink was taken across with him in the pilot boat. Today, the average Bay contestant never even thinks about refreshment. Even the Channel has been crossed on less than a couple of bottles of glucose and a few oatmeal biscuits. The pounds of thick grease once thought absolutely necessary have dwindled down to a matter of ounces. On many occasions, for many swimmers, an olive-oil rub suffices.

F.W.H.

Contents

APPENDIXES

Plates

Preface

> It can hurt no man to see these things practised by ancient commanders which may give good occasions both warily to invent new policies and wisely to use the old.
>
> ADVICE TO HENRY VIII 1539

In early 1957, I opened an earlier book by saying—'For many years long distance swimming has had a strong appeal for the British people. Right now interest is heightening and widening. Television, news-films, and radio commentaries are carrying it to an ever-wider public; the competitors, as always, stimulated by increasing notice and recognition, are rising to fresh standards of performance. Swimmers come here annually in ever-increasing numbers. Marathon swimming has, in fact, achieved a small but recognisable niche as an invisible export.' Six years have now passed. And that invigorating drive has accelerated most excitingly.

The sport—by the formation and initiative of the British Long Distance Swimming Association—has attained national status. That excellent body has itself organised four new championships between three and twenty-three miles in length. It has sponsored the resuscitation of the long-latent Amateur Swimming Association long-distance championship; it has also advised and part-fostered several local events. The Morecambe Cross Bay Swimming Association—senior marathon organisation in Britain—has also undergone a process of revivification; it has inaugurated new Twenty and Twenty-five Mile championships. Other clubs from the Solent to the Tay have redoubled their activities. To my knowledge, fourteen new championships have erupted. The Channel Swimming Association has become more influential than ever before. In one recent year, more than fifty swimmers, representative of every continent, waded hopefully into the Channel to try for the coveted 'blue riband' of swimming.

It thus became obvious that my former book was obsolescent. Although much of the material is evergreen, the rapid march of standards inevitably out-dated a considerable part of the contents. But much more aggravating to competitors was the fact that—because of new swims evolving—the whole field was no longer covered. For this reason, a simple revision and bringing up to date was quite impossible. The obvious need was for the evergreen matter to be extracted and joined to all the new information now available. And there was another extremely important factor to consider. In order not to produce an enormous volume (at an enormous price) my reportage must necessarily be limited. So with the exception of Bala—which is virtually a National championship—I have included no new event which has an approximate duration less than two hours. The Morecambe Inshore—which falls below this limit—has been retained from the previous book; it serves as a first-class example of a typical short tidal swim.

The tidal, navigational, and meteorological knowledge herein came to me the hard way through twenty-five years on the navigating bridges of ships; six of them in command. The swimming knowledge put forward has also been acquired the hard way—mostly with goggles on, head down, and forty-two strokes a minute. Since *Long Distance Swimming* was written, I have swum 3,632 miles; of that total, 451 miles were in record attempts or championships.

So much, then, for the origins, aims, and *bona-fides* of this new book. More important than anything else, I hope you enthusiasts enjoy it. A good deal of new material came in between writing the book and the final proof-reading. This has necessarily been somewhat squeezed in; I apologise for the telegraphese, the omissions and the blemishes.

GERALD FORSBERG

Acknowledgements

WHEN opening *Long Distance Swimming* in 1957 I wrote:—

First and foremost I wholeheartedly thank Dr. F. W. Hogarth for reading and commenting on each chapter while it was still in draft form. Dr. Hogarth has been Medical Officer to the Morecambe Cross Bay Swim Association for a considerable number of years. In addition to that, in earlier years, he pole-vaulted and swam besides playing Rugby and Soccer for Guys Hospital. It is that wealth of knowledge in athletics in general, and marathon swimming in particular, which—together with his medical experience—has been absolutely invaluable in producing this book.

In the collation of the historical material, I am generally indebted to the facilities of the British Museum and the Manchester Library. For certain interesting facts, I owe thanks to the *Guinness Book of Records*, and for several quotations to that ever-helpful writers' companion *Stevenson's Book of Proverbs, Maxims, and Familiar Phrases.*

For the section on Channel Swimming, I am tremendously grateful for the generous way that the *Daily Mail* and Messrs. Butlins gave me complete access to all their records. And, for details of some individual attempts, thanks must go to that enthusiastic and knowledgeable Channel officer, Inspector W. Floydd of Folkestone. The sketch maps were produced by Mr. B. E. Flood; by keeping out all unnecessary detail, he has made them of excellent value to swimmers.

Since the contents of that original book, amended and brought up to date, still form roughly 40 per cent of this volume, I can hardly do better than to reiterate those sentiments. But particularly extended to include the Editor of *Westmorland Gazette* who gave considerable assistance with the original Windermere material. Impolite oversight of this kindness has vexed me for six years.

And now, for the new material forming the remaining 60 per cent, much extra acknowledgement is due. Firstly, to various swimming officials for keeping me up to date with their events—John Slater of British Long Distance Swimming Association, Jack Brown of Morecambe Cross Bay Swimming Association, Billy Rowe of Hampshire Amateur Swimming Association, John Moorey of Solent Swimming Club, Derek Gill of Bradford Long Distance Swimming Club and most particularly J. U. Wood of the Channel Swimming Association. Secondly to Jack McClelland who has frequently drawn my attention to professional events which I might otherwise have missed. Thirdly to Wilf Toulcher and W. H. Lunt for supplying historical material or directing me to the right sources. Fourthly to Captain Bert Cummins of the *Swimming Times* for permission to use anything I required from that magazine. Fifthly to the many correspondents from all over the world who have written. Roughly four letters a week come in; it is thus evident that to name everyone over a period of six years is entirely impracticable. So sincere apologies and sincere thanks to all.

My great appreciation, too, goes to Colin Franklin of Routledge and Kegan Paul, for permitting me to ride my not very profit-making hobby horse for the second time. I can only think it is because he recollects me as a crusty cantankerous captain of a wartime destroyer when he was a newly joined Sub-Lieutenant in the same flotilla.

On another tack, I thank those who have helped me in the practical aspects of my researches. The friends who have oiled me down, rowed boats, fed me in the water, and carried my gear. Official observers who have spent many comfortless hours in wet small boats with stop-watches. These also are too numerous to mention. But I am deeply beholden to them just the same. Lastly I thank (and implore their understanding forgiveness) those whom I have stupidly overlooked: inevitably I shall recall the greatest debts at the very moment the book is finally printed! Sidney Smith, past President of Northern Counties A.S.A., drew my attention to the Bateman cartoon.

GERALD FORSBERG

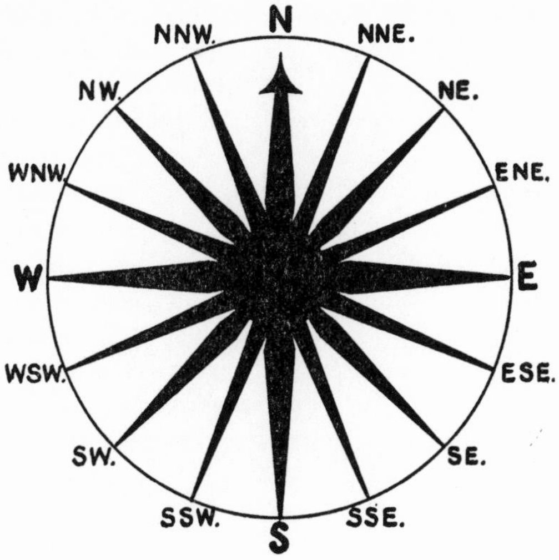

A Book on open water swimming must inevitably refer constantly to directions. This Compass Rose shows the 16 main compass points.

1

Through the Ages

And he shall spread forth his hands in the midst of them, as he that swimmeth spreadest forth his hands to swim.

ISAIAH

As a matter of necessity, swimming has been practised since earliest recorded history. Soldiers have always required to cross rivers to effect surprise or achieve safety. Swimming as a military proficiency doubtless swayed early campaigns as much as Commando operations in World War II. In the British Museum there are records *circa* 880 B.C. which show Assyrian soldiers, supported on inflated animal bladders, propelling themselves across a stream by vigorous leg-stroke. That set-up is no tremendously far cry from the frogmen and small battle units of present-day warfare. But, somehow, the addition of 'flippers', changing the animal bladder for a rubber bag, and the decision to swim underwater took several thousand years.

Knowledge of swimming history stems so much from Mediterranean roots that the result cannot help being blinkered. Available written records show the breast-stroke to be the style in common use. Yet had the Aborigines, the Polynesians and the Aztecs—to mention only a few examples—left permanent records, our ideas could be quite different. It seems inconceivable that such an efficient stroke as the crawl could remain undiscovered through so many adventurous and resourceful centuries. Even one of the Assyrian soldiers mentioned above seems unsupported by a bladder, and—although perspective in early diagrams can be all things to all men—may be doing an alternating over-arm stroke.

Early Greek mythology and legend abound with reference to swimming. Best known of these stories is the legend of Hero and Leander. Because of family disapproval young Leander was forced to extremes in his courtship of beautiful Hero. Each night he swam across the Hellespont to spend an hour or so with his girl-friend; shortly before dawn he swam back to his own side. To have been able to conceal all trace of fatigue from his watchful family, certainly marks him as an athlete of considerable stature. One stormy night Hero forgot to show the lamp towards which Leander steered and the unfortunate lad was swept away and drowned. These are the first recorded marathon swims and the incident may also qualify as another 'first ever'. Perhaps Hero is the forerunner of innumerable cinema hero*ines* who have—in Hollywood jargon—'carried a torch for their man'. Even today many torches sadly continue to flicker and die as other interests absorb the torch-carrier.

Even if that story is only partly true, it still remains as valuable historical evidence. It shows the sort of aquatic standard which contemporary Greeks considered worth building into a story. It indicates that such a feat carried something of the prestige nowadays attached to the Channel swim. So, better than any other clue, it points out the amount of improvement which has taken place through the ages of swimming.

The shortest possible crow-flight distance across the Hellespont is one and a quarter miles. But a two miles an hour current renders the direct route quite impossible; I calculate that a good average breast-stroker of today would require at least an hour to cross on the best practicable course. Lord Byron who, in 1810, re-enacted the swim for his own satisfaction, found even the single one-way passage exhausting enough. He wrote—after being in the water 1 hour 10 minutes—

My dripping limbs, I faintly stretch,
And think I've done a feat to-day.

Roman legends also tell of prowess in the water. Horatius, for instance, defended the bridge mightily, before plunging into the Tiber and swimming to safety. 'Even', according to Macaulay, 'the ranks of Tuscany could scarce forbear to cheer.' And—although the Tiber is a scant few hundred yards wide—the cheer was well deserved; for Horatius was clad in all the cumbersome equipage of war. Cassius went one better. Not only was it said that he swam the Tiber 'booted and spurred', but that he rescued a similarly clad but less expert swimmer—Julius Caesar.

In 35 B.C. we know that learners used water-wings—in the form of animal bladders—because Horace speaks of it in his *Satires*. Caustically commenting on the hard and soft ways of the art of learning, he makes a comparison. 'It is one method to practice swimming with bladders, and another to practice dancing with heavy shoes on.' Next century it is evident from the Bible that swimming was by no means uncommon. When St. Paul's ship was wrecked off the Maltese coast, the centurion commanded all those able to swim ashore to do so. Since the company survived, it points to water-proficiency in a reasonable proportion. St. Paul himself was, of course, one of those who reached shore safely.

At what period the British people learned to swim is open to conjecture. Knowledge could have come from the Phoenicians from whom we learned so many things. It could have come from Vikings or Romans. It is also at least possible for the art to have evolved naturally in Britain itself. A people who went to sea regularly in such relatively unseaworthy craft as ancient British coracles seem almost certain to have learnt the hard way. Despite the fact that knowledge must have arrived with the Romans, if not before, I have found no mention of British swimming until the fourteenth century. Then we were indebted to Geoffrey Chaucer (1340–1400) for mentioning the subject several times.

Sometime later, in 1538, Nicholas Winman established himself in history. He produced what is generally supposed to be the first book of swimming instruction. He was a German-Swiss professor, and his book *De Arte Natandi* was couched in the quaint dialogue form then in vogue. But despite that encouragement swimming as a recreation suffered an eclipse. As a military necessity it was still studied by noblemen, but the common people of Europe considered it to spread scourges. In certain cases there may have been much truth in the allegations. It would greatly depend where swimming was practised, for even today there are many countries where untreated sewage makes bathing dangerously unhealthy. Even in ultra-civilised countries, swimming-pools are sometimes closed during polio epidemics. When such things are possible in a modern day world, how much more likely for an indiscriminate swimmer to contract and spread disease in those rather unhygienic Middle Ages.

Beliefs and 'old wives' tales' die hard. As recently as my early days at sea there were coal-trimmers who refused, throughout their lives, to immerse their bodies in water. No doubt that scourge belief had been handed down, twisted and corrupted almost beyond recognition. Those shipmates of mine believed wholeheartedly that immersion in water would weaken their physical powers. In particular there was one six-inch streak down the backbone which was sacrosanct. That strip was never permitted even to be washed, let alone immersed. As they spent their whole working life among coal-dust the zebra-like streak ultimately became quite remarkable.

That aspect may well have been in an anonymous verse writer's mind when he penned the following in about 1880.

> Mother. May I go out to swim?
> Yes, my darling daughter.
> Hang your clothes on a hickory limb,
> But don't go near the water.

Before that, in 1818, Byron again startled the pundits by winning a ten-mile race. It started on the Venetian Lido and went up Grand Canal to finish at the present railway station. Swimming as a recreation was obviously, though slowly, returning to favour and England was leading the way. That swing was given extra impetus in 1828, by the opening of the first swimming-bath in Britain. At Liverpool, it was filled and changed from the river which was then luckily a good deal cleaner than it is today. Other localities followed suit and swimming-baths became, in the next few years, widely available.

Club swimming was the next advance. In the early 'sixties several clubs were formed almost simultaneously. I have no exact record of the earliest, but the Serpentine Club maintains that, by virtue of foundation in 1864, it is very nearly the oldest. Some of those early clubs, of course, withered and died before the end of the century. Otter Swimming Club is one that flourished. Formed in 1869 for the benefit of the Varsity 'blues' and 'ex-blues', it later welcomed members of the public schools and the Services. Far from dying, the club has won—in the last decade—every single National and Southern Counties team championship. As clubs became established, the next natural step was to inter-club rivalry. So, also in 1869, the Metropolitan Swimming Association was formed. Under that name it lasted a few months only before changing—apparently rather fastidiously—to London Swimming Association.

Competition led inevitably forward to greater speeds. Side-stroke evolved in the 'mid-seventies and gradually ousted old-fashioned breast-stroke from championship placings. Overarm side-stroke had further advantages, and was certainly in use by 1886. There was at that time little distinction between amateur and professional; cash prizes and the placings of bets were quite the order of the day. In that same year, 1886, the Amateur Swimming Association was formed as a national supervisory body. Slowly but surely it effected great improvement; in 1889, for instance, betting was prohibited once and for all.

After that era events moved fairly swiftly. In 1891 the Life-saving Society was born. In 1896 a most tremendous stimulus was given to speed-swimming by the re-commencement of the Olympic Games in Athens. Four years later Aleck Wickham made certain of lasting fame by introducing the crawl stroke to Australia. He brought it from the Solomon Islands where it was in everyday use. Almost simultaneously the Englishman J. Trudgen was able to cover one hundred yards in exactly sixty seconds; he used a method which was subsequently named after him. Although that time, half a century later, is no longer of national standard, it remains good going.

Richard Cavill brought the crawl to England in 1902 and won the national quarter-mile championship with it. By modern views it was an elementary stroke. One leg kicked while the opposite arm pulled through; that combined action was followed by the other arm and the other leg functioning similarly. With one leg kick for each arm stroke it very much more resembled an infant's crawl than the smooth present-day stroke does. It was of course from that striking resemblance that the name evolved. So the crawl had arrived and the A.S.A. was the governing body; with the grant of the prefix 'Royal' to the Lifesaving Society in 1904, the general swimming set-up approached the shape we know today.

Many stroke refinements followed. The crawl was geared up to a *four beat* leg action instead of the original *two beat*. Using this method in 1906 C. M. Daniels of U.S.A. and Otter Swimming Club won the National hundred-yard title in fifty-eight point eight seconds. To differentiate between this style and the older two-beat Australian crawl, the new speeded-up version was dubbed American crawl. Both those terms remain in popular use today, but now only among those having little knowledge of swimming. With the advent of six, eight, ten-beat crawls, the American and Australian labels should have dropped off. Personally, I have never seen a raw Australian version in the last twenty-five years. But names, like melodies, seem to linger on.

Long distance swimming was by no means excluded from these advances. The country abounded with professors giving exhibitions. One of the best known was Professor Stearne, a Manchester professional. In 1907, he carried out the first ever swim across Morecambe Bay, in three hours forty-five minutes. Soon after this time, swims through London, Rome and Paris drew excellent swimmers from many countries to thrill the crowds. That such swims have declined in more recent years is by no means due to loss of popularity; it is due to the decline in cleanliness and wholesomeness of the water in Europe's great rivers. Jack Jarvis and David Billington were at that time every schoolboy's heroes. Handicaps rather than championships were mostly in vogue, and, despite crushing penalties, those two giants came storming into the lead innumerable times. The year 1911 saw Windermere swum for the first time. The athlete was James Foster of Oldham and he took eleven hours twenty-nine minutes. Jabez Wolffe did Southsea Pier to Ryde Pier and back in 1913; time—6 hours, 5 minutes, 2 seconds. (Since writing this, I have discovered that this last swim was pioneered in 1884 by Horace Davenport who was later president of the A.S.A.; time 5 hours 25 minutes, in choppy sea.)

Back crawl evolved next. The 1912 Olympics began the eclipse of old English back-stroke. Nowadays the eclipse, in championship events, is quite complete; but at the seaside 'old English' remains the family favourite. Those same Olympics saw another revolution. In selected events, women competitors were allowed for the first time.

It has been seen how four-beat crawl proved faster than two-beat. Inevitably that pointed the way ahead to trials of six, eight and ten-beat crawls; some enthusiasts even kicked the legs as fast as possible without reference to the arms. Prolonged experiments proved that very few swimmers benefited by super-fast leg-strokes. As always, there were exceptions. Miss Gertrude Ederle, for instance, crossed the Channel in 14 hours 34 minutes with an eight-beat. But after the experimental stages most swimmers selected the middle-of-the-road six-beat. That proved to be a versatile stroke, efficient at every distance, and it has lasted till the present day.

As a direct result of the speeded-up crawl, brilliant new records were established. In 1927 John Weissmuller (U.S.A.) swam one hundred yards in fifty-one seconds, and Arne Borg (Sweden) achieved 19 minutes, 7·2 seconds for the fifteen hundred metres event. Both these great swimmers were so far ahead of their time that the records stood for many years; Weissmuller's for fourteen, Borg's for eleven. Even today those times remain well up to national competitive standards.

By this time breast-stroke had long been the Cinderella of the speed strokes, but it had retained many adherents. These enthusiasts spared no efforts to hot-up and streamline their favourite stroke. Instead of the traditional frog-kick, they tried undulating both legs together in the manner of a fish's tail. This method definitely produced faster results and the so-called 'dolphin fish-tail' leg-stroke came to stay. Underwater arm recovery was obviously inefficient and that was the next target for the backroom boys' attention. Over-the-surface recovery was introduced and—allied to the dolphin kick—it greatly increased speeds.

Still—although the stroke conformed to the then existent rules of breast-stroke—common sense made it clear that the amended style was really no longer breast-stroke. Nevertheless, controversy raged for years. National bodies and international federations ruled it legal or illegal until the swimming world was in chaos. Order was restored shortly after World War II by making the new style an entirely separate competition event. And so 'butterfly' was born—and breast-stroke was right back where it started.

Years of war rang down the curtain on swimming in every combatant country. But while the curtain was still descending a Mr. John V. Sigmund distinguished himself. In 1940 he set off down the Mississippi and swam for eighty-nine hours, forty-eight minutes. His total mileage was two hundred and ninety-two miles. He had the assistance of a current approximating to 2 m.p.h. and at the finish it was doing most of the work. Despite that assistance it was a formidable top-class performance which will long command respect. It is a great pity that war intervened; Sigmund might have been just the person for the first non-stop, two-way Channel success.

Back in England after the war, Tom Blower fought back to his pre-war supremacy. To his everlasting credit must go the first swimming link-up between Ireland and Scotland. In 1947 he traversed the North Channel in 15 hours 26 minutes. But behind the Iron Curtain Soviet athletes were turning in comparable or better performances. The 1949 Volga long-distance race was won by Vtorova. He completed the 95-mile course in 17 seconds under 28 hours. His stroke was reported to have been a regular twenty-two per minute throughout. The extreme slowness leads me to believe that the Russians work in stroke-cycles instead of strokes. For our reckoning the figure should probably be doubled to forty-four.

One of the saddest war casualties was the English long distance championship. It was immensely popular and attracted a tremendous sized entry from all over the country. It used to be swum over the reverse of the University Boat Race course with an extra half mile added on. The finish at Putney was always watched by large crowds; although it was barely on the fringe of marathon swimming, it brought in the marathoneers for their annual joust with the speedsters in a mid-way event. A fair time for the winner was an hour and a quarter and anyone within ten minutes of the champion was adjudged to have achieved standard time. Immediately post-war it was revived once only; then it lapsed again until 1962 when the Yorkshire and N.E. Counties' Swimming Associations staged it at York.

To confirm that swimming is a truly cosmopolitan pursuit a Mr. Navaratswamy blazed his own private Asiatic trail in March 1954. Braving currents and sharks he swam from Ceylon to India in 27 hours. Next year Professor Harry Briggs (U.S.A.) swam from Corsica to Sardinia in ten hours, twenty-nine minutes. And Jaime Cortazar swam the Straits of Gibraltar. As a matter of fact several other persons—including our own Jack McClelland—have also performed that feat. One of the fastest on record is Channel swimmer Periera who crossed in five hours four minutes. His diet—here's a thing for trainers and dieticians—consisted of port wine and fruit. I have much in common with Senhor Periera and share his regard for good swimming and good port. But I do feel that—to get the best enjoyment out of either—they should be indulged in separately.

The British Long Distance Swimming Association was formed in 1956. That body inaugurated a Windermere (10 mile) championship the following year, a Torbay (8 mile) championship in 1958, and a Loch Lomond (23 mile) championship 1959. The Morecambe Cross Bay Association put on a new Twenty-mile Championship in 1960. I had the good fortune to become first winner of all four events. Also in 1959, I just managed to beat Jack McClelland to the first-ever success in Lough Neagh (20 miles)—Ireland's largest lake. Abroad, during 1958, Greta Andersen swam the Catalina Channel both ways (42·8 miles) in 28 hours 25 minutes.

This chapter has galloped through 3,000 years in as many words. (Channel history being an entity of its own follows in the next chapter.) To the learned high priests of aquatics I apologise for dealing with the subject in such a curt and cavalier; fashion. To the novices of the order, more concerned with the future than the past, I apologise for delaying them with undue wordiness. Somewhere, somehow, between those extremes I hope it may prove nearly right for someone.

2

Progress of Channel Swimming

> The course of life is like the sea.
> Men come and go; tides rise and fall;
> And that is all of history.
>
> JOAQUIN MILLER

IT all started in 1862; merchant seaman William Hoskins rode a bundle of hay or straw, and scrambled his way from Griz Nez to South Foreland. Next came Captain Paul Boyton, who —wearing a life-saving suit—paddled over the same route on 29th May 1875: time twenty-three hours, thirty minutes. It was thus only natural that someone's mind should then fix on swimming the Channel without artificial buoyancy. That someone—as the world knows—was Captain Webb. At least, he was the first successful one—J. B. Johnson made a 63-minute 'attempt' in 1872. Contemporary observers did not however consider Johnson —one of the fastest swimmers of the day—was ever in earnest about a complete crossing.

Webb's first attempt failed, but as his fatigue faded he planned again. On 25th August 1875 he was successful. The start was from Admiralty Pier at Dover; the time four minutes to one on Tuesday 24th August. With the south-westerly stream running at considerable speed, he ran into difficulty from the start. Although ships had navigated the Channel for centuries, swimming it was a different proposition. Tidal calculations, accurate enough for ship-navigation, were by no means accurate for man-navigation. Therefore, in comparing Webb's effort with more recent ones, one great point must be constantly appreciated. Not only was the *swimmer* attempting a new and colossal task, but so were the boatmen and pilots. Their present specialised knowledge has been built on the experience of the preceding years. So, as a result of combined inexperience at that time, Webb was last seen from the English shore being swept vigorously westwards into the main English Channel.

For the main part of the passage, he swam breast-stroke at twenty-six strokes a minute. At one period in mid-Channel a jellyfish sting temporarily slackened his pace. And for the last two and a half hours he was so exhausted that his stroking became weak and irregular; indeed, much anxiety was felt about his ability to finish at all. His cross-Channel diet was beer, brandy, and beef tea. Lack of modern knowledge was in some little way compensated by the lack of modern rules. For instance, he had an attendant lugger and two rowing-boats throughout. And at the finish an outsize rowing-boat accompanied him on the weather side to keep the cresting waves from getting at him.

Webb finally reached the Calais sands at nineteen minutes to eleven on Wednesday, 25 August. A crowd of thousands massed on the French beach; they gave him a rousing welcome as he was assisted into a horse-drawn vehicle in shallow water and taken to recuperate. In England, of course, he became one of the greatest heroes that has ever arisen in peace-time. The whole nation was depressed eight years later when—at the age of thirty-five—he was drowned in an attempt to swim Niagara.

The maestro's England–France time stood supreme until E. H. Temme beat it in 1934. Fifty-nine years is an extraordinarily long time for any record to stand, and that interval spotlights the stature of the original champion. Together with Fred Archer, Steve Bloomer, W. G. Grace and a few others, he is assured of belonging to the select band of sporting immortals. He might even be considered greatest of them all, for even disregarding the record aspect, it was thirty-six years before anyone else crossed the Channel in any time at all.

During the intervening years numerous attempts were made by Monty Holbein, Ted Heaton, Jabez Wolfe and many others. The last-named made over a score of attempts; he once reached a point only a quarter of a mile short of Calais. It was said by on-lookers—but received with reserve by seamen—that he was washed back to sea by the opening of the Calais dock gates. 'Jappy' Wolfe was not only a great swimmer but he was a great swimming teacher. His book on swimming helped many people of that era to swim; it was one of my earliest and most treasured possessions.

Another sportsman swore that he would swim the Channel and smoke twenty cigars *en route*. I believe he carried out the second part of his vow successfully, but failed in the first. The first serious attempt by a woman was in 1900 by Madame Isacescu of Vienna who did ten hours from France towards England. Obviously, said the pundits—ignoring all the male failures—it was no job for a woman!

From local sources I heard that Burgess's successful swim was, in fact, his fourteenth attempt. That was on 22nd August 1911. When I belonged to the City of Westminster Swimming Club just before going to sea, his photograph dominated the entrance hall at Great Smith Street baths. Stern visaged, arms akimbo, and clad in knee-length costume he was regarded by the local citizens almost as a demi-god. His transit time was twenty-two hours thirty-five minutes.

After the Burgess triumph, another twelve unsuccessful years elapsed. Then Henry Sullivan (U.S.A.) made a conquest and a record. His time of twenty-six hours fifty minutes still stands as the slowest ever. And because of improved training, improved strokes, and improved knowledge, it is doubtful whether anyone will ever now take longer on a single passage. 1923 was a foreigners' year. Besides Sullivan, Enrico Tiraboshi, and Charles Toth completed the course; Toth was an American, Tiraboshi is variously listed as an Argentinian and an Italian. The historical point is that both these gentlemen swam a reverse course to all their predecessors. Their times (both under seventeen hours) pointed to the advantage of the France–England route, and their example was followed for many years to come. Webb's *absolute* Channel record was thus broken after forty-eight years, but the England–France record still stood in his name.

Following three more blank years (the interval lessens after each successful year) 1926 was another non-Briton's period. Two thoroughly outstanding swimmers came to the Channel with traditional marathon strokes wedded to the latest speed refinements.

As a result Miss Gertrude Ederle not only became the first woman to cross, but her time of fourteen hours thirty-four minutes—very temporarily—became the all-time record. She was closely followed across by the German swimmer Arnst Vierkotter whose phenomenal time of twelve hours, forty minutes again beat the record. That achievement officially remained supreme until the coming of the professional races, twenty-four years later. Georges Michel is listed as crossing in eleven hours five minutes in 1926, but it is not on the list of C.S.A. recognised successes.

1927–8 saw five more British conquests and the first of the Egyptians, in what was to become to them almost an annual pilgrimage. That era was my own first personal acquaintance with Channel swimmers. In training, Ishak Helmy was an extremely slow swimmer; I swam alongside him on one or two occasions and it was thoroughly hard work keeping down to his pace. Temme, on the other hand, was a real speed merchant; keeping *up* to his pace was, for me, almost impossible. He was able nearly to touch the even minute for a hundred-yard dash. In 1927 that placed him well up to the standard of good club sprinters. This versatile swimmer was also a water-polo international.

About this time Doctor Dorothy Logan caused a distinct flutter in Channel circles. She claimed to have completed the course, and was popularly acclaimed as having done so. Subsequently she said that part of the distance had been in a boat—and that the whole affair had been staged to spotlight the possibilities and loopholes for making false claims. The Channel Swimming Association was founded in 1927 with this aspect as one of the objects in mind. Use of their observers has simplified the procedure for swimmers, and has made sure of impartial reporting.

The first Commonwealth swimmer, Miss Duncan of South Africa, crossed in 1930. Four years later, Ted Temme with an England–France swim became the first two-way Channel swimmer. The pre-World War II era came to a close with two dozen persons having been successful and one having swum it both ways. It must be plainly stated that not all those Channel successes are recognised by the Channel Swimming Association. That is no aspersion on the unrecognised achievements; it merely means that the swimmers have omitted or forgotten to supply *all* the details required by the Association. In any case the pre-war C.S.A. was having difficulty in satisfactorily carrying out its Channel duties from a London headquarters.

Between 1939 and 1945 the Straits of Dover became—as will be remembered—extremely difficult for any form of waterborne activity. Hostile fighters, dive-bombers, E-boats and mines made even destroyer navigation a most unhealthy business; I can personally vouch for that. Almost the only swims taken during that period were involuntary but—especially during the Dunkirk evacuation—some quite long swims were covered by survivors. One soldier who started from the Dunkirk beach was picked up, still swimming strongly in mid-Channel. After the war two years elapsed before more normal conditions brought the marathoneer back to the Channel. The first post-war success was Daniel Carpio of Peru in 1947.

In 1949 Philip Mickman (at eighteen years of age, the then youngest success) crossed in twenty-three hours, forty-eight minutes, at his second attempt. He had appalling luck with the tides. Had he been fractionally faster, he might have caught tides to land six hours earlier. As it was, although advised by trainer Temme to retire and await a more suitable opportunity, he swam on with indomitable grit. He just missed taking Henry Sullivan's all-comers slow record, but made sure of the slowest time for the France–England trip.

As a speed contrast, the same year saw Pierre (U.S.A.) swim across in the astonishing time of five hours four minutes. Although accompanied by the regulation launch, small rowing-boat and trainer, Pierre's time was never ratified by the Channel Swimming Association. The reason was that he was an eighteen-months'-old trained Californian seal. After half an hour's rest and a meal, he was put into a box and taken back to France to celebrate.

Next year, 1950, brought a tremendous resurgence of enthusiasm. In great part it was due to the historic *Daily Mail* race. Because that race and its successor brought a brand new aspect to Channel swimming, I have given them an entirely separate chapter later in the book. It will suffice here to say that the competitive stimulus produced remarkably successful results.

The England–France route returned to some favour in 1951. Miss Florence Chadwick (U.S.A.) became the first woman to have swum this route. Her time was sixteen hours, nineteen minutes.

Another by-product of that swim was to make Miss Chadwick the only woman to have swum both ways. W. E. Barnie (Britain) further progressed the records of the Channel by crossing it both ways in the same year. He thereby carved a niche of fame by being the oldest successful Channel swimmer to date; he was fifty-five at the time. Brenda Fisher (Britain) during that year's Channel race brought the women's record down to twelve hours forty-two minutes. Both the last-mentioned athletes are professionals and both competed in the *Festival of Britain* Race.

The year 1952 saw four more British amateur successes, including again the dogged young Philip Mickman. That courageous swimmer tackled the swim 'the hard way' from England to France; he completed it five hours faster than his previous 'easy-way' swim. There was no professional race that year. The Butlin sponsored championship which commenced in 1953 is, together with the *Daily Mail* events given separate treatment later.

1953 also produced an unofficial record. Abou Heif (Egypt) is generally conceded to have completed the England–France trip in thirteen hours forty-five minutes. Unfortunately there was no Channel Swimming Association observer aboard, and the Association had reluctantly to refuse its ratification. That factor, of course, caused some little dissatisfaction when Bill Pickering (Britain) took the official record in 1955, and when Florence Chadwick went a fraction faster in the same year. Pickering's time was fourteen hours six minutes; Chadwick's thirteen hours fifty-five minutes.

It is a pity when controversy such as that flares up, but these things in some form or other are almost inevitable in any sport. The athletes themselves are often not entirely blameless. In this case, I think that might be the cause, for it does seem good sense when attempting a record to enlist the aid of an official C.S.A. observer. It fell to my lot—in 1957—to end that *impasse* with an officially observed swim of thirteen hours thirty-three minutes.

From that time on, standards have improved apace. Converted sprinters have increased the speeds. Better training methods and more skilful pilotage have produced better results. In 1961 we held our breath as Antonio Abertondo completed the first-ever 'there and back' swim, and watched Dorothy Perkins make an earliest ever success on 6th June. A decade before, these feats could not even have been seriously considered.

At the time of writing the formal records stand as follows.

England to France and back	Antonio Abertondo	43 hrs.	05 min.
France to England (men)	Brojen Das* (Pakistan)	10 hrs.	35 min.
France to England (women)	Greta Andersen (U.S.A.)	11 hrs.	01 min.
England to France (men)	Helge Jensen (Canada)	10 hrs.	23 min.
England to France (women)	Florence Chadwick (U.S.A.)	13 hrs.	55 min.

This chapter lays no claim to be a full history. To have deserved that title, infinitely more attention should have been given to the failures—for lost battles play a tremendously influential part in shaping history. Much more investigation of byways would have been necessary, instead of keeping to the broad highway. My object has been more concerned with a utilitarian aspect of progress, and the chapter has merely tried to show each step forward and to maintain the thread of continuity.

My own memory takes me back only to 1928, the remainder has been put together from verbal inquiries and much delving in old files. Even the evidence 'in the files' has caused me much worry. For instance, two different nationalities and two spellings are given to Tiraboshi (1923), two dates given for the Burgess swim, two times (only minutes apart) for several other successes; there were many other bewildering differences and I have selected the most favoured alternatives. Even the Webb swim is variously dated as 24th/25th August and 25th/26th August; I have altered my former opinion after reading his own book! If someone has thereby suffered an injustice, they have my sincere apologies; if someone received more than justice I shall be glad to meet them some time—preferably round about 'opening time'.

* Brojen Das has swum the Channel more times than anyone else.

3

The Lure of Long Distances

Man's capacity has never been measured nor are we to judge of what he can do by any precedent, so little has been attempted.

THOREAU

'WHAT on earth makes you do it?' That is a question which besets every marathon swimmer about twenty times a year. Seven short questioning words; they cannot entirely be answered with seven thousand. Sometimes the query is merely conversational stonewalling while the questioner looks for someone more normal to talk to. It is then permissible to score first by telling him it is done to get away from tedious people for a couple of hours every day. At other times inquiry comes earnestly from an interested and expert exponent of some other sport; for him there is only one way to crystallise the answer. 'The same as you, old boy. To be acknowledged expert and to do something better than most other people.' The whole answer, though, embraces both those ideas—together with a host of others. If I set these out in some detail, future sufferers need only refer their inquisitors to this book.

Probably the greatest delight about marathon swimming is the friendly atmosphere. Each swimmer regards every other one as co-member of a corps d'elite. After all, even the slowest swimmers who can complete a ten-mile course are persons reasonably out of the ordinary. Consequent on that mutual respect there is a minimum of back-biting and jealousy which often affects more mercurially temperamental athletes. Never have I known any marathon swimmer refuse advice, assistance, or material aid to any new participant. Healthy competition there is to the highest degree. Healthy beliefs, too, that 'anything he can do, I can do better'. But bad feeling between competitors is almost non-existent. Between strung-up and partisan supporters disharmony is occasionally inevitable but even that is usually forgotten by the date of the annual dinner.

For the well-being of every sedentary worker some form of physical exercise is a near essential. It develops and satisfies the body while simultaneously resting and satisfying the mind. Marathon swimming is an even paced, calculated, and sustained effort which is plainly more beneficial to heart and system than short concentrated doses of exertion as, for example, in squash. It is a clean, inexpensive, healthy and pleasant hobby. Most of all it is ideal for those of us who have discovered that we are not natural sprinters, but do always manage to finish a thing better than we start. 'Dogged does it', is a favourite north country adage. If marathon swimming ever required a motto no amount of searching could produce a better.

Personal reasons also bring many recruits to the marathons. Age may be one of these. When Ron Roberts (Otter S.C.) won the English 110-yard title a few years back, he was nationally hailed as the 'grand old man of the sport'. Most of the other champions were fifteen years or more his junior because Ron had reached the tremendous old age of thirty-four. For swimmers who have passed over that advanced milestone but who still unaccountably feel remote from the grave, long distance competition is the obvious answer. Ned Barnie, the sprig-of-heather Scotsman, conquered the Channel when he was fifty-five. And that points the way to twenty years more interest for obstinate thirty-four-year-olds not wishing to hang up their trunks for the last time.

I came to the sport rather similarly. Before the war I was an enthusiastic speedster, but six long war years cooped up in small ships without practice, left too much leeway to make up in 1945. Six years, barren of exercise, added three stones in weight too, and built me quite the wrong shape for sprinting. My first attempted avenue back to the top was in plunging. By the 1946 English championships I had achieved England's number four ranking but in 1947 the Amateur Swimming Association unkindly abolished that event from the National Championships. Two years hard ground-work elapsed before I was able to emerge again, as a marathoneer, in 1949. And a further two years after that before I even approached top-ranking again.

The wrong shape for sprinting? Yes. Just as the hammer-throwers and shot-putters differ from track athletes, so does the marathon devotee differ from the sprint swimmer. For sprinting, the ideal type is tall, slim, supple, thin-hipped, long limbed. Marathon champions, on the other hand, need an admixture of fat with their muscle. Because of lower speeds they need no be so streamlined; because style is not so all-important in open water swimming they need not be so supple. In marathon swimming—the 'good big'un will always beat the good little'un', but the dice are not nearly so loaded as in bath swimming. There a tall competitor with a height-reach excess of only twelve inches over a shorter opponent gains an obvious one per cent advantage in every length of a hundred-foot bath. In a seventy-five-foot bath, which is a very common length, the advantage is greater. That particular unfairness is ruled out in open water competition, but nothing can ever prevent a tall man with long limbs from being more mechanically efficient than a short one. Big hands and big feet are desirable qualities too. Obviously, the more nearly the feet resemble frogman's flippers the more efficient they will be. It is a whiskered and venerable swimming witticism that old swimmers always stamp frequently on their offspring's feet to ensure them a successful future. Those then are the necessary physical attributes. In temperament the champions are good sound, ordinary, stolid persons with a slow pulse rate.

'What are the advantages of open water swimming over bath swimming?' Fairer competition for small men with tall has been mentioned above; there is an abundance of other advantages. Much pleasure and feelings of real achievement result from completing a swim from one place to another. That feeling is entirely lacking in a bath swim. No matter what length the race, the same ground is covered time and time again. And the finish is usually right back on the starting point. Somehow, twenty-odd minutes hard racing over an indoor mile never can produce a feeling akin to the pride of having swum even from one pier to the next one along the beach. Open water swimming is self-evidently more natural, more useful and more healthy than the indoor variety. It seems unlikely, too, that the Almighty having created seas and estuaries, lakes and rivers, tarns and burns, intended men to exhaust their energy in steamy chlorinated hothouses.

For the materially minded there are strong attractions in the long-distance races held all round the country. The Press is more interested and so is the public. More general esteem attaches itself to a Channel swimmer than, say, a national middle-distance champion. Even to have *tried* the Channel ensures a *cachet* not available to someone who has tried for a county title. The wisdom of such a viewpoint is debatable but its existence is hard fact. Jabez Wolfe failed the Channel more times than any other man, but his name still brings a flicker of recollection to averagely well-informed sportsmen. Mention of a contemporary sprint champion would bring a flicker of recollection only to intimate connections, old clubmates, and to a professional 'memory-man'.

Other material benefits exist, too. The cups, shields and other trophies are quite fabulous by modern standards. In one good year I took out a £400 insurance policy to cover the season's returnable trophies. That is thoroughly attractive incentive when one sees the tinpot medals currently awarded in quite important short-distance racing. Despite that material aspect it is certain that the great majority of marathon swimmers race mainly for the satisfaction of achievement and not for 'pot-hunting' instincts. That is particularly evident in the Channel and Irish Sea swims for which there is absolutely no prize, but for which a fair personal outlay of money is necessary.

Satisfaction springs from the smooth combination of brain with muscle. In bath racing the brain can play little part in the constant repetition of identical lengths. In river, sea, or lake, the brain selects landmarks, works out courses, calculates short cuts, overtakes opponents on their blind sides and is constantly active. Pre-race study of maps, routes, tide-tables, weather forecasts can be worth many yards to the intelligent competitor. At the beginning of my long distance career I won the Otter Mile Handicap and the Willesden Mile Handicap, both in the Thames. Considerable pre-race study on map-reading, and on the general behaviour of running streams on differently shaped bends and in shallow edges, stood me in very good stead. It certainly enabled me to use the most advantageous courses and defeat physically superior swimmers. But I want particularly to emphasise that—although age is no bar—this is no sedate elderly person's pastime. Margaret White swam the Channel when seventeen; Susan Lynch won the Windermere Championship at sixteen. The young swimmer should always beat the old 'uns—provided they use their heads as well as their muscles.

In open water swimming the performance and not the stop-watch is all important. Doctor Roger Bannister, a year or so back, deplored the track athlete's modern tendency to race against the watch instead of against each other. In marathon swimming the stop-watch can be confounded by so many factors that it becomes unimportant. Times are at the mercy of tides, rough weather, cold weather, and shifting sandbanks; thus comparatively unfettered by record-breaking, all interest is focused on the clash of personalities in the race. Unlike bath swimming competitors' times can never be well known and pre-checked, so every marathon race produces its own big surprises. Each swimmer has his own favourite weather and hopes fervently for that. I will give one illustration. In the last decade Bill Pickering of Bloxwich, Frederick Oldman of Huddersfield, and John Slater of Otley have all been swimmers of fairly similar calibre on a six-hour swim. But given rough weather Oldman would probably have led the way home. In extra cold weather Pickering would possibly have triumphed. In fine and warm conditions Slater would have been a fair certainty.

It is curious how devotion to one's own sport blinds one to the good points of others. Some time ago I was talking to a young schoolmaster friend over Sunday lunch. He proposed to spend the afternoon on a racing bicycle with a cycling club.

'Good gracious', I said, 'what an absurd way to spend an afternoon. Flogging round the countryside with a mob of others. Just seeing how far and how fast you can get and never looking at the country. Four hours waste of time I call it'.

He just looked at me and laughed. I had only recently emerged from the swimming bath after a whole forenoon spent in a time trial.

When the penny dropped, I laughed too.

4

Breast-Stroke and Crawl: Marathon Twins

Success, remember, is the reward of toil.

SOPHOCLES

THE evolution of the main swimming strokes has been given in Chapter 1. Some of these *invite* the further attention of open water swimmers but only two positively *demand* it. The main objectives of serious swimmers are to swim faster and further than anyone else, and to save life when necessary. A combination of breast-stroke and crawl meets these requirements admirably. Back-stroke as used in lifesaving is almost exactly breast-stroke upside down; it requires no special mention, for breast-strokers will find it entirely natural.

Morecambe Bay and Windermere have been conquered by back-crawl. No doubt some day a swimmer will 'butterfly' across the Channel. But apart from individual swimmers wishing to improve and strengthen their particular style, those methods have no merit. Neither stroke attains the speed of front-crawl; neither approaches the all-round seaworthiness of breast-stroke. In fact, back-crawl and butterfly hardly deserve competitive status at all, but like Topsy they 'just growed and growed'.

That is, perhaps, a startling view but truth is often startling and unpopular. Similar artificialities are non-existent in track athletics. Certainly there are sack races where simultaneous action of arms and legs is similar to 'butterfly', but sack races are not regarded as serious championships. A 'running-backwards' race would be energetic and amusing, but the winner would hardly style himself champion. Back-*stroke* races lost their value when back-*crawl* evolved; before that they encouraged a lifesaving stroke and served a purpose. Devotees of butterfly and back-crawl emphasise that these strokes employ different muscles and are useful for change and relaxation. That is correct, and used as water-borne physical exercises they do have a part to play. As a means to an end they are excellent; as the end themselves, they are indefensible. Much more deserving of championship honours are underwater races or lifesaving races with standard dummy figures.

Marathoneers divide into two classes. There are those who regard completion of a long swim as an aim in itself; for those there is no better method than breast-stroke. Others wish to complete the swim *and* compare favourably with the best; for those, crawl is essential. Some years have now elapsed since a major championship was won on breast-stroke and it was then in curious circumstances. Edward James May used the stroke to win an early heat in the Morecambe Cross Bay in 1950. Due to atrocious weather, every subsequent heat was cancelled. May was therefore certainly the fastest man across that year and was judged champion. In very severe weather conditions breast-stroke swimmers might well beat crawlers. Unfortunately for the former, those conditions inevitably cause cancellations of races for safety reasons. Thus the point has never been put to test.

Marathon breast-stroke is second cousin, several times removed, from the 200 metres Olympic variety. Family likeness is there, but individual characteristics are strong. No underwater starting, copybook style, or practised turns are useful here. Strong, plain swimming is the 'be-all and end-all' of requirements. Stroke judges are non-existent; should the swimmer turn to the side to breathe, there is no objection. Should he wish to start or stop a 'dolphin-fishtail' it is quite in order—although it will not help a great deal. Since all the long-distance races are 'free-style', lopsidedness and originality are entirely permissible either for speed or comfort.

A flatter layout in the water is evident; a flat progress without undue up-and-down bobbing is a prime requirement. By the very nature of underwater arm recovery, breast-stroke can never be so evenly paced as crawl. Progress on the breast is necessarily a series of brusque accelerations and decelerations; car-users will readily appreciate that in these circumstances the power to performance ratio falls. Adding to that disadvantage, by making it three-dimensional with 'bobbing', is most undesirable. Furthermore, even-waterflow, skin-friction, and cavitation (all terms beloved of naval architects, but equally applicable to swimmers) become more unfavourable. Everything points to better results from flatter position; the limiting factor is of course raising the head to breathe. If breath can be taken to the side, little headlifting is required except for look-out purposes. In normal conditions it should be possible to complete thirty-or-so strokes between looks ahead and thus minimise interruptions to progress.

Actual performance of breast-stroke requires little elaboration. Almost everyone knows the arm and leg action of this style even if they know nothing else of swimming. Detailed description would in any case deviate from the aim of this book which is to discuss open water swimming in general, and not the elements of teaching. The traditional leg-kick—wide for short, narrow for tall swimmers—reigns supreme in the marathon. Recent sprint-refinements of screwing, rotating, undulating legs seem not to have arrived yet. That they will arrive some day, with a converted sprinter, is almost certain and assessment will then be possible, But so many 'guinea-pigs' are necessary for cast-iron proof that a decade must pass, and it has not yet even started. Such experiments are frequently confused by guinea-pigs who win, not *because* of their speciality but *in spite of it*. Meanwhile ship trials continue to show that, while 'gadgets' and elaborations work well in smooth water, sturdy simplicity is best in rough water. The analogy is most applicable to swimmers.

For that and other reasons, the old English arm-stroke is recommended. The more fashionable downward-cum-lateral action certainly grips more solid water, but it tends to jerkiness and bobbing. In sprint races it does facilitate breathing but, in open water, breathing rigidly geared to the arm-stroke is often impracticable. In seaway or river-popple, breath must be taken as opportunity occurs. One important aspect of the arm action is that, with a slow rate of stroking, it tends to become overlong. Like oars in a rowing-boat, the swimmer's arms give maximum mechanical advantage when they are within a few degrees of right angles to the body. So pulling too soon and maintaining the pull too late are wasteful of energy; surplus time should be spent laid out in the glide. But, in marathon swimming, comfort is of far higher importance than in sprinting. Extra comfort may well offset loss of energy in long stroking. Only a competent coach can tell each swimmer individually.

One part of the body particularly susceptible to discomfort is the neck. Muscles here are as vulnerable to fatigue as any others; they can become cruelly painful and cause abandonment of a swim. Bad weather conditions impose much extra strain on these muscles to more marked degree than others. Constant craning to sight a landmark, to keep in touch with boats, or just to breathe, combines with wave buffeting to make the strain almost intolerable. This is particularly the case with breast-stroke but remains true to a slightly lesser degree with crawl. First-aid measures are to work the head backward and forward, breathe to the other side for a short while, or to tread water and massage. Long term remedies will be set out when I deal later on with training, but these first-aid measures sometimes bring astonishing relief.

Crawl swimming was, as recently as thirty years ago, considered too exhausting for more than a few hundred yards dash. Gradually it extended its capabilities until nowadays the great majority of Channel swimmers use it. But British public opinion is slow to change and even today both Press and public still seem to consider its use surprising. Despite that it is here to stay; devotees of the stroke are adamant that it is no more energetic than walking. Mechanically it has the tremendous advantage of constant-speed propulsion, and momentum that is never completely checked. Naturally there are peaks and troughs on the speed graph but variation is relatively small. Even a motor-ship with a four-bladed propeller is subject to similar peaks and troughs, so it is evident that an absolute ideal is unobtainable—even with such a perfect machine as the human body.

In the marathon crawl, as in the breast-stroke, the body, once again, lies flatter than normal. Marathon speed is never sufficient for aqua-planing on the chest like Japanese sprinters; in any case rough water would detract from its value. A low-in-the-water attitude minimises resistance and gives buoyancy its maximum effect. Thus almost all energy can be used on useful horizontal forward propulsion and practically nothing on useless vertical effort for balancing. The head is lowered until the eyes are normally looking straight down, or at most 5 or 10 degrees ahead. A low position for the head allows its weight to be largely waterborne instead of muscle-supported; it gives immense relief to the neck muscles and general comfort to the body. In sprint swimming teenagers are advised to maintain the hairline at water-level; in marathon swimming only those of advanced age and receded hairline should obey that dictum.

There is much difference from sprinting in the arm-stroke; glide-to-pull ratio is much increased. The 'catch' is delayed, and the technical arm lift for recovery is similarly delayed. The result is that the arms work more exactly opposite to one another than in normal crawl. Sprint diagrams show, at certain phases, both arms well ahead of the face; in marathon crawl that is much less frequently the case. All in all, it boils down to the arms being proportionately longer immersed than in sprint crawl; once again this is good for buoyancy. As swimming speed decreases so does the importance of buoyancy increase; at nil speed, to carry it to absurdity, it obviously becomes the only important factor.

Women swimmers seem to swim in higher gear than men to attain the same speed. I have clocked Florence Chadwick, one of the world's finest swimmers, at fifty-six strokes per minute, while I only complete about forty-two. Those figures were both for a Channel-size swim; naturally one gets faster as the distances decrease. An easy, comfortable, and even rhythm is the hallmark of every good marathoneer. But just occasionally a few minutes of jerky stroking with extra emphasis on the pull is comforting. It seems to use different muscles and give relief in the same way as a good stretch after sitting too long. Leg-stroke being geared to the arm stroke becomes slower, wider and deeper.

Breathing is one of marathon swimming's greatest problems. Swimmers who can breathe either side gain tremendous advantages. Breathing away from wind and spray may, taking several aspects into consideration, gain a quarter of a mile in every hour from a competitor breathing into the weather. One-sided breathers must necessarily develop a monster roll to get the mouth above rough water. To the indoor coach it looks abominable, but to the outdoor swimmer it means the difference between carrying on or giving up. Even so, he often has to go two or three arm cycles before getting a chance. In extreme cases, oxygen deficiency turns the limbs into jelly; then stopping and coming to the surface is the only alternative to collapse.

There are many differences between open water swimming and bath swimming. But the greatest aspect of all needs no spotlighting; it is self-evident. Everything is for comfort. Relaxation, relaxation and more relaxation. The water is a friend even if it does have tantrums. It is to be coaxed, persuaded, and its aid enlisted. Sprint swimmers have no such feeling, they are never in the water long enough. During their short bursts, they literally fight the water away from themselves in dives, turns, push-offs and do-or-die bursts. They are the speedboats who punish the water, marathon swimmers are like yachts caressing it. Of course, there are exceptions to every rule. John Davis of Cardiff, formerly one of Britain's leading marathoneers, was the Zatopek of aquatics. Every stroke looked like his life's last, every twist of his head looked as if it would drop off. But to confuse the theorists, he was always up with the leaders at the finish.

5

Cold Water Comfort

Pleasure reaches its limit in the removal of all pain.

EPICURUS

THE human body is almost infinitely adaptable. A few examples will ram home that truism. Bakers, stokers and furnacemen accustom themselves to heat which would disable the average man. In winter, fishermen, agricultural workers and lightermen work in crippling cold. Foreign-going seamen have always alternated between one climatic extreme and the other. In days of sail this was a gradual process; today it is a matter of a week to ten days. Nowadays, too, with air transport, even middle-aged businessmen freeze in London one day and work in the sweltering Middle East on the next. The body will stand even more than that. Prisoners of war proved it in torture chambers; commando troops demonstrate it constantly with seemingly impossible physical feats.

This shows that no black magic is required to adapt the human body to immersion in cold water. Essential requirements are merely time, inclination, a reasoned scientific approach, and one other big thing: the conviction that the mind is the master of the body. Those who doubt it, and those who are 'comfortable lie-abeds' must forsake hope of eminence in this, or any other sport. Natural talent will often get its owner on to the championship ladder. Only will-power and guts will eventually enable him to climb that ladder to the top.

Normal body heat is 36·9° Centigrade (98·4° Fahrenheit). During the average swimming season the mid-Britain seawater or lakewater temperature approximates to 14·4° C (58° F), so three is a considerable gap to accustom the body to. In a fine hot summer, like 1955, the Channel in July–August can rise to 17·8° C (64° F) and Windermere to 19·5° C (67° F). But that is only one time in one year. Even on 18th June of that year, before summer really took hold, it was a very different story. The first heat of the Morecambe Cross Bay Championship was swum in 11·7° C (53° F). (As a matter of interest all six competitors did finish, although some took 3½ hours.) But both these quoted cases are extremes. The swimmer who aims at comfort in 14·4° C (58° F) will be at his ease in most United Kingdom competitions.

First preliminary conditioning is usually carried out in an indoor pool; most of these are maintained at about 22·2° C (72° F). That, of course, is high above open water temperature but serves as a very painless first step. Naturally, ability to swim the intended distance in this temperature is ultimately an essential. With practice there should be a feeling of complete 'at-homeness' in the water. To feel 'at home' in the water sounds an exaggeration but is truly no such thing. I, for one, always feel that way. Faced with a five-mile swim, and time to do it, I regard it as a real pleasure. Twenty times more so, for instance, than spending the equivalent length of time watching a Hollywood masterpiece from a comfortable stall. On the other hand, faced with a 2½-hour walk, excuses and alibis would come thick and fast.

From the indoor pool a further temperature step-down will eventually be required. Part-heated outdoor pools are the ideal easy stage, but for economy reasons, these ideals are few and far between. Many fine luxurious swimming stadia are fitted with excellent heating apparatus which is currently unused. Usually, therefore, the next step is into unheated pool, sea, river or lake. In mid-Yorkshire, where all these facilities are lacking, they use reservoirs on cold high moorland. Needless to say, after such tough indoctrination these Yorkshiremen are hardly ever beaten by any sea temperatures during the competition season.

Londoners may feel that, with polluted rivers, distance from the sea, and shortage of outdoor pools, they are far worse situated than all others. That is not so, for the Serpentine Swimming Club itself was formed in 1864, caters specially for open-water swimmers. Competing in the Club handicaps is an ideal method of acclimatisation to cold water. Prize-racing adds stimulus and supplies incentive just where those qualities are most needed. Being under starter's orders is also a certain cure for the 'shall I get in now or wait a few minutes?' waverings. These events are open to swimmers of all speeds, really of all speeds, not just champions and near champions. Mr. A. J. Goffrey, an enthusiastic and relentlessly efficient handicapper ensures almost simultaneous fishing of up-and-coming seventeen-year-olds with sprightly seventy-year-old evergreens.

The first race is during the Easter week-end; probably with the water temperature around 7° centigrade. Racing then continues throughout the year until the 'season' finishes on Christmas Day. After the winter 'lay-off' that first Easter dip is often excruciatingly painful to old hand and novice alike. Cold strikes different people in different ways. Personally, my face is the most vulnerable part and it is a great temptation to revert to old-fashioned trudgen-stroke, thereby keeping the face out of water. But these earliest races are only fifty-five yards in length and are completed in a few moments.

A brisk rub-down afterwards makes Mr. Average-Man feel a king amongst men. It is sheerest pleasure; it has to be experienced to be believed. At that moment the swimmer is certainly more physically and mentally alert than the vast majority of his fellow beings. It is a complete invigorator, and gives life, energy, and the mood to tear a morning's hard work to pieces. From the cold-water conditioning aspect it is invaluable. Anyone who can swim fifty-five yards in a temperature of 7·2° C (45° F) will find at least the initial entry into water of 14·4° C (58° F) no bother at all.

As the season progresses, races lengthen and the water warms. The maximum length of races is half mile, 1,000 yards and the mile. These fall far short of marathon distances, but are all extremely useful in tuning the body to open water swimming and to open water temperatures. Racing also sharpens up stroke-timing and that aspect belongs to another chapter. Long training swims can be carried out here in water not much warmer than the sea. In very hot weather when *bathers* crowd out *swimmers* from almost everywhere the Serpentine is one of the few places capable of dealing with both sects. Unhampered swimming exists nowhere

The cartoonist Gus has a go.

Captain Webb reaches French soil after exactly 21 hours and 45 minutes in the water, on August 24th, 1875; the first man ever to swim the English Channel.

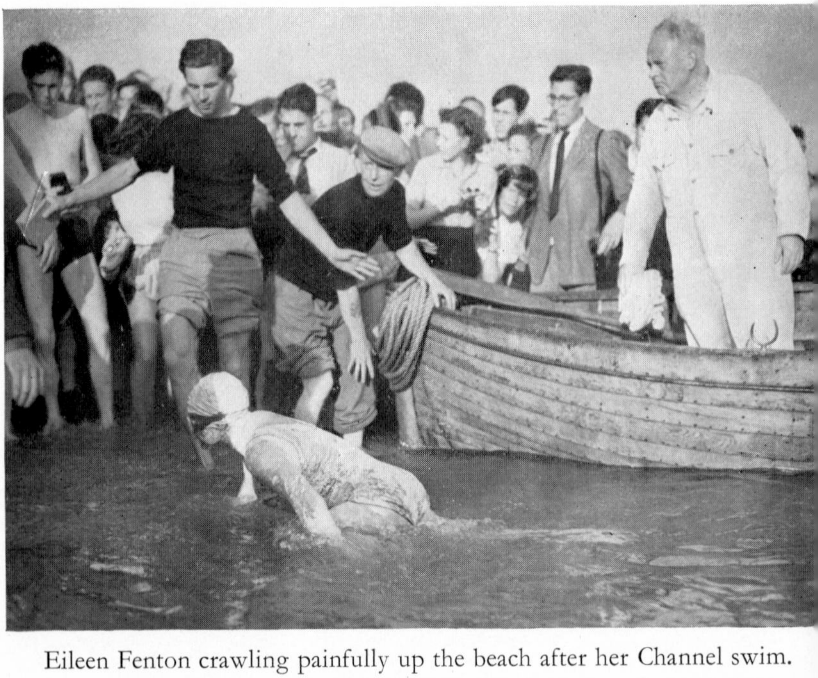

Eileen Fenton crawling painfully up the beach after her Channel swim.

in London during a heat-wave, but on the Serpentine deep boundary one can swim with the minimum of collisions. In cold weather it is still better, and it is then possible to get two or three hours uninterrupted swimming and pacemaking closer inshore. With diving-boards conveniently set 110 yards apart and an easily visible clock-tower, it gives extra point to swimming.

All these activities are preliminaries to the stage of highly specialized race-training; they are essential for forming a sound basis on which to build that training. Knowledge of one's ability to stand cold is half the psychological battle of the marathon. The other half is, of course, knowledge of one's ability to *swim* for the requisite time. One half is extremely closely related to the other because the physical effort of swimming raises the body heat. Nevertheless, in the earlier stages the two halves may, if necessary, be developed separately. For scrutiny and analysis that division is most desirable and helpful.

Later, it is essential to complete, at least once, a swim of similar duration and temperature to the one being trained for. But even failure to complete such a trial is not absolute failure because it brightly spotlights the weak points of physique.

As an example I give a personal experience. Early one season my right leg cramped badly after only two hours swimming in a temperature of 11·1° C (52° F). It was the first time such a thing had happened and I scuttled for the bathside in alarm. In very few minutes the cramp passed off with self massage and I then swam for another hour. Nevertheless, I was terribly dismayed that such a thing should have happened only a week or so before the onset of the racing season. I sat down that evening, thought hard, and analysed it on paper. The layout is given on the following page; it might serve as a pattern on which to base other sorts of failure-analysis.

As a result of that study there was no recurrence of the leg cramp. Which particular point remedied the failure will never be known. It is rather like an aircraft manufacturer putting two hundred modifications into an aircraft to prevent repetitions of an unexplained crash. In both cases every modification, however tiny, probably contributes something to the efficiency of performance. It may be one point alone which bears major responsibility; or responsibility may be shared amongst many. But if a recurrence *is* prevented, the apportioning of blame is unimportant except to the extremely tidy-minded.

QUESTION	REMARKS	ACTION REQUIRED
Legs my most vulnerable part?	Self-evident, nothing else was affected.	Extra grease to try and maintain warmth in calf muscles.
Calf muscles too stiff?	Very possible. I had been walking about six miles every day.	Cut daily walking to minimum in swimming season.
Circulation faulty?	Possible, but unlikely not to have been discovered before.	Loosen waistbelt. Perhaps that is slightly restricting circulation.
Transition from Mediterranean to English temperature has left me unprepared?	Very possible. Luckily 11·1° C (52° F) is a low temperature for England and should improve weekly.	Persevere with cold conditioning. Body will become more accustomed. Water will become warmer.
Some bodily disorder lowering physical condition?	Unlikely, but should be investigated.	Consult doctor (He provided some anti-cramp medicine.)
Overdoing leg drive?	Possible. I have an over-vigorous screw kick with the right leg. Muscles have not recovered from winter lay-off.	Relax leg stroke in race. Carry out 30 minutes' legs-only practice daily.
Chill wind and rain final straw to body only just coping with water temperature?	Air temperature was 10° C (50° F). That is almost certain to improve as summer progresses.	Persevere with cold water conditioning and remember that according to statistics sea and air temperatures must rise weekly. Such unfavourable circumstances are unlikely to occur again.
Can cramp be treated in water?	Confirmed with other swimmers as occasionally possible.	In any recurrence try self-massage for at least ten minutes before leaving the water.

Other methods exist for accustoming the body to low temperatures. Mr. E. H. Temme (first both-way Channel swimmer) once told me that in winter he reduced clothing to a minimum. He also advocated sleeping without bedclothes even in winter. Everyone to his own taste. Such Spartan routine is not to mine. Surely the swimmer who has worked hard all spring, summer and autumn must let up some time. And the ideal time from many points of view is over the Christmas–New Year period. After a month or two of rest and comfort any athlete returns much refreshed to his labours.

Critics may contend that unnecessary emphasis has been placed on conditioning to temperature. They may even point to successful marathon swimmers who have not carried out careful conditioning. But it must be remembered that on certain isolated calm and warm days the sea is little different to an indoor pool. On those special occasions a good bath swimmer can excel in a marathon. Such a case again occurred in my experience. I swam in my first big sea race without having swum previously in the open air. Beginners luck held, the Solent was flat and calm and at 20° C (68° F), and I was able to put up a good time. But no swimmer of calibre ought to gamble on those conditions. Channel aspirants who have wasted whole summers waiting for such an ideal combination will confirm sadly that it is too rare for ease of mind.

There are artificial methods of temporarily raising body-heat (alcohol, camphor, nicotinic acid tablets), but they are very transient aids. Their use is described later in the book. They do not, and can never, replace 'at-home-ness' in the water and good healthy circulation. If there is any doubt about the latter an early visit to the medical officer is the obvious course.

Summing up as simply as possible is often the best aid both to perception and reception. So here it is:

> January to April, bath swimming. April to June, gradually decrease bath swimming. Start and gradually increase distance of open air swimming. July to September, 100 per cent outdoor swimming. October to December, decrease outdoor periods, increase indoor proportion again. Then re-commence the cycle.

Mention of re-commencing the cycle reminds me that cold water immersion has other uses besides marathon-conditioning.

A friend of mine had an annoying stammer. He had a fund of anecdotes, but his unfortunate speech defect often thwarted or delayed general conversation for long periods. Quite frankly, despite all our sympathy and understanding he was in grave danger of becoming regarded as the club bore.

A kindly and interested doctor suggested that cold water swimming might cure the affliction. Year after year Mr. X persevered with the treatment. Year after year his speech improved until it became entirely normal. Now he converses fluently with the best. It was a complete and resounding success for the water cure.

That is where this particular cycle re-commences. Quite frankly, despite all our sympathy and understanding, he is in grave danger of becoming regarded as the club bore. He now talks of nothing but cold water swimming.

6

'Roll on My Twelve'

The life so shorte, the crafte so long to lerne.
CHAUCER

I

THIS chapter deals with preparation and training for marathon swimming. Because it deals with all twelve months of a swimmer's year, it is necessarily a longer chapter than usual. Royal Navy sailors, when particularly fed up, love to cry 'Roll on my twelve'. It means that at the end of their twelve-year engagement they are having no more of it. Marathon swimmers in the middle of twelve-months' toil sometimes echo those feelings. But when the release date arrives the Royal Navy sailor often 'takes-on' for another period. So does the marathoneer. Once the bug is in the system, it is almost always there for ever.

There is generally more than one good way to do anything. This chapter does not claim to describe the only way to success. An intelligent, experienced, understanding coach could chart another course and win championships for his charge; there is no doubt about that. But this is my way, and for that reason it is written on a more personal note than other parts of the book; the methods have been tried in the water and not found wanting. Channel training is in a class by itself and qualifies for a section of its own later in the book.

Many aspects of marathon preparation have common denominators with other sports. Reasonable living is one of those denominators. Inexperienced athletes often think that improvement can only be achieved by some highly spartan and inconvenient routine. The exact reverse is true: to avoid overstraining and boredom, the least inconvenient routine consistent with efficiency, should be the aim. Rising at 5.30 a.m., for instance, and turning in at 9.30 p.m. is no more beneficial than doing the same things at 7 p.m. and 11 p.m. Even nightwatchmen have been champions before today.

Probably few athletes will ever be fitter than during their schooldays. We may later be better swimmers, better footballers or better ping-pong players—but only because we have channelled our energy into one sport instead of many. The superb physical fitness of schooldays was laid on the solid bedrock of regular hours and regular food. That is vital point number one. No fancy food and no fancy hours. Hot-pots and not *hors d'oeuvres*; bedtime at eleven and not bebop at twelve.

What is the best diet? Captain Webb liked red meat. Bill Pickering put up a world channel record on green salads and raw peaches. For the ordinary competitor I suggest once again that they return to schooldays. To porridge, bacon and egg, soups, stews, puddings, and all the good things that 'mother used to make'. Doubt it? Then consider a hospital diet scientifically selected to inject new health into the patient. One day's menu will probably include all the above; next and succeeding days will only ring the changes on similar items. And the hospital cook is probably no better than 'Mum' or the 'better-half'. *No* fancy food? Well, as the Radio Doctor used to say, 'a little of what you fancy does you good'. But make sure it is a little. In 1949 a man was admitted to hospital who had consumed nothing but beer, bread and cheese and pickled onions for fifteen years. He liked that diet, but it nevertheless made him feel rather poorly.

Regularity's virtues are not confined to food and sleep. It applies equally to elimination of body waste. Presentation of oneself at the 'littlest room' at a regular time each day works wonders. Non-presentation of oneself, because of late rising, disinclination, laziness and bad organisation also works wonders—but in the reverse direction. Father Bear could be no more grumpy than an irregular eliminator—in fact, he probably was one. Many successful athletes arrange the remainder of the day's programme around this little act and I thoroughly agree with their emphasis. The idea is to make a plan and to stick to it. Consider the human body as a pendulum operated machine. Give it a little swing by missing the daily elimination and it will take days to settle down. Give it a big swing with a riotous 'Saturday night at the Palais', and it will take weeks. The analogy is not inappropriate.

In short, I repeat that hoary advice about eight hours sleep, with half an hour extra after a particularly hard work-out. If you can lie down or sit with your feet up, for thirty minutes in the middle of the day, that is a wonderful recuperator. If you can doze, too, it is better still. Sleep is good medicine but once again guard against the overdose. Too much sleep makes the body and mind lethargic. Practically every coach will emphasise that angle, and it was once given extra emphasis by a keen legal brain. The late Mr. Justice Shearman, a prominent athlete in earlier days, wrote that 'young athletes grow slack and torpid from the amount of lazy sleep to which they are condemned'.

Weight charts fit the regularity schedule, too, for every athlete should know how his body is shaping. The measurement should be made at the same time and on the same day each week. (I personally do it every Saturday forenoon at eleven, after breakfast, after elimination, and on the same scales.) A sudden increase or a sudden fall is an immediate indication of a defect in the body. Training should not be resumed without medical permission. Gradual increase may mean the body is getting too much fuel for the work it is doing. (As the work is increased so will the body weight usually fall.) Gradual decrease means the reverse, and is generally beneficial in the early and middle stages of training. Every athlete has a 'fighting-weight' and it does good to get down to it. Reduction below 'fighting weight' results in staleness, fatigue, 'couldn't care less' attitude and boils. Exactly where the dividing line is situated must be found by experience individually in each athlete. By logging weekly weights and performances, the ideal weight should soon become apparent. You may be caught by staleness once, but next time the danger signals will be recognisable.

I experimented for four years to find what bearing extra weight has on speed through the water. Manifestly thousands of different experiments on thousands of different persons are required for an exact figure. Results would also differ at short and long distance because of the different stance in the water. My experiments were necessarily conducted on one body—mine—and on the middle distance, the mile. It astonished me to find that added weight and added time seemed to go tidily in the same proportion. For an example—take an easy mathematical case. Mr. X weighs 12 stones and does a 24-minute mile. If he lets his weight rise to 13 stones, but remains at the same state of fitness, he will then do no better than a 26-minute mile. Doubtless, future investigation will modify my theory for more accuracy but I am sure my general principle is correct. In the meantime, it will serve as a very good rule-of-thumb guide for swimmers, where no guide of any sort existed previously. Speed is affected by the carriage of extra weight by the same muscles; but more especially by the change of streamlining, the extra volume and surface area, and the increased skin friction which results from that increase of weight.

Performance against the stopwatch must also be a routine matter. Trials, like weight measurements, should be at certain times of certain days. Only by these methods, coupled with identical conditions and on identical course, can comparison be illuminative. Only by further use of logbook and pencil can the illumination become permanent. It is often instructive and useful to refer back to the corresponding time last year. Memory is fallible; but the logbook tells the truth for ever; I, for one, like to see my progress year after year as well as month by month. My small logs—only pocket diaries—take me back through routine and highlight to 1950.

Still on the subject of time trials, I emphasise the necessity for similar conditions in each trial. Weather conditions are beyond our power to alter, but other factors are within them. If the same pool is not available for each trial, then try for the same *size* of pool. A short course one week and a long one the next will give no useful comparison. Changing from fresh water to salt must sometimes be done, but that affects true analysis too. It is not helpful to do the trial alone one week, against an opponent the next, and with the pacing machine the third. Select one method at the beginning of the season and stick to it. The pacing machine, if available, is the best. The lone trail the next best and the temperamental human pacer least reliable of all. This instruction applies to the weekly recorded time trials only. For other training, any method that makes you interested and fast is good.

Those preparations are basic factors. Almost without exception that advice would be useful to the exponent of any competitive sport. Now comes the separation of swimming basic from general athletic basic. Long, slow, muscle-building swims are the first requirement. (Exact routines are tabulated later.) Time is unimportant on the first swims, but in about mid-March the stop-watch should emerge from its winter hibernation. The first timed swims should be carried out without too much exertion. It is all part of planned and gradual build-up of muscle and breathing with no great strain. Doctor Hogarth has neatly summed up the differences between sprinting and marathoneering. 'One', he says, 'is breathlessness without exhaustion. The other is exhaustion without breathlessness.' But the lack of breathlessness in marathon swimmers is only achieved by much practice towards the improvement of 'wind'.

In April much thoroughly enjoyable work will have been completed. Apart from the thrills of competition, most swimmers find the early, easy own-speed swimming the most pleasant part of the year. From now till September it will be a battle of mind against matter; indeed, the immediate task also includes a battle of wind against water. Sprints, sprints, and more sprints. This is a real jerk out of the complacency of winter. One length dashes, two-length dashes, timed and untimed, paced and unpaced. A few seconds rest, and then start again. Racing, too; most clubs have at least one race a week. If you belong to more than one club there will be more than one race a week. I personally belong to four. Racing is good, it brings out that extra ounce reluctantly the first time; on subsequent occasions it comes more readily. Be the race back-stroke, breast-stroke, or freestyle, it is all good for the wind.

If your club has a training scheme for orthodox-distance swimmers, this is the time for the marathoneer to use it. Chief Petty Officer Ogden of the Royal Naval School of P.T. is the harshest, slave-driving coach I know—and the best beloved. A typical evening with him usually includes a half-mile loosener, a two-twenty yard sprint, legwork, armwork, a dozen individual one-length dashes, starts, turns and a relay race. And woe betide the slacker. Ogden's boys work hard and reap remarkable results. I have derived much benefit, and have been lashed into action with as sharp words as the ordinary seaman next to me. Quite right, too. Commanders' stripes don't show on swim trunks.

But the long-distance swimmer must look ahead, for most top-line races are in July–August. Even his basic *swim* training is now almost over; he must get down to solid application, to specialise in his own marathon training. By mid-June specialisation should be under way. At this point, half-way through the year, and on completion of basic training, it seems reasonable to pause and take stock. Training goes straight forward; the chapter heading does not change, either. But because we are marathon swimmers, we need not be marathon readers too. Stop and have a breather. Then we will dive in for the next lap.

II

Now to advanced training. We have built up muscles and shaken the system out of winter laziness. From mid-June onwards there must be one of two plans.

Plan No. 1 is super efficient. It aims at achieving peak form on one certain date for one certain race. It gives great mental and physical advantage in that selected race distance. Plan No. 2 aims at a wide coverage of dates by coming to a peak on about 1st August; that allows for swimming in July races on the way up to the peak, and in the August races while trying to maintain peak form as long as possible afterwards. Wider coverage in distances is obtained by training for the five-mile event. That is a sort of half-way house between the high and low marathon levels; it is altogether a reasonable compromise.

Each plan is good—so long as it is maintained throughout the season. Changing ambitions in mid-season is the five-star way to achieve nothing. I have used both methods, and on the whole prefer the second. Nothing is more annoying than training a whole year for one race and then seeing it cancelled on account of bad weather. Postponement for even a fortnight can see one competitor slipping off his peak form and another one climbing up to his. Postponement and cancellation are the twin bugbears of specialisation. The more general approach ensures many good races and often achieves victory in unexpected places. For instance in a three-mile race on a rough day, the reserve stamina on a five-miler may prevail even over the three-mile specialist. Again on a calm smooth day a five-miler may be able, with his extra speed, to challenge the specialist ten-miler over his own distance. And should injury or loss of form attack the specialist, Mr. Jack-of-all-distances is there to take the advantage.

Whichever alternative is chosen, the swimmer's pace must now be sharpened up. The schedule given later in the chapter refers to the five-mile peak on 1st August method. To train for a different date is easy; it requires only to start the advanced training so many days earlier or later than the dates given. To aim at a different distance, it is also necessary to vary the advanced training. Keep the 'shock' training according to my schedule, but in the other session increase or decrease the distance as requisite.

The finest method of speeding up a swimmer is by use of a pacing machine. Such machines have now achieved almost world-wide recognition. One type consists of an electrically driven trolley which runs from one end of the pool to the other. Another type is simply an endless wire running through pulleys and having distinctive marks painted on it. Yet another is a system of electric lights flickering up and down the bathside. All will run at different speeds according to the control setting, and the swimmer endeavours to keep abreast the trolley, paintmark, or flickering light. All methods are capable of fine adjustments and all stop short of the bath end to allow for extra speed at turn and push-off.

'Pace' is the linch-pin of advanced training. There is only so much energy in any one human body and 'pace' governs the speed at which it is expended from a fit swimmer. It is the swimmer's aim to find the exact pace which will exhaust him after exactly the right duration of time. Obviously, if some energy still remains at the end of a race, that race should have been swum faster. On the other hand, too fast a pace would have exhausted the competitor before reaching the finishing post. *Constant* pace is also the aim. Like an automobile the human body burns more fuel in accelerations and decelerations than when at cruising speed.

The great delight of a pacing machine is in its lack of temperament. It will turn out a constant pace (and any pace) for as long as required. If that is its greatest delight, its greatest use is to drill the human body into being an even paced machine, too. The method of using the machine is to adjust it to somewhere near the swimmer's best time for a given distance; then set them both off and watch. It is likely that swimmer will beat machine at first, then machine will beat swimmer, and finally swimmer will sprint hard to catch the machine on the post. That is, of course, object lesson No. 1, the swimmer's uneven pace has been exposed.

As soon as the swimmer can withdraw faith from his own pace-judgement, and replace that faith in the machine, improved results will come like magic. Ironing out inequality of pace first enables the competitor to complete the same distance in the same time with *less effort.* To further the improvement, the machine is set a few seconds faster on each occasion. Like a carrot in front of a donkey, the machine lures the swimmer inexorably on to hitherto unthought-of times. Naturally each human body has its limits. It is the responsibility of the intelligent swimmer to recognise these limits. The danger signs are undue and persistent fatigue and a falling off in performance. The remedy is change of routine or a complete rest for a few days. Each case must be dealt with entirely on its own merits. Good common sense, and the swimmer's own feelings, coupled if possible with the experience of a coach or medical officer, must solve every 'staleness' problem separately.

Do not lose heart if you have no access to a pacing machine. Neither did I have access until the fag-end of my career. They are a comparatively recent innovation and most of the reigning champions have achieved top-ranking without such assistance. Having been exiled in Gosport and the Gulf of Suez, Ipswich and Istanbul, Beirut and Bayswater, I had never seen one till a year or so ago. Now it is far too late to be of use to me, for 'old dogs cannot learn new tricks'. But there are other good ways of checking pace. A coach or a friend walking up and down the side can soon, with the aid of a stop-watch, become a reasonable pacer. My own way is to plan the swim beforehand. I note down the estimated times for each two lengths, and the progressive times also. Then I situate a timekeeper in a convenient position near the even-length turning point. This ensures that after emerging from even-numbered push-offs, I am able to see the timekeeper when taking my first breath. If I observe five fingers held upwards I know that my pace is faster than it should be by five seconds and adjust accordingly. Fingers held down mean the reverse and the speed must be speeded up. Alternatively, a slate, plainly chalked, can be used instead but it is really unnecessary. If the timekeeper needs more than the fingers of two hands to signal the deviation from the estimated pace there is something radically wrong. Eihter the planning or the swimming is bad and they both ought to be done again.

For several reasons, the mile distance is the most useful for weekly standard time trials. Firstly, it can be used satisfactorily from March throughout the year, and it is thus encouraging to see regular recorded improvement. Increasing the trial distance in mid-season would leave one guessing at the value of relative performances. For instance, is a 55-minute two-mile swim as meritorious as a 26-minute mile or more so? As many words have been wasted in such arguments as a soap-box orator wastes on his Hyde Park audience. It is better, therefore, to stick at one distance throughout. Secondly, no matter how many sprints are included in his training, the swimmer tends to hold too much in reserve on his long swims. Fast-miling is therefore always an excellent livener. Thirdly, the ability to swim a competent mile opens up a new vista of competition. And the more races (even as short as a mile) competed in, the greater grows the confidence, experience, and fitness of the competitor. Finally, twenty to thirty minutes is the greatest time that one can reasonably ask a kindly bath-attendant or friend to devote to a stop-watch. Even when self-timekeeping by the stadium clock, it is astonishingly difficult to remember with certainty the number of lengths swum if that time is exceeded.

Self-timing is an art on its own. It is not quite so satisfactory as having assistance, but it effectively safeguards against the natural tendency to slack off when unobserved. First plan your swim again. Know what times you hope to achieve at quarter, half, three-quarter mile marks and endeavour to keep to them. To defeat boredom, I also enter the realms of mental arithmetic. Normally, I train in 110 yard pool, and now think nothing of forecasting my final time mathematically at any point in the swim. Take the easiest example. At the ten-length mark the clock shows sixteen minutes; sixteen divided by ten gives one point six minutes per length. Multiply that by sixteen (lengths in a mile) and it shows a forecast of a twenty-five minute thirty-six second mile.

Rather boring, you say? In marathon swimming, boredom threatens alike those who do think and those who do not think. But as thinking is useful, it may as well be done—there is plenty of time.

Naturally a clock with large centre second hand is quite the best for self-timekeeping. But there is another type by which accurate results can be obtained; the half-minute or minute 'jerkers'. Wait until the minute hand jerks to a clearly marked minute, say ten past twelve; then dive in and carry out the swim. At the end of the mile, pull up to the bar and count slowly as you wait for the jerk. Suppose the next movement carries the time to twelve thirty-six just as you have counted up to thirteen. It is now exactly twenty-six minutes since starting the swim, but you may already have been waiting thirteen seconds for the jerk. Fairly accurately then, your time for the mile must have been twenty-five minutes, forty-seven seconds. The type of minute hand which revolves continuously is definitely the worst for this particular purpose. Nevertheless, delaying the start until the exact hour or half hour will reduce calculations to a minimum and increase readability to a maximum. Then, too, if there is a slight error in reading the clock it is likely that the same error will occur on each and every occasion. So, because any error is constant, comparison with previous swims will remain possible and valuable.

Many young marathon swimmers ask about the value of P.T. exercises. My advice (which may not apply to a short-distance swimmer) is to leave them alone. For us, the best form of P.T. is swimming itself. Swimming stiffness can best be cured by more swimming; it is then quite certain that only the right muscles are being tackled. By incorrectly using the right P.T. exercises, it is possible to ruin one sort of muscles while another sort are being mended. There are exceptions to every rule; neck-twisting, neck-bending strengthens neck muscles and guards against the rough water agony previously described. This is an exercise which may conveniently be carried out many times a day. P.T. is also a useful gap-filler when, for some reason, medical or otherwise, the athlete is barred from the water. For really full-time athletes, like some of the foreign 'shamateurs', P.T. is also useful for gap-filling to avoid overdoses of waterwork. But for ordinary spare-time athletes time is precious, *and the best training for swimming is swimming.*

There are two forms of recreation valuable to the swimmer; one of these is walking. In the basic training period it is impossible to walk too much. If clean, good, country or sea air is available, so much the better. If not, walk anywhere, even up and down the back garden. Swing the arms and try for five or six miles a day. I do it regularly. But as the competition season draws near, walking must be scaled down to a minimum. It hardens the calf muscles and tends to cramp them. It is fortunate that water-polo, the other recommended recreation, can be continued longer. Having a side-line activity maintains interest and fends off staleness to a remarkable degree.

Water-polo is an admirable game to break the monotony of training. It ensures half an hour of continuous swimming liberally interspersed with sprints. Fatigue is held off by interest and it breeds stamina and guts twin virtues which are pearls without price in the marathon. Occasions arise when one is swum to a standstill—then the ball is passed, and out of the bag comes a twenty-five yard sprint in twelve seconds or so. In my swimming 'log' I always consider a water-polo match as equivalent to a half-mile swim and enter it as such. Apart from possible injury and strain there is one particularly valid reason why even water-polo should be discontinued in the actual competitive season. All the most important matches will, it seems—inevitably occur on the day of your big championship, the day before (when you require a twenty-four hour stand-off), or during your organised rest days. To avoid constantly recurring difficult decisions between team and self, it is best to opt out of the club team at the very outset of their league competition and rejoin them when it is finished.

The rest-day just mentioned is an absolute necessity. Most machines need a rest one day a week, and the human machine is certainly no exception. When marathon swimming first took charge of me, I tried to keep every Sunday free. Unfortunately, because of business engagements and travelling I was often cut off from swimming on certain weekdays also. Too many rest-days being even more detrimental than too few, another plan was obviously required. Now my business days-off have become rest-days and I swim, as requisite, on Sundays. This is not ideal because of irregularity; it *is* however a good second best which I fancy most of my readers will have to adopt. In case the Lord's Day

Observance Society is critical, it should be pointed out that Sunday has enough hours to encompass a swim *amd* a visit to church. Since embarking on this new routine I have never—apart from necessary travelling and seagoing—missed Divine Service any Sunday.

Little has been said of coaches or trainers. That is because few of these gentlemen have their hearts fully in long-distance swimming. For sound financial reasons they prefer to keep to the indoor pool. The greatest number of guineas come from the shallow-end swimmers with one foot still on the bottom; it is only natural that, with a living to make, the coaches should gravitate thus. Britain's number one marathon coach is therefore an amateur. Wilfred Toulcher of Huddersfield talks, thinks, reads, writes, and has his whole being in the sport. He has assisted more successful long-distance swimmers than anyone else in the country. Such a coach is of tremendous importance and no amount of theoretical knowledge can equal on-the-spot interest and attention. Any good coach knows the signs of staleness, the elimination of stroke faults, and variations of routine to maintain interest. A marathon coach knows, in addition, that style takes a back seat to stamina and guts, but he will be on the look-out for bad faults, wriggling and crooked swimming. As usual, a compromise may be the solution to the coach problem. I have always rigidly obeyed the club coach for the six winter months, and directed my own operations for the six summer ones. This is most satisfactory so long as there is understanding and goodwill on both sides, and one retains the same coach for several years.

One last important general point before switching to greater detail. What about a glass of beer and a smoke? Ideally, they're out. But by Doctor Hill's 'little-of-what-you-fancy' principle they are 'in'. I personally smoke two or three cheroots and average one or two glasses of beer a day. Medical opinion is pretty unanimous that such slight indulgence is harmless. To check that opinion I asked F. G. Milton his idea, as I could hardly think of a more valuable one. Freddie is a member of Otter Swimming Club, has won five national freestyle titles, won the Allied Forces in Europe Victory Championship at the age of forty, and competed in the national championships with distinction at forty-two. He smokes little, and is emphatic that beer in moderation is beneficial. Al-

Tough swimmers break the ice at the Lee Dam, Lumbutts, near Todmorden before taking a dip. *Left to right*: Cyril Huggins, Derek Turner, Donald Myers, Kendall Mellor, R. Thompson, G. Thompson, Michael Oates.

Channel finish. A swimmer may land on shingle, on a slipway, on slimy rocks or at the foot of cliffs.

Excellent conditions in Lough Neagh. The author out for a record.

though that last opinion was slightly biassed (I discovered that he earns his living by importing Danish lager) it was indeed borne out by a lady doctor at an official A.S.A. lecture. She said emphatically that beer was preferable to tea, coffee, and even milk. There was considerable fluttering in the official dovecotes that evening!

None of that means that you must *cultivate* a taste for hops and nicotine. If the enjoyment is not there, neither is the benefit. Success in marathon swimming is due to a score of different factors; abstinence from tobacco and alcohol may just make the difference of winning or not winning a race by a few all-important seconds. It is quite certain that marathon performances will improve yearly. More devoted high-priest outlooks and less fallible human indulgences is the way to excellence in many spheres of life. Swimming is one of them. There is no room in the future for (I quote Dr. Bannister in the *Sunday Times*) 'the leisured light-hearted spirit of the Olympic Regatta of 1908, when the Belgian eight tossed their cigars in the water as they stepped into the boat'. Even in those days they only came second. Jim Peters, Britain's marathon runner of imperishable memory, had one main slogan for slashing world records.

'The more you put in, the more you can take out when wanted'.

Here is more detail. The sketch programme that follows is intended as a guide and not as a rigid instruction. Many variable factors affect its application. One athlete may revel in work which only blunts the keenness of another. For business reasons you may have a fortnight's gap in your programme. Holidays sometimes intervene. The corporation even closed my London bath for re-boilering one year. In all such eventualities common sense will enable you to rejoin this sketch programme at an appropriate point or improvise a parallel one from where you left off. One thing requires more emphasis than any other—the approach work must be gradual. A jump into the middle of the programme is a jump into real trouble. Strains will inevitably result and may persist throughout the season.

January: Slow swims of increasing length. This is to acclimatise to water and to build muscle. There is no set distance at each swim. Quarter, half, and one mile swims are equally acceptable, so long as monthly mileage reaches a total of twenty. Walk up to six miles daily. Plan and commence regular habits of eating, sleeping, exercising, eliminating and weighing.

February: Continue as for January. Gradually lengthen the average training spin. Thirty miles swimming is the aim this month.

March: Continue as for January and February. Forty miles is the month's target. Commence time trials over a mile course once weekly. For this purpose try and select a time, day, and place which will serve throughout the year. Commence logging weights against times.

April: Continue mile time trials weekly. Continue distance swims. Add in repeated sprints over twenty-five to two-twenty-yard courses. Leg practice. Arm practice. Starts and turns, etc. Enter all club races in all styles and distances. Maintain the monthly mileage at forty-five miles.

May: Unlikely that all training can be carried out in one session from now onwards. Suggest two sessions (but you can spread into three if more convenient). One session devoted to continuance of April's shock training. Next session, two mile swims with no loitering. Monthly total should be sixty-five miles. Continue mile time trials weekly. Enter all club races.

June: First half of month as for May. Begin to cut walking gradually. Enter all club races. Second half of the month. One session to include fairly fast mile. Other session to include fairly fast three miles. Except on day of weekly mile time trial. Monthly mileage should reach eighty.

July: Continue weekly mile time trials. Cut walking to minimum. One session should consist of any arm work, leg work, etc., considered necessary. Second session, fairly fast three- or four-mile swims whenever possible. Discontinue races below the mile, but enter every mile race possible (without interfering with marathon races as they occur). Club, county, area, national championships—you may come last over this short distance but it is all good experience. Get one five-mile swim a week done to give you confidence. The quality of swimming, and getting race experience is more important this month than mileage. Nevertheless, not less than fifty miles should be achieved.

August: Differing stages of training should have built you up to peak form. Now the problem is to retain it. *Cut out all slow swimming* except where necessary for loosening or massage. Once again enter every race possible of a mile or upwards. Practice sprints whenever there is an opportunity. Your 'big' races will be this month so all other swimming must be arranged round those races. Arrange your rest day to come the day before important races. Continue weekly time trials. Monthly mileage should be near the fifty mark.

September: Continue as for August until after your last race. Then *gradually* work down to half a mile or so daily. A complete break will throw body and mind quite out of gear. Seven days after beginning the work down, try a last mile time trial. Relaxation of all seasonal strain and anxiety should produce the fastest time of the year. Monthly mileage not less than thirty-five miles.

October, November, December: This is the swimmer's stand-easy, but there is plenty of work to be done in easy stages. Correct stroke faults. Develop any part of the body which has been a weak link. Practice bilateral breathing or any other useful attribute. In general, put to good use all the season's lessons, and lay the foundation for next year. Any new innovations must be practised until, before January, they become entirely automatic. Recommence walking up to six miles per day. Monthly totals should work down to thirty, twenty-five and ten. December should be really an easy month before starting again.

That programme is one that served me well in several very good years. With it I was runner-up in the Ryde to Southsea race twice, and first and third in Morecambe Bay besides several other successes. It is good practical advice and requires only to be adapted to other swimmers' special circumstances. My total those years was over five hundred miles annually. (This was before I stepped up training to tackle Channel distances.) In four early years I, indeed, completed the equivalent of a trans-Atlantic crossing from England to Newfoundland. Perhaps that is the nearest approach to a trans-Atlantic swim since the nineteen-twenties. Then, a now unknown swimmer dived into the *Aquitania's* pool when she left Great Britain and swam until she arrived in the States. He claimed a trans-Atlantic record which has lasted till now. There will be a good chance for someone to break that record when B.O.A.C. decides to include a swimming-pool in the amenities of its future airliners!

In Britain at present a new trend is emerging in that some major championships are being programmed for June. If you wish to excel in these, the schedule I have given must be advanced and telescoped. Personally I prefer to use June championships as 'training swims' on the way to the seasonal peak.

7

'Don't be Fright!'

> Your labour is for future hours.
> Advance. Spare not. Nor look behind.
> Plough deep and straight with all your powers.
>
> R. H. HORNE

THE illustrious comedian who used this chapter title as his trade-mark, evidently knew much about the human make-up. Almost everyone has suffered from some kind of stage-fright; likewise most competitive swimmers have had 'butterflies in the stomach'. Despite many years of competition, I still suffer slightly, even in quite unimportant club events. Obviously only deep hypnosis or a stiff slug of sleeping draught could completely rout these loathsome lepidoptera. But by more natural means their activities can be curbed considerably. No one will complain about a mild flutter, but they do object to mass aerobatics. Incidentally, the sleeping draught is not recommended. Because the medicine had worked at the wrong pace, one Channel contender snoozed off during the swim and had to be taken out of the water.

The keynote to confidence and ease of mind is—perhaps you have guessed it—regularity. If the swim is many miles from home, some mental and physical disturbances are bound to result. But with thought and good sense those disturbances can be cut to an absolute minimum. Unless you are a near-millionaire, you can hardly take your own bed for pre-race sleeping. The point is semi-facetious but wholly relevant. If it is possible, by dint of early rising, to sleep in your own home, do so. Regularity will then have been maintained to the last possible moment, in familiar surroundings, with familiar people, and on familiar food. I even advocate all-night travel as preferable to spending the previous evening in idleness among strangers. Travelling keeps the mind well occupied with matters other than swimming. And so long as the body can be well rested sleep is—for this one night only—unimportant. (As a matter of fact, sleep is likely to come more easily in a warm railway carriage than in a strange cold bedroom.) There may also be a chance to stretch out and snooze for an hour in the dressing-room before the race. Such a cat-nap is not 'worth its weight in gold' as some trainers aver. The saying is outmoded and is an understatement as well. A relaxed hour of sleep just before a race is at least worth its weight in Uranium 235.

Next best thing is to travel several days before the event so as to get thoroughly used to the place. The advantage of acclimatisation, having met some of the officials, found the rendezvous, and explored the dressing-room, compensate in great measure for the uprooting from familiar surroundings. Morale is boosted high by the most curious things. Knowing the local ropes better than one's rivals is one of these important trivia. The early arrival's mind has already disposed of many problems which his rivals are just beginning to find worrying. Should it be impossible to travel early and just as impossible to travel the same day, only one alternative remains. The brief overnight stay is the last and worst alternative, but common sense will go a long way to surmounting this obstacle too. Some advice from personal experience may help in doing so.

It is vital not to think aimlessly, and at length, about the forthcoming event. Certainly it will ease the mind to ascertain a few specific details and to lay out and check the gear which will be required. That is sensible preparation and will save appearing on the morrow minus some important item. Some such minor calamity inevitably befalls some swimmer in every race. For instance, one of my rivals in the Morecambe Inshore arrived without trunks on one occasion. That sounds laughable and impossible, but is really quite easy to do; indeed I had an exactly similar misfortune on arriving for a swim in the Sea of Galilee. I was forced to borrow an olde-worlde garment from the organisers which considerably restricted free limb movement. Even worse, it supplied me with a great number of active and irritating souvenirs of the district. Subsequently my Medical Officer was polite but sceptical; his voice took on that 'heard-it-all-before' tone when I blamed the borrowed bathing trunks, and implored his assistance. Not a very pleasant memory of the Holy Land, but it could have been worse, one supposes.

After the preparation and checking of gear, try to forget the race altogether. That is more easily said than done, but several things will help. An accompanying parent or friend to talk to—even a telephone conversation with home. A visit to the cinema is good for two and a half hours' distraction; if required, two visits and five hours' distraction will do no harm. Do not go to bed specially early to 'get plenty of rest'. Such dislocation of routine is fatal and the result will be wakefulness into the wee sma' hours. Go to bed at the normal hour and let habit help sleep to come. Keep the diet as normal as possible and plan for arriving at the starting line two hours or so after the last meal.

Should sleep not come quickly, it is annoying but not a disaster. Switch on the light and reach for a book. Not this one, which does not claim bedside charm, but a really absorbing thriller. One or two such volumes in paper backs are a must for every competitor's bag. Thrillers to ensure keeping the mind engrossed; paper-backed, so as to be expendable. Grease and oil plays havoc with more pretentious books, and although there is no valid reason why grease and oil should ever come into contact with books at all, the fact remains that they do. After half an hour's reading, switch off the light and try again. Repeat this process as many times as necessary, and never lie unsleeping in bed with your thoughts and worries taking charge. When my ship was running backwards and forwards to Tobruk in a particularly bad period of the war, I successfully filled in all the gaps between one dive-bombing raid and the next with a book of poetry. And the most gruelling marathon is no worse an ordeal than the 'beef-and-spuds-run' to Tobruk was.

Back to the marathon keynote. Observe the regularities and normalities of life and then the big tests will only worry one during their actual happening. To worry before and after the big tests is the way to stomach ulcers and anxiety neurosis. If used to a pipe and a glass of beer, take them and enjoy them. Doing without at such short notice cannot be of physical benefit and will certainly be of psychological harm. Mental disturbance has astonishingly quick effect on the body. Shortly before writing this I read a medical report of a girl whose arm had been afflicted to the point of requiring amputation. But once the origin was tracked to a distressed state of mind, skilful *mental* treatment restored the arm to normal physical condition in a few weeks. Mind and matter are indissolubly connected; Eastern fakirs and yogi-men have long known this, but here in the West we are only beginning to realise it. Cheerfulness, in fact, goes a long way towards championships. Despite that body and mind hook-up, do not alleviate sleeplessness or worry by long walking or pacing. Soft and welcome relief will undoubtedly result, but so will hard and unwelcome calf muscles. Sit down as much as possible; lie down as much as possible. Calf muscles are most vulnerable to cramping, and must be looked after. This minimum walking rule applies from that last training swim to the big event itself. All necessary walking—for buses, trains, and up and down stairs—is acceptable as light exercise. Anything extra is unacceptable. Remember the elder statesman's advice to the younger. 'Never neglect an opportunity to sit down or to relieve yourself'. This advice is equally applicable to the swimmer on the brink of a championship.

Travel—whether by road, rail, or air—is a dreaded stiffener, but one extremely elementary precaution will help greatly. If travelling by car, stop for a short stretching period every hour; even a change round of seats will help if pushed for time. Rail travel is similar, a stroll along the corridor once an hour will save stiffness from becoming set. On arrival at the destination, any residual stiffness should be swum off immediately. Half a mile or so—even on the big day itself—causes negligible loss of energy to a fit marathoneer, and will benefit the muscles tremendously. In any case, an athlete, trained to swim daily, sorely misses that routine if it is cut off. Once again routine is best continued to the possible moment. Naturally, tearing oneself to pieces in a time trial is not recommended, but the customary immersion and a little exercise is. Massage is also on the not recommended list. Bad massage is a menace at all times; good massage is unnecessary. In fact it will leave the uninitiated wearier than after a five-mile swim.

On the actual day of the race it is at last permissible for the mind to dwell on the event. But constructive thought, not aimless wondering, is imperative. It is good to take stock and assess chances before mixing and talking with the other competitors. Much ill-informed chatter circulates before any race; by being well informed it is possible to be immune to many of the worries and jitters that are generated. Being well-informed about weather conditions is of prime importance. If possible, take a look at the course from the starting point. Note the direction of wind and waves, and find out from knowledgeable locals how the tide will be running. The 'average' time for the course is already known and has been allowed for in training. Now, after checking the weather, fairly accurate additions or subtractions can be applied to the average duration.

The method is elementary in the extreme. Nevertheless, I have seen otherwise intelligent competitors literally at sea in the application. Briefly stated, the system is unforgettable. Wind blowing with the swim makes it shorter, against the swim longer, and directly across the course average. That applies to all strengths of wind in which a competition is held. Obviously, a gale from any direction would slow down a swimmer but races are not swum in gales. The most advantageous following wind is about ten miles per hour; more than that tends to chop up the water too much for efficient stroking. A head wind of twenty miles an hour would nearly double the length of a swim, if it did not cause cancellation altogether. All these adjustments to the average time are subject to tidal conditions. Although all the races I know are swum on a similar tide every year, there are inevitably minor differences which need consideration, and this will be explained in the chapters dealing with particular races.

This wind-advantage is not obtained, as in a runner, by direct affect on the body; it is because the top layer of water is influenced along by the wind. Disregarding tides, which are entirely separate, a ten-miles-per-hour wind will drive that top layer about two hundred yards in an hour or the equivalent of nearly 3½ minutes swimming. So with a following wind of 10 m.p.h. 3½ minutes may be subtracted from every hour of average time. To be more specific, take the particular case of the Morecambe Bay Championship. The average winning time by the current course is two hours forty-five minutes. A light breeze from behind would therefore enable it to be completed in two hours, thirty-five minutes; from right ahead it would retard the time to two hours fifty-five minutes. An obliquely favourable wind or an obliquely adverse wind—i.e. not from dead ahead or dead astern—would have a reduced effect which must be estimated by trigonometry. It is possible to tabulate the advantage/disadvantage for every direction and force of wind; but that development seems more suitable for a paper read to the Institute of Navigation than for a swimming book.

All these pre-race pointers are helpful. Not only do they allow a new and adjusted pace to be worked out, but they build up a defence against the Dismal Jimmies. These lookers-on-the-black-side, of whom one is inevitably present, always forecast a difficult swim. Possibly they may be right, but the intelligent swimmer will know from observations the precise degree of difficulty and be forewarned. More often they are wrong and then the forewarned competitor is able to discount the dire prognostications altogether; leaving his less fortunate rivals to wallow in this war of nerves. A typical Dismal Jimmy remark is on the subject of wind. 'It will be a terrible race with the water blowing into the nose and mouth all the way'. But investigations may have shown that—for rightside breathers anyway—the conditions are most favourable.

It is always comforting to know the exact temperature. A reasonable bath thermometer costs only a few shillings and, for ease of mind only, is worth pounds. Take the water temperature if possible in open water. From a boat is best, but off a pier or jetty is good enough to obtain reasonable accuracy. If forced to measure the temperature from the edge of a beach, subtract two degrees, because in summer inshore water is always warmer than offshore. It gives a great feeling of superiority to know the temperature for certain, while other competitors are testing with the tips of their fingers and guessing. Air temperature is interesting, too. Once again knowledge gives confidence, and apprehensive guesses only lead to gloom and despondency. Information about the course is also valuable. Ideally this should be gleaned from a boat trip at the same state of tide as the race. Second best, and much more usual, is study of a map or chart. It is a great thing to recognise land-marks, know where the next course leads, and generally know what to expect next.

Another useful pre-race occupation is a study of form. It is extremely heartening to know that, by the 'form-book' one may finish not far behind the favourite, or might even beat him. In most sports form is computed over *distances*, but in marathon swimming, the distance basis is impossible. The Windermere Swim and the Morecambe Cross Bay swim are, for instance, both about ten and a half miles. But the former takes roughly six hours, and the latter—because of tide—takes three. Therefore form based on distance must be inaccurate, and form based on *race durations* is the only alternative. Here is a personal example on which to base other form calculations.

The race in question was the Morecambe Cross Bay. On heat times Barry Woodward (Leander S.C.) led me by a few seconds. But, as my swim had been done in a cross-wind and his on a following wind, I retained hope and wanted another advance check on how we should match up in the final. Luckily we had both swum, in different races, against Gordon Hill (Oxford S.C.) and he was thus available as a yard-stick. Gordon was probably the greatest of the middle-distance marathoneers in the country at that time; he had beaten Barry Woodward by twenty-seven minutes in roughly a two-hour swim and me by eleven minutes in roughly a one-hour swim.

Without very great calculation it can be estimated that the figures were favourable to me by a fair percentage. Reducing both swims to a common denominator of two hours it made me five minutes faster than Barry. Furthermore, I always seem to improve relatively to others as the distance increases. So as the Final would be a two and three-quarter hour race in September, the omens seemed good for keeping well up with Barry and perhaps pipping him on the post, if lucky. I checked the records of all four other finalists, too, and decided that things looked quite good.

There is much difference between pugilistic 'I'll moider de bum' bragadoccio and reasonable confidence based on hard figures. It makes plenty of difference to easiness of mind at the start of a race and that in turn affects the early performance. Unfortunately, in this particular case the calculations were quite in vain. They were never put to the test, because the final was ultimately cancelled on account of bad weather. Perhaps not a bad thing really; the day was so cold and rough that lion-hearted Bill

Pickering, then an amateur, would probably have completely upset the form-book and out-lasted us all.

Many elementary efforts at form-reading always go on in the dressing-room. I feel that competitors who have not studied newspapers, have not smuggled stop-watches into the rivals' training sessions, and have not 'tapped' mutual acquaintances, do not deserve to have information handed to them on a plate. When interrogated about my training times I therefore prefer to be evasive. If pressed, I always remember the fantastically fast swim that occurred once only during training. The fact that it was a midget bath, that possibly there was a miscount of lengths, and there was doubt about the minute hand of the clock does not bother. It is not a lie, even a white one, but merely a personal contribution to the war of nerves. Or what Stephen Potter might consider a good example of 'one-upmanship'.

Other problems arise in the dressing-room. They are really no more difficult than deciding whether to take a raincoat when it looks like rain, but to beginners they seem like real epoch-making decisions. They are certainly not that, but are of some importance. Sound judgement in the dressing-room lays a firm foundation for the swim. Anything left undone at this point must necessarily remain undone—unless much good time is sacrificed—until the finishing post. Greasing up for instance is easy on land, incredibly difficult at sea. It is a good idea to make a list of things to be done, and then to tick them off one by one. That expedient will save swimming a mile before remembering that one's earplugs are in a bag aboard the mark boat. Which happened to me on my Channel swim!

Opinions differ about the necessity to grease-up at all. The Channel has been conquered without grease, and I can vouch for doing Windermere, Morecambe Bay and the Solent without it. This is a question that every swimmer must solve individually. If grease is not used in training, it is not likely that there is need to use it when racing. Remember, every pound of grease is another pound of weight to carry through the water. Swimmers are, indeed, the only class of athletes who voluntarily award themselves weight handicaps. For well-covered individuals an olive-oil rub all over should be sufficient, with vaseline slashed liberally on the main chafing surfaces, i.e. crutch, armpits, chin, and creases in the back of the neck. Besides vaselining the chin, an extra good shave is recommended. A bristly chin, over a passage of hours, rubs the inner shoulder red raw. And red-raw flesh in salt water is by no means comfortable.

Goggles, earplugs and helmets are an unholy trio. They cause more trouble sometimes than even the weather. Once again the Channel has been crossed without them. But easily irritated eyes must have goggles, and the need will have become obvious during training. For those dependent on them it is too bad. Many, many minutes have been wasted by goggles filling with water, goggles steaming up, or goggles requiring adjustment. Without them, one is not only clear of these ever-present snags but has better look-out facilities. Ear plugs are essential to some, but other lucky ones are happy without them. A good compromise is a little cotton wool to keep warmth in and cold out; if the wads drop out *en route* they can easily be replaced if necessary. Helmets appear to serve no useful purpose. My strong advice is to wear a plain water-polo cap to facilitate identification, or nothing at all. Whatever is decided, one thing is of over-riding importance. It is absolutely imperative not to get grease on the buckles of goggles, helmets, or trunks. Grease ensures that these items lose all fastening or gripping power; they are then entirely useless until after systematic and painstaking cleaning in hot water.

Swimming trunks are not frequently remembered as items of equipment, but they are obviously important. Thin nylon or silk trunks gain undoubted advantages over thick woollen garments even in sprints; over any marathon distance, the difference may well amount to several minutes. It is inadvisable, however, to train in wool and subsequently to race in nylon; the difference in warmth is quite phenomenal. It is necessary to train in the thin trunks and they will then feel entirely natural on race days. It is important not to detract from this weight advantage by sewing on club badges in heavy absorbent material. Besides being detrimental to the speed, they may be rather a worry when spectators are interested in them.

I shall remember to my dying day a swimmer sporting an enormous and splendidly ornamental badge standing on the high board at the Sporting Club, Alexandria, Egypt. He was obviously tremendously pleased with the attention his badge *seemed* to be receiving from the mixed audience below. Mercifully he was unaware that his rather loosely fitting trunks had slipped sideways. Other and more embarrassing aspects were now claiming the real attention of the audience.

From dressing-room hints, now to the starting point. Some swimmers relish tablespoons of glucose to give lasting energy. Doug Payne (Otter S.C.) sometime Southern Counties and Solent champion is one of these. Others swear by a mouthful of whisky to raise last-minute warmth. Huddersfield coach Wilf Toulcher is amongst these. I like neither, but have respect for the performances those persons have achieved in the marathon world. (It should be noted that alcohol is forbidden in B.L.D.S.A. events.) A smart and purposeful start is recommended, for—although there is a long race ahead—seconds often count at the finish. (I lost the Solent Championship by 90 seconds in 1951.) From a lackadaisical frame of mind a lackadaisical pace follows.

Whether the start is crowded or well-spaced-out, the confident and experienced swimmer should never be bustled out of his planned pace. Excitement sometimes leads a young swimmer to put his head down and 'bash it out'. That will only result in uneconomical loss of energy and an abominably zig-zag course. A straight course is worth twenty years of age sometimes. I remember managing to beat a very good fast swimmer in a needle championship in Malta Grand Harbour solely because of that factor. If Leading Writer Wilkin reads this he will no doubt red-facedly confirm the importance of straight steering. The spectating sailors of his ship did mention the matter to him at the time.

The straight course is achieved by following the boat if there is one, or by steering for a prominent landmark. If those are not available sun and wind will help. Take an extreme example. If the sun ought to be ahead, but instead shines in the eyes when breathing there is obviously a ninety-degree error of course. Or if breathing has been away from the wind and becomes into the wind, it is also likely that an unintentional change of course has occurred. It is best to note the directions of sun and wind in relation to the course before starting the race. They will then stand in good stead throughout the competition, although in a long race it must be remembered that the sun shifts westwards several degrees each hour. The important direction in which to keep a lookout is ahead; this does not entail stopping and scanning the horizon like a homecoming sailor, but does mean snatching a quick glance ahead as frequently as possible. Backward lookers of the 'how far have I gone now?' type are unlikely to meet with much success, and are quite certain not to meet with the boatman's favour.

Finally, be of good cheer. Remember the racing maxim about 'horses for courses', for this may be your course. Remember also that there are fifty-one million people in the British Isles. Even if you only get half-way, you will be better than fifty million, nine-hundred and ninety-nine thousand of them at least.

Don't be fright!

8

The Way to Start Competing Outdoors

Hast thou entered into the springs of the sea?
Or hast thou walked in search of the depth?
BOOK OF JOB

IF thou hast not done either, this very short chapter will assist thee. A good proportion of my correspondence is from sprint swimmers seeking to graduate to the marathons. So I now suggest some of the primary and intermediate tests before taking your 'finals' in Morecambe Bay, Windermere, or the Channel. In advance, I apologise to those selfless and enthusiastic organisers of the smaller races for giving them such short shrift. Each one is dear to my heart and many of them I have swum in myself. But, as explained in the preface, space inexorably confines the main aim of this book to the swims taking over two hours.

The first step, then, is to transfer from indoor competition to outdoor competition somewhere, somehow. It is a totally different world, and a better one. I have already mentioned competitive swimming with the Serpentine Club. There are other all-the-year-rounders—for example Hampstead, Bournemouth Spartans, and City of Rochester. During the summer, many club and open half-mile championships offer themselves. The Bedford river swim is one such. At the thousand-yard mark, is the Ulph Cup swum in the pool at Great Yarmouth. Next in range come open-sea Pier-to-Pier events such as at Brighton and Southsea. These are no more than random examples. At Dover, Weymouth and Plymouth there are 'breakwater' swims. Completion of these courses will certainly not achieve national recognition. But it ensures much local esteem. Poole and Exmouth have sea events.

At Windermere, there is a Cross-Lake of about a mile; at Dundee, the Tay Swim is 1¾ miles. Douglas Bay, I.O.M., is also 1¾ miles. The Clyde Firth—Gourock to Dunoon—is 2¾. A two–three miler is available at Whitby. So you can see that opportunity exists in most parts of the country. Inquire from members of your own club. Inquire from members of visiting clubs. The Bradford Long Distance Club and the Solent Club welcome members.

Naturally, I cannot cover—even briefly—every local swim in Britain. So those given merely indicate a pattern. Your own inquiries and common sense must elaborate the pattern to your own fancy. Venues for individual swims are as numerous as sea-gulls on the white cliffs of Dover. It's up to you to 'walk in search' of the legendary difficult feats in your own part of the kingdom. Then to destroy the legend for all time!

The big prizes and the big reputations may be associated with places hundreds of miles distant. But smaller events are available and local reputations to be made probably within the range of a bus ride. This is the normal way in to the 'big time'. But not the only way. A barrister friend of mine, John Kay-Mouat, asked advice one year. After which he swam daily with resolute aim and assiduity. In his first race he came third in the Otter Mile against distinguished opposition. In his second race, he swam into second place in the Windermere Championship. His third outing was a rough tidal crossing from Alderney to France through the notorious 'Alderney Race'. His fourth decisive act was to give up competitive swimming. The only marathon swimmer in all my experience to 'get off the line' when once hooked.

So choose the way into the first season. After that can come the Morecambe Inshore, Bala, and the A.S.A. Long Distance. The following season could bring the Channel within reach. But stop now and consider whether the great effort is worthwhile for its own pride of achievement alone. One particular overseas gentleman had not gone through this thought-stage before he knocked at the Channel secretary's door. 'How much,' he demanded from that long-suffering individual, 'does the Channel Swimming Association pay people to swim the Channel?'

The answer to that—in plain North Country—is nowt. Or to be exact, minus nowt. There is a certificate and a blazer badge for successful contestants. They pay for 'em both!

9

Lake Bala

> As the South-West that, blowing Bala Lake,
> Fills all the sacred Dee.
>
> TENNYSON

THERE is no need to study the direction of water flow in this lake. A former Poet-Laureate has done it for us. The inlet is at the south-west end and the outlet into the Dee is at the north-east. The flow is accelerated by south-west winds and retarded by the reverse. But I can tell you—which Tennyson neglected to do—that the movement is not very great: that is in any weather conditions suitable for swimming. The average of my swimming times for this course is the same as my still-water times for the same distance; other swimmers have confirmed this lack of current. Something less than ¼ knot has been the maximum encountered.

The Welsh championships of the British Long Distance Swimming Association for men and women, were inaugurated on 1st August 1960. To meet administrative convenience it is not quite an 'end to end' swim. The course starts from a promontory just offshore from the Glanllyn boathouse. From there the finishing point at the north-east extremity of the lake can just be seen. A straight line from start to finish scrapes clear of all projections of land and keeps the swimmer less than 250 yards away from the northern shore all the way; this close proximity naturally makes it a good race for spectators. The distance—as near as can be measured—is 3 miles and 80 yards.

In a short straight race, like this, tactics are quite unimportant. Steer straight and dig hard! Victory goes to him—as an early

American General said—'who gets thar fustest with the mostest'. So the end-product is an event on which it is absolutely perfect to cut one's marathoneering milk-teeth. Lake temperatures are within a degree or so of 16° C (61° F) during the first week in August.

The first recorded swim of the single length was by John Slater (Todmorden) on 31st July 1960; time—1 hour 24 min. The first two-way swim was by Arthur Endersby (Coventry) on 22nd May 1961. Brrrr! Time—3 hours 40 min. The Men's record is held by Malcolm Humphreys (Church Crookham) in 1 hour 15 min. 08 sec. The ladies' record is by Dilys Beynon (Sutton Coldfield) in 1 hour 26 min. 40 secs.

Just a tip or two in closing. The championships are held on August Bank Holiday Monday and Bala is a particularly attractive and popular holiday area. Therefore book accommodation early; I started three months beforehand one year and achieved no success. Besides the B.L.D.S.A. championships, successful individual swims are recognised by a certificate from Bala Urban District Council. That body appreciates at least seven days' notice, in order to send 'Application for Recognition' forms and arrange official observation.

By road, Bala is easily and enjoyably reached through magnificent country. It is 55 miles from Liverpool, 51 from Shrewsbury, and 205 from London. But don't ask me how to get there by rail. I drove a senior and most experienced British Railways inquiry clerk up the wall by putting exactly that question.

Men's Championship

1960 J. Smith (Rochdale) 1 h. 21 m. 03 s.
1961 M. Humphreys (Church Crookham) 1 h. 15 m. 08 s.
1962 W. J. Kennedy (Otter S.C.) 1 h. 17 m. 20 s.

Ladies' Championship

1960 Jean Oldman (Huddersfield) 2 h. 08 m.
1961 Dilys Beynon (Boldmere S.C.) 1 h. 26 m. 40 s.
1962 Susan Lynch (Stanmore) 1 h. 33 m. 30 s.

Junior Men

1962 K. Juba (Otter S.C.) 1 h. 33 m.

Junior Ladies

1962 Linda Bell (Pool-in-Wharfdale) 2 h. 30 m.

10

Amateur Swimming Association Championships

If you can force your heart and nerve and sinew,
To serve your turn long after they are gone,
And so hold on when there is nothing in you,
Except the Will which says to them 'Hold on!'

KIPLING

THIS race, for many years swum in the Thames, is comparatively short by marathon standards. But it is fiercely competitive and therefore demanding in the extreme. As an A.S.A. championship, the event carries much personal kudos for individuals and valuable 'national points' for their clubs; it thus attracts a top-class entry. Many competitors are more at home in sprint races—and it is for this reason that the pace of the leaders is inclined to be ill-judged and over-hot in the early stages. Old rivals try to 'bust' one another without thinking whether they are also going to bust themselves!

Because the Thames became somewhat unclean for swimming, the race went after World War II to the Serpentine. This venue proved unsatisfactory and the trophies went into the vaults for fifteen years. Finally the British Long Distance Swimming Association—aided by Yorkshireman Henry Dixon, the then President of the A.S.A.—managed to revive the event in 1961. At least, it was then given a trial run by the B.L.D.S.A. under 'action conditions' and proved popular and practicable. The A.S.A. championships were officially re-commenced the following year.

The course is now down the River Ouse at York. It starts at

Poppleton Lido and goes to the Blue Bridge, York. By virtue of being in confined waters, the event is capable of being held in all but the very worst weather. The same confined conditions, combined with the shallowness, ensure that in summer the temperature is reasonably high. In all normal summer circumstances, it should be appreciably warmer than the sea. Say—in July–August—about 18° C (64½° F).

A good average time for men is 2 hours. And for women 2 hours 10 min. The records are respectively—Jim Kennedy (Otter S.C.)—1 hour 36 min. 20 sec. Susan Lynch (Wealdstone)—1 hour 52 min. 30 sec.

Some of the greatest swimmers in the world have competed in this championship. The following Olympic gold-medallists have won it—Jack Jarvis (eight times), Paul Radmilovic (three times), Henry Taylor (three times); silver-medallist Jack Hatfield (seven times); bronze-medallists E. P. Peter and T. S. Battersby. International swimmers, Green, Cavill, Springfield, Champion, Pascoe, Milton, Deane and Hale have also held the trophy.

Amongst such a galaxy of talent, a choice of the greatest must be a personal opinion. But with four gold medals spread over three Olympics, 'Raddy' Radmilovic is hard to surpass. In 1961 I saw a curiously confident old-timer plunge into my local pool and reel off a quarter mile in six minutes. This proved to be Raddy taking his lunchtime exercise. He was then aged 72 or so. There's hope for you chaps yet!

For full details of all winners—men and women—the A.S.A. Handbook should be consulted.

11

Coniston Water

With the earth and the sky and the water, re-made like a casket of gold.

YEATS

SWUM in the late afternoon sun, Coniston is an unforgettably beautiful experience. I came to the locality semi-accidentally during an afternoon drive through Lakeland; it was positively impossible to pass by without adding the jewel to my 'collection'. The Water has this distinct advantage of being the right size for one to play 'off the cuff' without elaborate preparation. The views of wooded foreshore and the unfolding of the fell scenery is spectacularly rewarding. The sightseeing appeal cannot be better emphasised than by my scandalous swim-time of 3 hours 5 minutes. Too much looking: not enough working.

Here are the vital statistics—Coniston's, not mine. First its position—23 miles from Keswick, 11½ from Windermere. Depth ranges from a couple of feet in a few weedy places to 184 feet. Overall length is 5½ miles. Swim course begins from a boat pier on west side of lake at High Nibthwaite (south end) and goes to the extreme shore at the north end. Or vice versa. This distance is 5 miles and about 700 yards. Temperatures are similar to Windermere—which see. But being smaller and shallower, it is slightly more susceptible to fluctuations of adjacent land temperatures, i.e. it will be a degree or so warmer than Windermere in hot weather and correspondingly less in cold conditions. The predominant winds are westerly, but this aspect is relatively unimportant. The lake is nowhere more than a half-mile wide, and

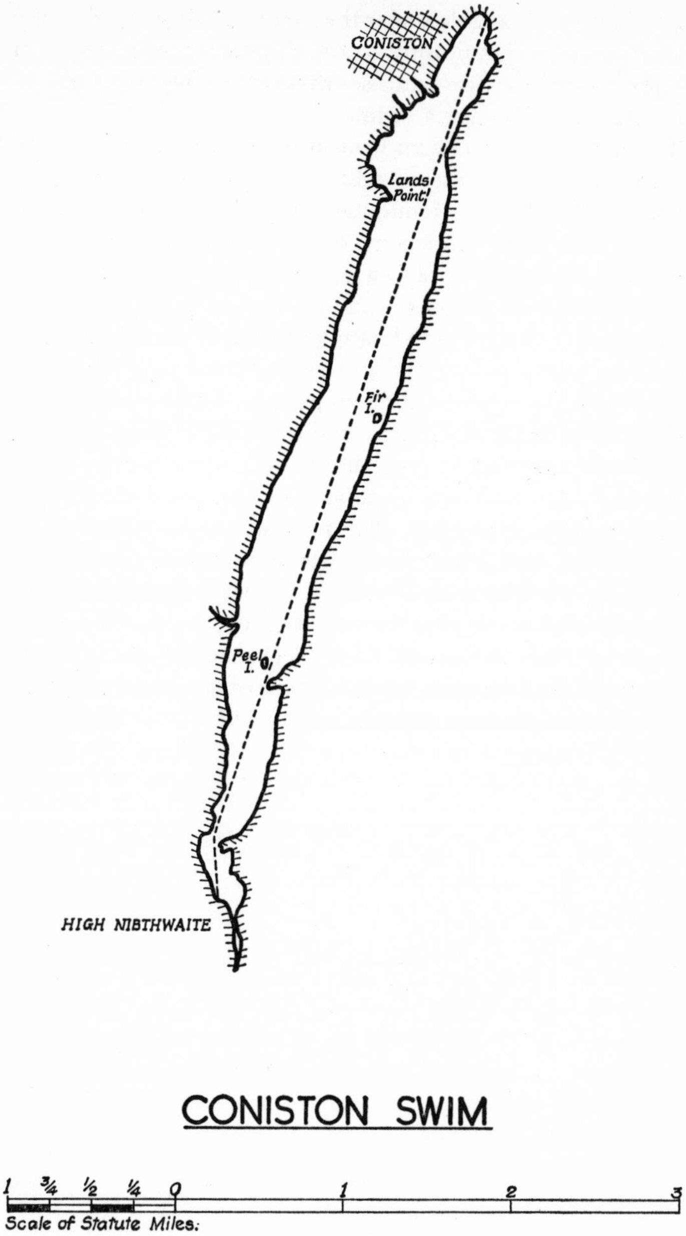
CONISTON
Lands Point
Fir I.
Peel I.
HIGH NIBTHWAITE
CONISTON SWIM
1 ¾ ½ ¼ 0 1 2 3
Scale of Statute Miles.

much shelter is available under the lee of one shore or the other—without adding significantly to the distance. Strong winds from the north-north-east or south-south-west are the only ones which can effectively sabotage a swim.

The first person to swim Coniston was Jack Kerwin of Bradford in 1958. The present record is held by Bryan Finlay of Coventry in 2 hours 33 minutes, 56 seconds. Ladies' record is held by Veronica Anderson of Warrington; time—3 hours 55 minutes. First two-way swim was in 1961 by Derek Gill of Bradford; time—8 hours 56 minutes.

Boats are obtainable at a boating station on the west side of the lake about one mile from the north end. Which reminds me of one other reason for my slow time on passage. I said at the beginning that it was an impromptu dip—and therefore it was impossible to obtain local oarsmen at such short notice. So—for the first time in her life—my wife took command of a motor-boat. At times it headed perilously towards shallow water and indignity—if not disaster; only by my shouted instructions was it turned away at hair-raisingly last moments. At other times it shaved close across my path at full speed, like a promotion-conscious destroyer captain showing off to his admiral at Fleet manœuvres. We successfully tamed the boat after a half an hour or so. But it was exciting while it lasted. Both in the boat and out of it.

12

Ullswater

Long distance swimming is an excellent way of seeing delightful scenery. And in addition it's most cleansing.

DOCTOR LEON WALKDEN

THE sentiment expressed above by a dedicated swimming doctor is, like many medical pronouncements, a mixture of the aesthetic and the hygienic! But it is not universally correct, as witness the changing colour of one's bathwater after a swim in the Thames or Lough Neagh. But in respect to Ullswater, the quotation is entirely appropriate. The water is so good that the Manchester Corporation endeavoured, in 1962, to acquire it as a drinking water reservoir. The scenery ranges from picturesque to majestic. I am not sure how dead that proposed Manchester take-over bid is; better 'collect' this swim while there is yet time.

Geographically, Ullswater is one of the eastern lakes, roughly midway between Windermere and Penrith. The village of Glenridding, at the south end of the lake, is 13 miles from the former. Pooley Bridge, at the north end, is 6 miles from Penrith. Several boating stations exist in the height of the season; one at the south-west corner by Glenridding seems to work longer and more regularly than the others. There is a pleasure steamer in which non-dedicated swimming friends can embark. In this, it is possible to carry out an up-down-up voyage while the swimmer plays his 'one-up'. I recommend this for all spectators except the devoted small-boat enthusiast.

The swim course is now well established as starting at the steamer pier, Glenridding, and finishing at the steamer pier,

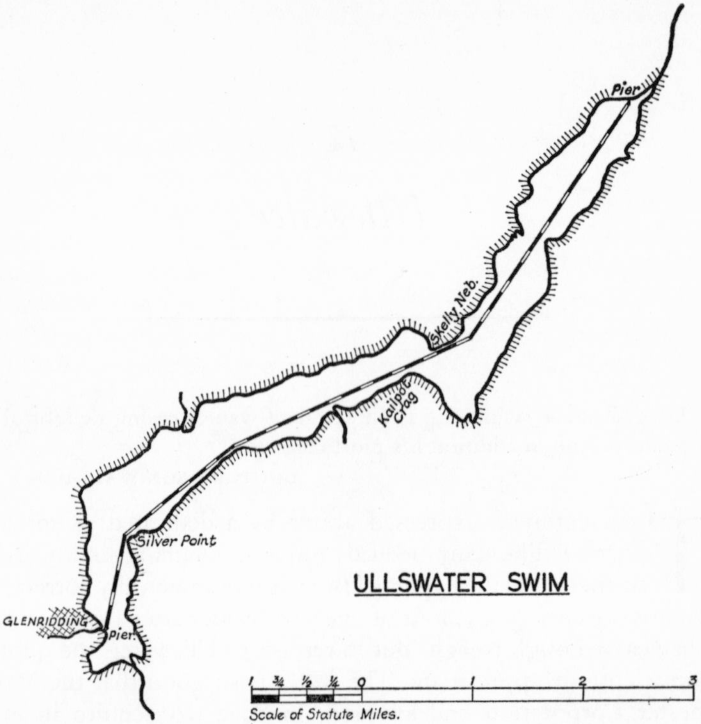

Pooley Bridge. Or vice versa. Navigationally perfect courses make the distance 7 miles and 100 yards. But more practically, it is 7¼ miles. There are three main courses. From Glenridding Pier to Silver Point is roughly due north for just under a mile; then roughly east-north-east for 3¼ miles to Skelly Nab; thence north-east all the way home.

Since the lake is nowhere greatly more than a thousand yards wide, there is abundant shelter; the swim *can* therefore be carried out in almost any weather. But the very crookedness of the reaches puts much distance on for shelter-seeking swimmers. Unless time is all-important, it is best to wait for more moderate weather. Gales cool the water down by vigorous mixing and by surface heat-losses. Normal temperatures are naturally—by virtue of proximity—akin to Coniston and Windermere. So are the winds. The lake is comparatively shallow (one deep spot of 205 feet) and, so far as surface swimmers are concerned, virtually weed-free.

The first known conquest of this stretch of water was by Jack Kerwin (Bradford) in 1959; time—4 hours 49 minutes. The first two-way success came from Ruth Oldham (London University and Grange-over-Sands) in 1961; time 10 hours 40 minutes. Records are—*Men.* Geoffrey Wilson (Bradford) in 3 hours 40 minutes. *Ladies.* Dorothy Perkins (Bradford) in 4 hours 18 minutes. The reason for Yorkshire predominance—or partial predominance—is that the Bradford Long Distance Swimming Club now holds its annual championship over this course.

13

The Windermere Swim

Be ye strong therefore and let not your hands be weak; for your work shall be rewarded.

CHRONICLES

FOR many years Lake Windermere has been an irresistible target for marathon swimmers. It thoroughly deserves the highest esteem because it is one of the most arduous swims in the United Kingdom. Conquerors join a very *élite* band of swimmers; these only are entitled to wear the blazer badge of the British Long Distance Swimming Association. And that is a much cherished reward for being strong in purpose as well as in muscle.

By map measurement, the length of the course is apparently nine and three-quarter miles. But although rulers and pencils have no difficulty in navigating close inshore, swimmers do not find it so easy; they need three or four feet of water to navigate in. For that reason corners cannot be cut as sharply as the map suggests; the shortest practicable distance is actually just over ten miles. Inevitable navigational errors, and unavoidable wiggles, further raise the distance to the most popularly quoted figure of ten and a half miles. There has always been much debate about the actual distance swum, and the average of the foregoing is the nearest possible approach to an accurate answer. No doubt swimmers, trainers, journalists, and raconteurs will continue to pick their own favourite! The northern mark is a boating pier 50 yards north of Waterhead Steamer Pier; the southern mark another boating pier 100 yards north of Lakeside Steamer Pier.

Since James Foster of Oldham (and later New Zealand) first

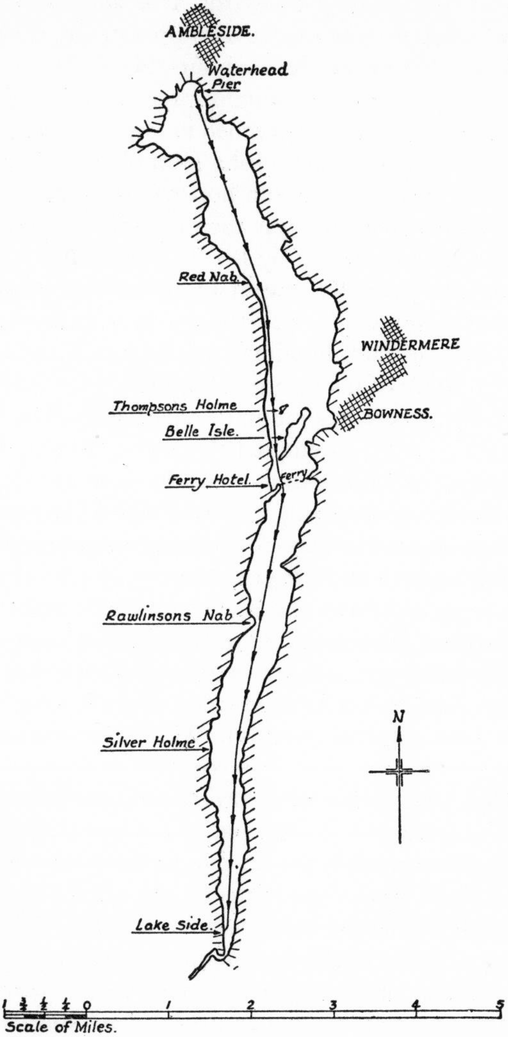

Windermere Swim.

conquered Windermere in 1911 there has been a remarkable improvement in swimming standards. It is an interesting sidelight on that advance to note that several present-day contestants have halved Foster's time of eleven hours twenty-nine minutes. Yet Foster in his era reigned quite supreme. Although there were many challengers no one succeeded in even completing the course until twenty-two years later. John Humphrey of Preston then, in 1933, lowered the record to ten hours four minutes. For a breaststroke swimmer that time was then remarkably good. Next year, of course, Charles Daly set up his shattering time that was to last for twenty-one years. (He swam a four-beat crawl with sixty arm strokes to the minute.) He held the record of six hours twenty-two minutes from 1934 until Oldman pipped it in 1955. As a matter of fact, the breaking of his record at long last, gave fresh stimulus to aspirants. They were beginning to regard it as quite impregnable. Captain Webb never attempted this swim, although he did give an exhibition in Millerground Bay in July 1877. Major Jason Zirganos of the Greek Army swam the lake no less than four times in one year—1951. The prize for good attendance comes, I believe, to me with seven lengths notched up.

Pilotage up and down the lake can be done most efficiently by one's boatman. Nevertheless, personal knowledge of the route adds tenfold interest, and well repays previous map-study. More important, it allows the boat, for long periods, to follow behind in its most advantageous position. When the boat is abreast the swimmer, there is a light but constant bow-wave disturbance. Such minor interference when protracted becomes a major annoyance and distraction. If the boat is stationed ahead, a similarly annoying disturbance is set up due to the wake turbulence. Not only are these things upsetting to the mind, but they lead to mechanically inefficient and fatiguing stroking. A boat following behind, is well out of the way of interference; it is also in an ideal position to keep watch on the swimmer and, if necessary, to effect rescue. On one occasion an oarsman rowing abreast chopped my neck with his oar three times; this also tends to detract from one's equable outlook.

Passage times along the course can be checked at several conspicuous points. A few selected distances are tabulated below. The figures in brackets indicate the times that a swimmer should take at a pace of one and three-quarter miles per hour. The place names appear on all good maps. As I first swam the lake from north to south the figures go that way. But it is not difficult to reverse them!

Waterhead Pier to Red Nab is	2·3 miles (1 hr. 18 min.)
Red Nab to Tommy Holme is	1·8 miles (1 hr. 3 min.)
Tommy Holme to Ferry is	0·8 mile (0 hr. 27 min.)
Ferry to Rawlinson's Nab is	1·7 miles (0 hr. 59 min.)
Rawlinson's Nab to Silver Holme is	1·6 miles (0 hr. 56 min.)
Silver Holme to Lakeside (keeping west of steamer track) is	1·9 miles (1 hr. 5 min.)

That makes a total of 10·1 miles in five hours forty-eight minutes. That is slower than the record but is a good time to aim for. Before sprint swimmers turn up their noses at this speed, there are some factors to consider. No lines on the bottom for straight steering and no turns and push-offs. Grease—if applied—has a retarding effect. Open water is often rough, and any stops for food naturally decrease average speed.

Feeding stops are, of course, most important factors in the make-up of every long swim. Any possible economy in passage time is most valuable. For that reason, pre-race feeding should be as late as possible before the start. This may not entirely obviate the need for feeding stops on passage, but will certainly reduce the frequency. Medical opinion varies about pre-race feeding. Dr. F. W. Hogarth, medical officer to the Morecambe Cross Bay Swim Association is probably more knowledgeable on this subject than most. He believes that, provided the meal is not excessive, it is in no way dangerous for a fit and experienced marathoneer to swim quietly after a meal. No more so, in fact, than a housewife walking to the High Street with a shopping-bag after lunch. A championship race is slightly different; it is as well to have at least an hour's gap between meal and commencement.

Whether feeding stops are necessary at all, in a six-hour swim, is a matter of conjecture. Workers in several walks of life can manage a hard six-hour stint without refreshment. Perhaps not so many nowadays as before, but it is still by no means uncommon. Feeding stops are certainly a great mental comfort, because they provide something to look forward to. They are physically comforting, too, while they last, but starting again detracts a great deal from their pleasure. Re-starting takes a tremendous effort of will, and no little time and energy before the previous rhythm can be regained. For efficiency I recommend the minimum number of stops. One stop after three hours, to split the swim in two, is perhaps the best compromise, but if one stop is still insufficient for individual cases, the remaining time could again be split similarly. Whatever the decision, one should at least start with a good long uninterrupted stretch of swimming. Methods of feeding and types of food are discussed later in the chapter on Channel training.

Interference from current is negligible, although several small streams do enter the Lake. These gradually flow towards the outlet at the South but—even after heavy rainfall—the resultant southerly drift is hardly perceptible. In dry warm weather, twenty or thirty yards an hour would be a generous estimate of assistance to a swimmer. Even light southerly winds will, however, more than cancel the slight effect of current. So much land shelter is available that a championship has been successfully held in moderate gale conditions. Whichever way the wind blows, the landlocked lagoon west of Belle Island gives nearly half an hour of calm-water swimming. It is first-class stand-easy nearly in the middle of the course. As a point of interest, the actual middle of the swim is just south of the Ferry.

Lake swimming is an invigorating and refreshing change from sea competition. Progress is necessarily smoother because there is insufficient length for a swell to build up; there is also much shelter even from short choppiness. Something of interest is always to be seen, and that greatly adds to the enjoyment. I happened one day to be talking to John Slater (a former record holder) about it. 'Wonderfully interesting scenery,' he said. Recalling memories of lush green woods, formidable peaks, long vistas and picturesque islands, I heartily agreed. But when he went on to talk about boulders, weed, dark patches and eels, it began to appear as though he and I had been on different swims. In further conversation it became quite evident that we were definitely at cross-purposes. For while I had enjoyed the orthodox landscape—albeit from an unorthodox level—he had worn goggles and revelled in the underwater views throughout. After which I took to goggles myself and now enjoy the best of both worlds.

There used to be no organising authority for this swim. But since 1957 the British Long Distance Swimming Association has staged annual Championships for men and women. They also recognise and issue certificates for individual swims. When taking part in B.L.D.S.A. events boats are arranged by the Association. And in recent years—due to the drive and zeal of William Anderson of Warrington—an increasing number of trained pilot-life-savers have become available. These facilities much ease the burden on the swimmers themselves.

On individual swims I have always hired a motor-boat from the Bowness Bay Boating Company. Bowness is half-way down the lake, and it is very convenient to start from there. The boat trip to the start at either end allows time for taking water temperatures, for on-the-course study, and for pre-swim preparations. The trip back at the finish is long enough for rest, recuperation, and leisurely dressing before arrival. The boatmen have made their living throughout many seasons on Lake Windermere; they therefore have a vast fund of valuable local knowledge and of interesting stories about past swimmers.

They are of great assistance on the swim. Besides their watermanship and navigation, they 'know all the right people'. It was as the result of a friendly hail that the Ferry courteously gave me right of way. That very civil gesture saved much time and energy. The passenger steamers, too, were informed by 'bush telegraph', about my attempt on the record. They, in turn, obliged by giving me a wide berth; in that way wash and bow-wave gave minimum trouble. The captains of the two ships in service gave an encouraging toot on the syren and a friendly wave each time they passed. They completed about three trips apiece whilst I laboured away at one.

Despite all this there are sturdy individualist swimmers who prefer to get their friends to row. This is satisfactory if one has friends who like rowing. Mine don't. Rowing-boats can be obtained from Bowness and from both ends of the lake.

Windermere has the reputation of being inordinately cold. That is unfair. In winter it does occasionally freeze, whereas the sea customarily does not. But in prolonged sunny periods in summer it may rise above sea temperature; the highest I have known is 20° C (68° F). That temperature is only slightly below indoor swimming-pool standards, and will hardly be excelled anywhere else in Britain. The bottom water in such a deep lake must always remain cold, but only the top three feet affect swimmers—except when gales give the whole volume a thorough mixing. In settled weather, however, the top layer reacts fairly rapidly to average air temperatures. Thus if the average air temperature over several days is 15½° C (60° F) the surface water will be somewhere around that figure too. It is important to realise that one singling sizzling hot day will have very little effect. In sunny weather it will be warmer close inshore than in the middle; in cloudy, rainy weather there is little to choose. Compared with lake temperatures, the incoming becks will be warmer in warm weather, and colder in cold. The coldest, personally experienced, in the recognised swimming season was on 7th September 1957. That day, water temperature averaged 12½° C (54½° F).

This type of swim has great advantages. Because of almost still water, all results have to come from the swimmer himself; canny pilots cannot find favourable tidal streams. For that reason it gives better and fairer comparison between performances of various long-distance swimmers than any other. Strength and direction of wind does influence performances, but it would not be beyond the ingenuity of man to compensate for that. A table of wind force and direction co-efficients could be calculated; that in turn could be tabulated to give a time-correction to apply in all conditions. The actual time plus or minus the corrections would give a fair time for comparison between rivals who had swum in different weather. Perhaps on the whole though, it is more English to permit the slight element of luck which now exists. Incidentally wind directions and strengths are notoriously fickle on inland waters; so many bending and intensifying influences are present. But my analysis of wind conditions in the Irish Channel (which see) will serve as a very reasonable rough guide to Lakeland expectations also.

In spring, and early summer, Windermere could be an excellent training for the Channel. Fairly rough water would be obtained on occasions and the temperature could be Channelish. Later, of course, would-be Channel swimmers must train in the actual lash and splash of salt water.

Windermere is a stern hard marathon test, but to the real enthusiast a pleasurable voyage. Some not quite wholehearted marathoneer may possibly contemplate an easy prestige trip. Mr. Punch's advice to persons contemplating marriage is equally applicable to them. Don't. Other marathoneers who *are* wholehearted may even consider doing it both ways non-stop. Philip Rising (Rotherham) who later became president of B.L.D.S.A. was, in 1952, the first person to succeed in this. To date only four people have copied his example.

Records are:

Championship Men	Gerald Forsberg	5 hrs.	19 min.
Championship Ladies	Susan Lynch	5 hrs.	37 min.
Individual Professional	Helge Jensen	4 hrs.	58 min.
Individual Two-Way Men	Gerald Forsberg	12 hrs.	57 min.
Individual Two-Way Ladies	Jean Adams	15 hrs.	09 min.

14

Lough Neagh

Men will not win battles unless their training has been hard.

FIELD-MARSHAL VISCOUNT MONTGOMERY

LOUGH NEAGH is a 'natural' for the ambitious marathon swimmer. Accommodation is cheap. The people are enthusiastic. The chances of getting a swimmable day in a fortnight's holiday are good and the food is magnificent. This is the only U.K. swim which goes through three counties—which is good for lineshooting. But take a tip from me, this is not an ordinary swim, it is a battle against nature; the area is notorious for sudden storms and severe squalls. Then—having taken my tip—take another one from the great Field Marshal.

The Lough is the largest enclosed stretch of water in the British Isles. It is roughly 20 miles long by 10 miles wide, and covers 153 square miles. In poorish visibility, it is possible to be out of sight of land for considerable periods. Through being so large it sometimes whips up quickly to sea roughness but it equally quickly calms down again after a blow. Depth along the swim route is between 20 and 50 feet. Water is dark brown and unpalatable. There is a plague of lake-flies but these affect boats' crews more than deeply immersed swimmers. When I swam it the temperature of water averaged 16° C (60½° F); this is probably slightly more than normal summer temperature. Wind directions and strengths are roughly similar to those I have tabulated in the Irish Channel chapter. But as stated above there are occasional vicious local tantrums.

From Maghery (bottom left-hand corner) to Antrim (top right-

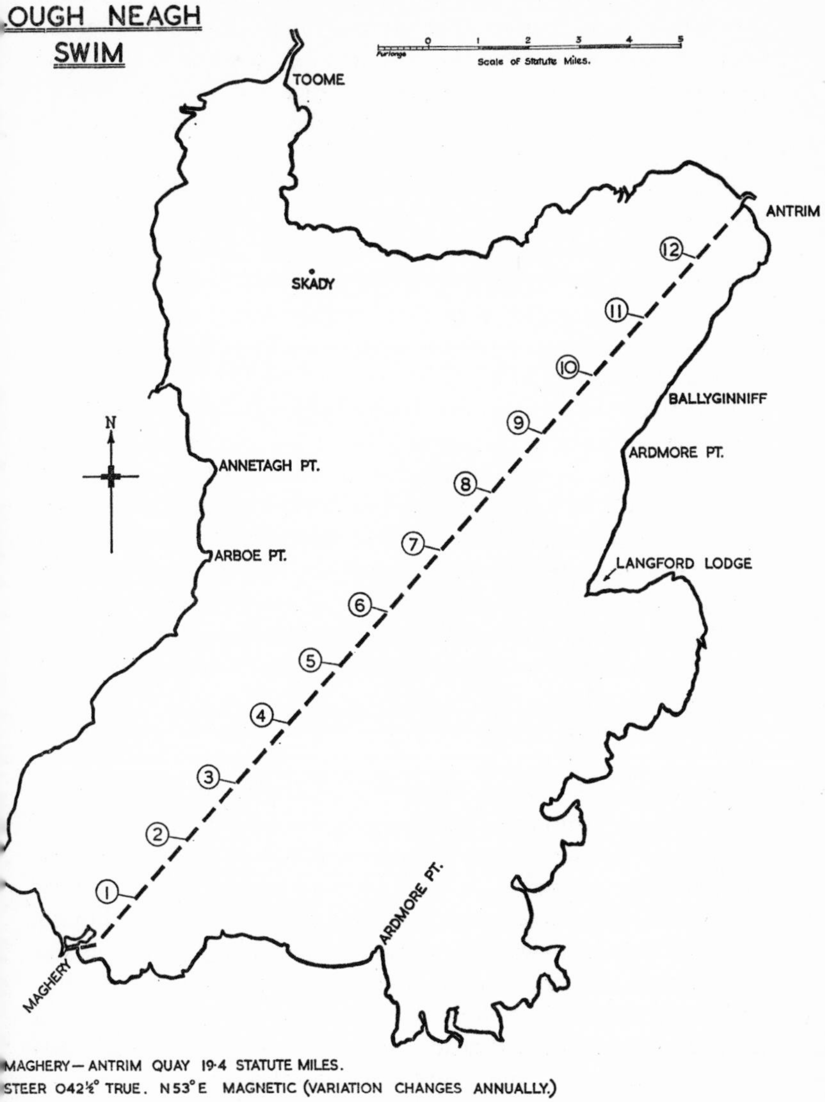

Inaugural record swim 1959. Figures in circles indicate hours on passage.

hand corner) is 19·4 land miles. Like other swim distances, that must be qualified as the shortest distance on a calm day; it assumes no swim-wiggles, perfect boat steering, and no wind to blow the boat sideways away from the swimmer. As weather is rarely perfect and human beings never, the distance always tops 20 miles. The other diagonal looks longer but this is an optical illusion. That's my story and I'm sticking to it!

Pleasure boats are non existent, so hire of a fisherman's boat is essential. There are none too many of these either. Because the best swimming season is also the best fishing season, a fisherman requires adequate compensation for switching tasks. A figure of around £25 will suffice at present, perhaps less if you are a good haggler: that is for motor-boat with crew. Presumably one could borrow a rowing-boat for less.

Legendary Finn MacCoul, Irish god-king, hurled a lump of earth far out to sea. The earth became the Isle of Man and the hole left behind became Lough Neagh. From that early date until 1959, nobody had ever swum it. Channel swimmer Mercedes Gleitz tried it in the 'twenties. The 1956 Butlin champion, Jack McClelland was unsuccessful in early July 1959. I succeeded in mid-July, and Jack also succeeded in August. My time—13 hours 12 minutes. Jack's time—greatly incapacitated with cramp—was 17 hours 58 minutes. That is the present state of play; two men, no women.

Local swimmer Jim Bradford of Lurgen had twice tried to get *across* without success. In 1959 fortune smiled on him also. He breast-stroked across nine miles in nine hours. He is thinking of switching his swim-axis lengthways some time. One other thing pleased me tremendously. It concerns one of the independent observers on my swim—Bobbie McVeigh, of Crumlin. Inspired by a wonderful summer and by all the activity on his native Lough, he jumped in and swam seven hours on the breast. This is just one example of how contagious the marathon 'bug' is. Congratulations and hard luck, Bobbie! It is a bug from which practically no one ever recovers. Perhaps—we hope—these local boys may notch up numbers 3 and 4 on the lengthways route.

Admiralty Chart No. 5074. Lough Neagh.

15

Loch Lomond

The bonnie bonnie banks o' Loch Lomon'.

ANON

LOCH LOMOND is the largest enclosed loch in Scotland with an area of 27 square miles. The northern extremity of the recognised swim course is the beach at Ardlui adjacent to the Ardlui Hotel. The southern extremity is the beach at Balloch fairly close westward of the B.R. steamer pier. This latter place is no more than 18 miles from Glasgow and one gets to the other end by 27 miles of driving along the winding lochside road.

Prior to 1959 no one had swum the length of the Loch. Tradition has it that Rob Roy the noted highland freebooter swam across once about 1700—presumably to avoid capture. A flurry of correspondence in the local papers disclosed no other names. In 1959 the British Long Distance Swimming Association conceived a championship race. Naturally the swim was said to be impossible by the pundits; every new swim is greeted by the same declaration! After the event many thousands of words were written, and I have cuttings ranging from British National newspapers to the *Gibraltar Chronicle* and *South China News*.

However, since I competed in the event my own reportage may be more factual. An extract of what I subsequently wrote in *Swimming Times* follows. It is of historical interest; it also serves to point out typical conditions in a summer that was neither downright bad nor downright good. At the time of writing, no other man has completed the course so my time of 15 hours 31 minutes remains a record. See the Loch Lomond chartlet

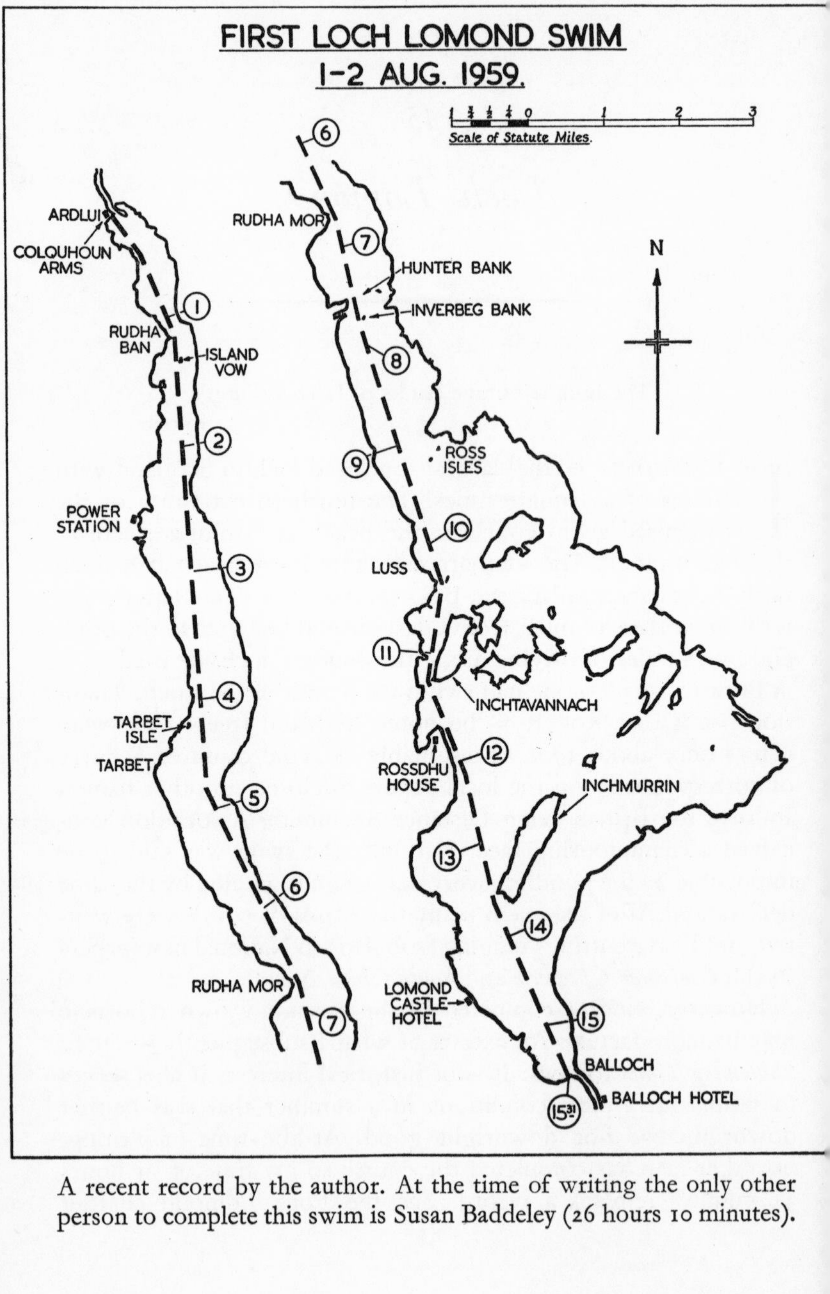

A recent record by the author. At the time of writing the only other person to complete this swim is Susan Baddeley (26 hours 10 minutes).

for the actual course taken. The best Admiralty Chart, by the way, is No. 2021. Loch Lomond.

'This event—if every course is impeccable and every corner cut to the maximum—is over a distance of 21·6 miles. But, because of the night swimming factor and the strong cross-wind, accurate navigation was impracticable. It would therefore be far from exaggerating to count the distance as 23 miles; most newspapers plumped for 24. The start from Ardlui was at 11.35 p.m. Saturday, 1st August 1959, and daybreak was not until about five hours later. Between these times water temperature was around 14½° C (57–9° F) with occasional small but painful patches of intenser cold. Air temperature dropped to 10° C (50° F). It was at this stage that my old Huddersfield rival, Trevor Smith, seized up and had to withdraw. Much later in the day both air and water rose reluctantly to 16½° C (62° F).

'Until 8.30 a.m. there were no more than ripples to contend with. But at that time the wind began to freshen across the course from right to left; it continued to do so throughout the day. For a considerable distance it was possible to hug the coast and gain a little shelter; this relief was welcome despite the extra mile or so it put on. The last five miles were different; there was nothing to do here except brave the elements and bash right across the wide exposed basin with viciously cresting waves. This final unkindness caused the withdrawal of Channel swimmer June Gilbert after nearly nineteen hours' swimming and within clear sight of the finish at Balloch. She is an indomitable girl and in calmer weather would undoubtedly have completed the course. A much deserved special certificate was awarded to her for completing 19·1 miles.

'This swim is fractionally harder than the Channel. Water is less buoyant; air and water temperatures are less. My time of 15 hours 31 minutes for this event compared with my Channel time of 13 hours 33 minutes supports that view. So does June Gilbert's failure. It is a mile longer and in still unhelpful water I count it as my sternest test to date. Incidentally, Mrs. Dorothy Brown meticulously timed my swim to tenths of a second. During the night section she made history by being the first A.S.A. time-keeper to sleep while officiating, or, anyway, to admit it!'

After one year had elapsed another onslaught on the giant loch was made. This time there was no championship but a pair of sturdy individualists entered the water.

Dr. H. Baddeley (Medical Adviser to the B.L.D.S.A.) and daughter Susan together attempted the swim in early August 1960. Susan succeeded in 26 hours 10 minutes. Although time endurance records are not recognised, it is worthy of passing note that no British woman swimmer has been in the water longer. Dr. Baddeley accompanied her for 21 of those miles before being taken out. On the part of both swimmers, this was determined, dogged, plucky swimming. It deserves far more than this brief mention. The worst hour—said Susan—was just before dawn. From experience, I concur. Towering mountains, black uninviting water, excruciatingly cold patching, and chill winds down the Highland slopes. At this time Lomond's banks are definitely *un*bonny. Press-interviewed later, it transpired that dawn morale was (*sic*) sustained by a supporter in the boat. He played the guitar and sang—time after time—'Itsy-bitsy, teeny-weeny, yellow polka-dot bikini.' Thus warned, I shall certainly and very thoroughly search *my* boats for stowaway guitarists.

After a winter's consideration and hindsight I jotted down a few notes. My opinion is still unchanged so I put them below for the use of those 'with serious intentions'.

Route. The one we used is the best for either north-bound or south-bound swimmers. It any calm water exists at all, it is usually on this side of the Loch. You *might* cut off a few yards in distance by going further east but so little as not to be worth while.

Time of year. Mid-August produces the maximum water temperatures anywhere in Britain—except in freak summers early or late. 'Some time in August' is the best planning assumption.

Cold patches. Frequent in the northerly half of the Loch, scarce in the other half.

Currents. Negligible. In enclosed waters, what goes one way in one place must go another way in another place. It cannot get out and go anywhere so it all cancels out in the end. The best plan is to ignore water movement and if there does happen to be an extra half-mile to do at the end it is just hard luck. Scientists with scale models might be able to calculate something but there is no practical rule-of-thumb method. It is of course foolish to swim against any strength of wind.

16

Loch Ness

Read not to contradict and confute, nor to believe and take for granted, nor to find talk and discourse, but to weigh and consider.
FRANCIS BACON

LOCH NESS is a most distinct challenge to top swimmers. But two things ensure that it will never vie in popularity with, say, the Channel. First is the comparative inaccessibility and second is the extreme cold by U.K. standards. Fort Augustus (at the end furthest from the Arctic) is 541 miles from London; it is even further from the outpost of empire where I am stationed. The great depth of the loch—754 feet in places—ensures that the bottom layers of water hardly vary in temperature winter or summer; approximately this is 5° C (41° F). This would not affect swimmers if that water stayed tidily down below. But at many places up-wellings bring this abhorrent stuff to the surface—fortunately, it mixes slightly with other layers on the way. As a result, one may reasonably expect the following August state: warm spots (*sic*) of 13½° C (56½° F) and cold spots of 10° C (50° F). Transition is sharply defined; on my own swims, I measured a 2° C change in 10 yards. This patchwork quilt of temperature makes it difficult to attain the desirable mental detachment.

Length is 19·4 nautical and 22·6 statute miles. The course from Fort Augustus to Lochend is so straight that on clear days one can see most of the way ahead. Breadth is astonishingly uniform throughout—between ¾ and 1 mile. Steep mountains on each side make a kind of wind-tunnel which bends and intensifies the wind. On a bad day, the steep waves driving up the loch are easily

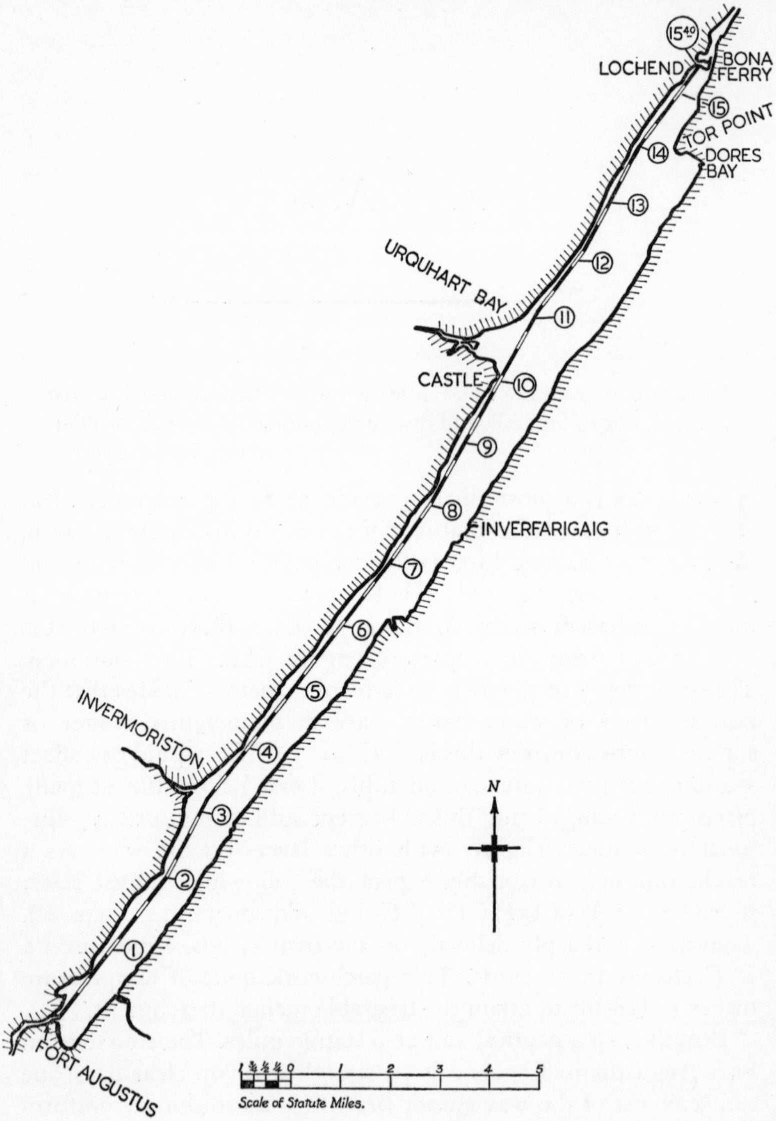

LOCH NESS SWIM

equivalent to open sea conditions, and bring up the cold water to the top for a frigid mixing. In August, the *direction* of the wind should be satisfactory for a south–north swim threequarters of the time and the *strength* satisfactory for half the time. That is according to statistics. During my stay in the area, it was too rough throughout and blew frequently from the reverse direction. The water, although pure enough for drinking, is peat-brown. Through goggles, the maximum visibility is about two feet. Very gloomy!

Last, the Monster. There are believers and disbelievers. I belong to the former—there are too many sworn statements from reputable persons to disbelieve. August has most sightings but this may be because of more people then about the lochside. Eighty-five per cent of sightings are before 9.30 a.m. I have read seven reports of seeing it on the shores. Nobody has recorded an attack on a human in the water since A.D. 565, and on land since 1527. But when swimming, I did not feel particularly reassured. One feels that there has to be a first time for everything.

A soldier swam across, fleeing from the opposing army, in 1746. The Roman Catholic Abbot of Fort Augustus repeated the feat in 1938. Then nowt until 21st August 1961 when I swam across and back in 47 minutes. Next day, on a training spin, I covered exactly five miles from Fort Augustus Pier to Invermoriston Pier in 2 hours 50 minutes. In 1962 Derek Turner was forced to abandon an end-to-end attempt due to low temperatures and roughness; he had done nearly 12 miles in 11 hours 30 minutes. That's all so far.

The best Admiralty Chart is 1791 (Caledonian Canal). price 7s. 6d.

17

The Morecambe Inshore Swim

Time and tide will wait for no man, saith the adage. But all men have to wait for time and tide.

CHARLES DICKENS

THIS race is one in which brainwork really plays a large part. To my mind it is an absolute 'connoisseurs piece' for nice judgement can easily snatch victory from a faster but less thoughtful swimmer. A good average time in which to win the event is sixty to seventy minutes; so, although the actual length of course is nearly three and a half miles, it cannot quite rank as a fully blown marathon. Nevertheless, it is an extraordinarily interesting affair which all prospective marathoneers would do well to utilise in preparation for bigger events. Fast milers, in particular, will find it an excellent stepping-stone. And on the theory of 'more races the better' even every established marathoneer should try to include it in his training schedule.

The organisers put on several heats and a final in every season. Occasionally weather intervenes, but—being a close inshore swim—there is partial shelter from north-east and south-west, besides complete shelter from east and south-east. Winds from other directions should—according to the form book—rarely reach the prohibitive force during the July/August season. There is therefore a good chance of a completely satisfactory annual programme. In theory that chance should be about eighty per cent, and in practice the calculation seems to be borne out. On really rough occasions—to avoid disappointment to the assembled athletes—the final is staged in the local swimming stadium. And, although pool swimming completely scuppered my own chances on one occasion, it was extremely rewarding to obtain accurate lap-times of those taking part. So that readers can assess their own, or their protégés, chance of success, I am going to summarise those performances. An opportunity of timing distance swimmers in 'action conditions' occurs so rarely as to be very worthy of note.

Gordon Hill (Oxford) and Raymond Holmes (Lancaster) swam neck-and-neck to gain A.S.A. gold medals over the first mile of the course. They both passed the mile post in twenty-four minutes forty-five seconds, a pace that even many club-standard milers would be proud to achieve. Still swimming side by side until the last length, they finished the two-and-a-half-mile course in one hour four minutes and one second. Holmes just managed to produce a fraction extra to draw away from Hill at the finish. A race of almost exactly similar calibre was swum again in 1961; this time Holmes was beaten by fellow-clubman Brian Winn.

However, there is plenty of encouragement for the 'not so fast'. A competitor needs the ability to swim thirty-minute miles endlessly, the speed to produce occasionally a twenty-six minute mile, and an intelligent knowledge of tides. Then, especially in the sea, he has a chance of being well up with the leaders in any race. Even if he falls short of these qualifications he may still complete the course with distinction. No navigational difficulties arise with this event, because every swimmer is provided with a pilot; incidentally, the pilots' and swimmers' names 'come out of the hat' and are thus fairly paired off. Unlike maritime commercial practice in big ports it is not permitted to nominate a 'choice' pilot.

Tide runs fastest in deep channels and slowest on the shoals. There may even be weak reverse currents on the edge of some channels. Some strips of ebb tide start running before high water. But local knowledge is of tremendous value and these worries are best left entirely to the pilots; they can be relied on to navigate to best advantage. Although, as a master mariner, I know a fair amount about tidal phenomena, I would require two or three years' practical study to be able to challenge the pilots' knowledge of this particular locality. (Or much comprehensive theoretical study of a set of aerial photographs taken at short intervals throughout a complete tidal cycle.) Apart from their tremendous personal enthusiasm, there are also pilots' prizes as added inducements to skill. One can be assured that they are using every sinew and every particle of grey matter in picking the best courses. To go to the Green Street landing-stage for the pilots' heated post-mortem of every race, is to know that they, at least, have put one hundred per cent effort into the contest.

But the most important factor in this race is outside the pilots' brief. I make no apology for returning to the subject of pace; in all races it is important, in this particular race it is *all-important*. That is because tide (and, to a lesser extent, wind) can reduce the duration of this event to under an hour or increase it to over ninety minutes. That is an important enough point, but the really vital aspect is that tide can treat every swimmer in the same race differently. Many eyebrows—but not the pilots'—will undoubtedly be raised at that statement. It needs careful elaboration and it shall have it. By use of that knowledge I reduced my own time from ninety-seven minutes to sixty-six minutes in a fortnight. That is the real proof of the pudding, the explanation follows.

There are two factors out of human control and one within it. Centuries ago, tides were proved beyond the powers of even illustrious King Canute; they remain the same masterful elements today, and winds are equally intransigent. So, although the authorities try to stage each heat and final in identical conditions, it can never quite be done. For convenience, swims must be staged at alternate week-ends; tides—although running *roughly* in fortnightly cycles—are not entirely so exact in their habits. Further, although there are two sets of 'big tides' every month, one of these sets is bigger than the other. That inevitably brings about a difference between conditions in one heat and another.

Winds also inject their influence into tidal conditions. A blow from west or south-west drives water into the Bay, increases the depth, and delays the high-water turn of tide. Wind from the north-east has an opposite, emptying, effect, and consequently accelerates the tidal turn-round. Those are the non-controllable factors; the human controllable one is punctuality in starting. A race started fifty full minutes before high-water produces a compact and exciting tussle throughout. One started thirty-five minutes before high-water strings out the competitors into an elongated procession, and causes many retirements. That is only fifteen minutes in time, but it makes an enormous difference in race appeal for competitors and spectators alike.

The course is roughly 'U' shaped but with one side considerably longer than the other. The outward leg is about two and a half miles, and the homeward leg about one mile. The idea is to swim the first leg with the last of the flood tide, get round the turning mark at slack water, and come home quickly on the gathering ebb. But there is a snag to this theory of all favourable tide. The period of absolutely slack water at the turning buoy rarely exceeds two or three minutes, so any swimmer who fails to reach the turning mark by that time faces an increasingly swift ebb-tide. As all swimmers are in the water together, it appears—at first thought—to be equally annoying to all, and no advantage to any. That idea is quite erroneous as further thought shows.

Here is an example of a race starting only thirty-five minutes before the tide turns. Inexperienced tidal swimmer A sets an ordinary prudent well-judged pace to last seventy minutes. Experienced tidal swimmer B sets off at a tremendous clip, and hopes his calculations are correct. In fact, he does just manage to complete the outward leg by the very last slack water, and therefore rounds the mark buoy a quarter-mile ahead of A. He is much exhausted and has to reduce speed, so that—through the water—he is now swimming no faster than A. *Through the water*, *through the water*, *through the water*. That is the absolutely vital point, because as the tide ebbs, the whole body of water is moving. Thus the ebb tide now hits inexperienced Mr. A unkindly in the teeth, while—at the same time—pushing experienced Mr. B kindly up the stern. *For every one hundred yards of tidal movement the gap between A and B opens two hundreds yards, despite the fact that both are swimming exactly the same pace.* And the speed of tide increases noticeably every minute, thus further assisting B and further retarding A. In fact, the tidal speed will soon be sufficient to 'kill' any competitor more than a quarter of a mile short of the turning mark. That last point explains the reason for many retirements in late-started races.

So the hot tips for this race are as follows. For a late start (thirty-five minutes before high water) sprint away to bursting point. The race will be virtually finished at the turning mark; whoever gets there first can almost certainly free-wheel home to victory on a roaring tide. For a punctual start (fifty minutes before high-water) swim a planned and judged race throughout, because there will be equal opportunity on each section of the course. Although tide is a factor beyond one's control, it is of absorbing interest to know exactly how it is behaving. During the race a glance at the anchored boats along the course will help. Except in very strong winds they will always be pointing into the tide. If they are pointing in diverse directions the tide is entirely slack. There is also one other opportunity to check the tidal flow, and that is at the turning point. There is always a 'slick' downtide of a moored buoy so the direction can easily be seen. The rate of flow is disclosed by the amount of turbulence around the buoy.

My explanation was rather lengthy. But I have often found that when explaining maritime matters to even the smartest non-maritime minds a little extra length pays great dividends. No one could have been more alert, more quick-witted, or more keen to learn than the seamen boys of H.M.S. *St. Vincent* when I was training officer there. But the omission of one line of explanation left them completely in the dark, whereas one extra line engraved the answer on their minds for ever. Even right now I am not sure whether the 'different tidal effect for different swimmers' point has been emphasised sufficiently. My wife has read this manuscript. She still says, 'You're all in the water together. Why isn't it the same for all of you?'

In this quite short swim, grease is definitely unfashionable. So are goggles and ear-plugs, although just occasionally an ultra-cautious competitor can be seen sporting the whole works. For the ordinary swimmer, a touch of olive oil or vaseline on the chafing surfaces will suffice. The 'Inshore' is a warmer swim than the 'Cross Bay'. It is always held at high tide when the warmer sea water is holding the colder river and lake water in check; the rather shallow depths can also help the temperature. But neither of these factors produce a tremendous difference; one or two degrees is all that can be expected. However, together with the shorter duration, it does make a less Spartan introduction to Morecambe Bay than the longer swim. To my mind, in order to cut down the Cross Bay failure rate, an 'Inshore' certificate might well be made a compulsory qualification for the bigger event. But such regimentation would most assuredly be regarded unfavourably as un-English. We are a peculiar breed of people who have higher regard for the gallant loser than for the efficient winner. 'Have a go, Joe' is an attitude of mind more deeply ingrained in the character than we realise.

The 'Inshore' is an extremely popular swim with the ladies. For them, competitive long swims are fairly few; they show appreciation of this one by coming hundreds of miles to compete. The ladies do not actually race against the men, although—for convenience—the competitors all start together. Thus a men's championship and a women's championship is fought out simultaneously on the same course. The Press occasionally—also for convenience—forgets that there are two separate races. When a woman competitor arrives before the first man it is always newsworthy to headline 'Slim eighteen-year-old blonde defeats tough Yorkshire veteran.' It does not occur very often but is inevitable every now and then. Women athletes have improved so much nowadays that—in almost any sport—a 'national' class woman can do better than a 'club' class man.

Revenue is derived from entry fees, donations, and sale of programmes, so the swim is entirely self-supporting. The organisers are persons who—for the love of swimming—decided to combine with swimmers to produce one of the most attractive near marathons in the North country.

The best Admiralty Chart is No. 2010, Morecambe Bay. But a chart is not particularly necessary or useful.

The declared aim of the Morecambe and Heysham Swimming Club is—according to their rules—'to promote and encourage distance swimming in sea water'. Swimmers from all over the country are grateful to the club for doing it so efficiently. Spectators, too, enjoy the close-to-the-promenade swim. If there is a local lad beating a Yorkshire lad it is wonderful; if Yorkist is beating Lancastrian it is terrible. The Wars of the Roses still goes remorselessly on in these parts—even when the respective champions are in swimming trunks.

RESULTS

Men's Championship

1951	Anthony Keenan (Lancaster)
1952	John K. Slater (Tod'n. Yks.)

1953	John K. Slater (Tod'n. Yks.)
1954	Ray Holmes (Lancaster)
1955	Ray Holmes (Lancaster)
1956	Ray Holmes (Lancaster)
1957	Ray Holmes (Lancaster)
1958	Joe Smith (Rochdale)
1959	Joe Smith (Rochdale)
1960	Joe Smith (Rochdale)
1961	Brian Winn (Lancaster)
1962	Brian Winn (Lancaster)

Ladies' Championship

1951	Joan Carr (Barrow)
1952	Betty Scott (Cleckheaton)
1953	Shirley Dunbar (Nottingham)
1954	Hazel Wilkinson (Shipley)
1955	Hazel Wilkinson (Shipley)
1956	Hazel Metcalf (*née* Wilkinson) (Shipley)
1957	Pauline Barraclough (Bradford)
1958	Barbara Blenkinsop (Coventry)
1959	Joyce Bricknell (Coventry)
1960	Dorothy Perkins (Bradford)
1961	Dorothy Perkins (Bradford)
1962	Brenda Evans (Middlesbrough)

18

Solent Swims

Behold, we count them happy who endure.

ST. JAMES

THIS is one of the great marathon courses of Britain. In the South Country it is probably the most active of them all. The course is from Ryde, I.O.W. to Southsea on the mainland; or vice versa; or both ways non-stop. The actual single direct-line distance is almost exactly 4½ miles but—because of tide—it is usually necessary to add a few hundred yards with a curving course. The Cross-Solent championship is in temporary abeyance due to lack of boats. But during its existence it was once won in as little as 1 hour 49 minutes; on another occasion it took 2 hours 37 minutes. From those figures of absolute top-class swimmers, it is obviously a hard swim throughout. There is no free-wheeling on the tide anywhere. And times are dominated by weather.

The first recorded transit was by George White of the Portsmouth Swimming Club in August 1883. His time is not known. But on 21st August of the following year Horace Davenport swam from Southsea Pier to Ryde Pier in 2 hours 13 minutes. For comparison with present-day shore to shore times it would not be unfair to add 20 minutes to Mr. Davenport's time. The same year he did the two-way in 5 hours 25 minutes. Probably the next two-way success was by the ever-to-be-remembered, 'Jappy' Wolfe. He also swam from pier to pier, thus meriting a 20-minute addition to each leg. Actual times were, Southsea to Ryde 2 hours 44 minutes 50 seconds, and Ryde to Southsea 3 hours 20 minutes 12 seconds. Total 6 hours 5 minutes 02 seconds.

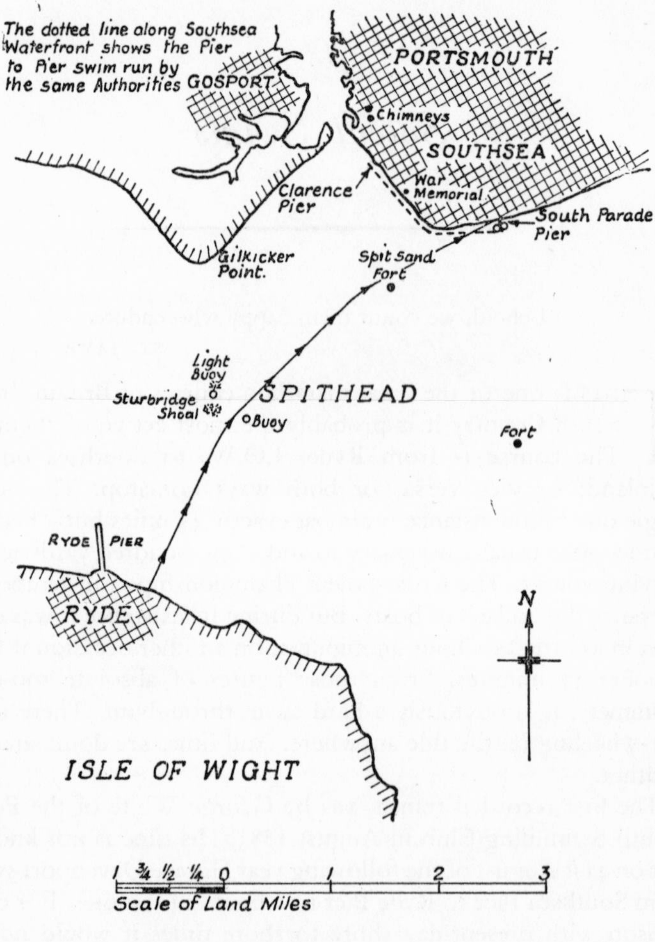

Ryde to Southsea Swim.

The track shown may require some adjustment in differing tidal conditions.

A full list of successful Solent swimmers is not now available but a list of race champions is given later. They form an able, colourful and diverse body of men. But they are not the only characters in the story. In recent years one elderly lieutenant-colonel devoted almost the whole of his retirement to conquest of the Solent but never succeeded. It is all these personalities who go to make marathon swimming such a fascinating sport. One very memorable 1961 day was when Chairman John Moorey and President Jim Bland of the Solent Swimming Club swam briskly across together to show an example. Time 2 hours 32 minutes. Ages 48 and 57 respectively!

This is an absorbing event for the thinking swimmer because there are no professional pilots available to advise. A good deal of expertise has built up among the officials of the Solent Swimming Club. But they may not at short notice always be available. So thoughtful planning and skilful operation can mean the difference between success and failure. Or between slow times and fast. And even if a volunteer pilot is available, enjoyment of a swim is augmented by understanding.

The tidal situation in this part of the Solent is complicated and confusing. Water flows in around both ends of the Isle of Wight. Quite a fierce tide flows in and out of Portsmouth Harbour. Sandbanks and shallow patches distort the tidal streams in different directions. That makes the swim sound impossible but naturally it is not. By steering a good course one should never be within a mile of the Portsmouth Harbour entrance. And in other vicinities of the swim course, the tidal stream is much less strong. At neap tides the maximum rate of stream is about two knots and that only in special places and for a total of about one-third of the time. The other two-thirds of the time it is less than that—decreasing of course to zero at times. Then, additionally, the conflicting streams sometimes cancel one another out and produce an area of artificial slack water.

So to sum up. A first-timer would do well to await the slackest neap tides of the month. Then, by steering as near as possible straight across, the difficulties are minimised. If you can get an experienced pilot, other times of the month are by no means out of the question. But it does mean more turbulent water. And skilful interpretation of the tidal information which is comprehensively set out on Admiralty Chart No. 394 (Solent—Eastern Portion).

A word about Admiralty charts. At ten shillings or so, they may seem expensive luxuries but in fact they are not. They add great interest to the event in planning beforehand. They also add great interest in re-telling the story afterwards in the swimmers' equivalent of the 'nineteenth hole'. This particular chart expands the distance between start and finish to about 12 inches which is a vast improvement over most maps. Besides the large scale, it has other advantages over land-lubberly maps. Tidal positions are indicated in various places and connected with those positions are tabulated directions and rates of tidal stream for every hour. The buoys are named and described, and many other useful details shown.

One swimmer whose active days are over, has made a lampshade from the relevant portion of chart. Every night when he switches on the lounge lights, he re-illuminates the scenes of his past triumphs. Of course, the swim may be done without recourse to a chart; in fact, it often is. I recommend it entirely for interest value. Some help may be necessary from a nautical friend at first but chart work can soon be mastered. It is by no means a black art.

Now a bit about the course to be steered. I have done this swim four times from Ryde to Southsea and never in the reverse direction. For that reason the 'sailing directions' now given are in that first direction but they will suggest a pattern to be employed for the reverse route if necessary. But since Ryde–Southsea is popularly supposed to be the 'easy way', the new arrival at the Solent would be well advised to use the directions as they stand. There is a specially drawn chartlet on a nearby page; study of this in conjunction with the instructions will make things easier to understand.

The swimmers' task is to navigate accurately along the advised path. From an eye at water level there is rather a lack of navigational aids. Fortunately, there is one extremely prominent landmark to be seen almost all the way from Ryde. The Portsmouth Power Station twin chimneys are a godsend to trans-Solent swimmers. Although they may not be exactly on the correct course they can be extremely useful. It requires only an approximate calculation to know how much to one side they ought to be kept.

After something more than an hour's swimming it should be possible to transfer attention to Southsea Castle. This is a fairly prominent mark further along the sea-front towards the finishing point. Then if the sun is shining, the gleaming light paintwork of South Parade Pier should stand out plainly, forty minutes from the end. On a dull day this final landmark will not show until slightly later. Perhaps it is not quite correct to describe that at the final mark. As the beach is approached individual houses and hotels begin to show. Then buses and cars. Then—unbelievingly and thrillingly—the crowd standing at the finishing point. That is the really satisfactory and final steering mark. Occasionally, for an intermediate mark, one may be able to use a ship at anchor. Such a ship can be of great assistance providing it really is at anchor. It can be perplexing and frustrating to try aiming at a moving ten-knot steamer!

Those are all 'leading' marks. In other words they show the longitudinal correctness of the courses to be steered. Distance marks to indicate progress *along* the track are few and far between. However, for the first one and three-quarter miles, there are several buoys which may be used as indicators. The buoys are well described on the Admiralty chart of the area, and they also have names painted on them. It is possible, therefore, to make a list of their distances from the starting point beforehand. Then, on passing them, there is some indication of speed and distance swum. Unfortunately, from such a poor vantage level, one may pass between two and three hundred yards away and never notice them. On the 'blind' side, one can, of course, pass much closer without seeing them.

Nevertheless, every piece of knowledge may come in handy. I have therefore worked out a few distances for memorising. The south-west Mining Buoy (green and white, can-shaped) and the North Sturbridge (black and white, conical) are both roughly equidistant at three thousand two hundred yards from the start.

After leaving that first cluster of buoys behind, there is a two-mile stretch with no reasonable marking at all. Once again the only exception is a conveniently anchored ship, the position of which has been noted on the boat trip across. There will rarely be an opportunity to take bearings and to plot such a trip accurately on a chart. An approximate and more easily carried out method will therefore be helpful. Note the time of leaving Southsea in the boat, note the time of passing the selected ship, and note the time of arrival at Ryde. As boats proceed at different speeds to swimmers, those times cannot be used 'raw' for information. But in the form of a proportion they are immediately useful.

For instance, say the boat takes one hour for the complete crossing, and passes the anchored ship twenty minutes after starting. That ship is therefore obviously anchored *roughly* one-third of the total distance from Southsea to Ryde. As the total distance is four and a half miles, the ship must be anchored one and a half miles from South Parade Pier, or three miles from Ryde. The time proportion will rarely be so convenient even as that example, but can easily be worked out in a few moments with pencil and paper. Besides being navigationally informative, it keeps the mind gainfully occupied.

Towards the end, there is one distance mark which needs no calculation at all. Spit Sand Fort sits in a prominent position, almost exactly one mile from the finish. It sticks up out of the water, as prominently as a sore thumb, and cannot possibly be missed. Like the final bell which track athletes receive, it is a very welcome signal for the last lap. Some swimmers use it as a leading mark, but I strongly advise against that. Swimming towards a relatively close mark becomes a fixation. One becomes so attached to it, that it is retained long after its usefulness is past. Worse still, one may—in an effort to pass it on one particular side—even start swimming into the tide. My advice is to use *distant* landmarks for steering, and to let the tide take you which side it likes round the intermediate marks.

All this navigation is extremely elementary, but it is the best that can be expected from an almost completely immersed swimmer. He has no compass, chart, or any other navigational aid. And all his bearings have to be taken from water level in a split-second glance. Another useful navigational aid is the time. Work out the expected duration, and split it into convenient fractions. Say the expected time is two hours twelve minutes. Then one should be half-way in one hour six minutes, or three-quarters of the way in one hour thirty-nine minutes. That method is as effective as it is elementary. It will be entirely satisfactory in that two-mile stretch in the middle. And Spit Sand Fort will come along enough before the end to allow a final, not too drastic adjustment of pace. Unless one has a waterproof wristwatch the times must be requested from the attendant boats.

The tide between Spit Sand Fort and the finish is the most important tidal factor. In that section, a competitor is committed to one course; he has no alternative. At that juncture he is also tired and least fitted to deal with difficulties. Tide does cause some retirements here but it need not do so. The stream *never* runs faster than a swimmer's speed and normally at this point in the race does not exceed half that pace. Crossing the deep-ship channel is worst, but it is no more than five hundred yards wide and can soon be edged across. Many retirements are caused by the lack of the knowledge that the worst is already over. For once over the ship-channel, the water shoals and the stream ease.

There is still hard swimming ahead, but conditions improve as the shore is approached. There is no real relaxation though, until one's hand begins to scrape the pebbly bottom. Incidentally, that stony bottom is regarded by many as the final straw. Rather than torture the soles of their feet, they prefer to crawl out the last few yards on hands and knees.

I remember especially one championship occasion when Channel swimmer Fred Oldman beat me by no more than ninety seconds! That was a good beating by a good swimmer. That day was so rough I was only too pleased to land anywhere at all. It had been over two and a half hours of the hardest possible swimming. It was sheer ecstatic luxury to subside on that stony beach with breakers still breaking over me. Other swimmers will be interested in the experience for they doubtless have it coming to them some time or other. My condition was in no way a black-out collapse, but the muscles had been pushed to more than the 'extreme operation load' and could take no more. My brain was clear throughout, and after three or four minutes my muscles felt back to normal. There was even no subsequent stiffness.

As I lay collapsed, it was satisfactory to think that although beaten into second place, I had in turn beaten the sea. Already seven of the fourteen starters had been forced to give up, and the thought made me feel rather self-satisfied. Fortunately that bubble of self-satisfaction was pricked before it got to any size. Out of the crowd of spectators came Fred Gill with outstretched hand. He was the previous year's champion and a wonderful swimmer. Before turning professional that year he had been an England water-polo triallist. But with all those attributes, tactfulness was not his strong point. 'Well done, Commander!' he said, pumping me vigorously by the hand, 'Actually, in this weather I wouldn't have done *much* better myself.' If looks could have withered, Fred would have turned into a pretty sere old gentleman at that moment The evening papers restored some of my equinimity when they stated that 'conditions ranked among some of the worst known for the swim'. Even that seemed an understatement.

Inevitably, that reminded me of another Fred Gill story. Two consecutive stories about the same swimmer may smack of bad management, or a paucity of anecdote. But strong personalities always foster strong memories, and Fred was a personality if anyone ever was. During the course of a distinguished swimming career he had won many championships, but the Solent championship had somehow eluded him. One year, to his delight, he won it at last. But in the moment of pride and achievement, fate struck him down.

At the ceremonial prize-giving, Billy Rowe, the Hampshire A.S.A. secretary, always made a speech. He gave the placings and the times together with a very brief review of each swimmer's attainments. Every swimmer was presented with some small memento if he crossed successfully. Knowing Fred Gill's pleasure at this long-awaited victory, Rowe asked the new champion to say a few words. Across the room Fred shook his head. Rowe repeated his offer more persuasively, but received another head shake. 'Speech', we all shouted encouragingly, thinking that Gill was overwhelmed by the great occasion. He signified refusal more emphatically than ever. It was not until the evening papers came out that we discovered the full reason. 'Londoner Wins Swim,' headlined the Press, 'But Loses Dentures on Way'.

The list of past champions makes fascinating reading. A water-polo international, national champions, and Southern Counties champions. Three Channel swimmers have triumphed; two others, Sam Rockett and myself, have been runners-up. Here comes the 'Who Was Who'.

1933: E. H. Temme (Plaistow). 1934: M. G. Connor (St. Martin's S.C.). 1935: E. C. Jones (Bristol Police). 1936: E. C.

Jones (Bristol Police). 1937: C. Rogers (Gosport S.C.). 1938: C. T. Deane (Penguin). 1939: C. T. Deane (Penguin). 1947: E. J. Guast (Portsmouth Dockyard). 1948: A. N. Other. 1949: A. Hoad (Royal Navy). 1950: F. Gill (Willesden). 1951: F. C. Oldman (East Ham). 1952: D. J. Payne (Otter). 1953: G. Hill (Oxford). 1954: D. J. Payne (Otter). The races from 1933 to 1938, inclusive, and 1947 were from Southsea to Ryde; all others were in the reverse direction.

Despite many hardships it is a most interesting and sometimes amusing marathon course. Besides the natural difficulties there is also a variety of man-made ones. Paddle steamers rock the swimmers in turbulent wash; diesel launches dose the competitors with obnoxious gases on passing. There are deep-sea ships, pleasure-boats and fishing-boats going about their lawful occasions. Even indignant yachtsmen shouting testily for the right of way. On one classic occasion the Navy, presumably to show it works on Saturdays, carried out a landing exercise through the middle of a dozen swimmers with squadrons of landing-craft.

Meteorological conditions do not differ sufficiently from Dover to merit special mention. A chapter on Channel weather follows later, and that may be applied equally well to the Solent area. There is only one significant difference. Because of more sheltered water, swimming is possible on a greater percentage of days than in the open Channel.

Records to date are:

Southsea–Ryde	A. Moorey 1 hr. 54 min. 48 sec.
Southsea–Ryde	Jean Ramshaw 2 hr. 34 min.
Ryde–Southsea	C. T. Deane 1 hr. 48 min. 51 sec.
Ryde–Southsea	Andrea McHutcheon 2 hr. 43 min.
Two-Way	M. Jennings 5 hr. 07 min.
Two-Way	Jean Ramshaw 5 hr. 47 min.

19

The Torbay Championship

> The Arte of Navigation demonstrateth how, by the shortest good way, by the aptest direction, and in the shortest time, a sufficient ship, between any two places (in passage Navigable) assigned: may be conducted: and in all storms, and natural disturbances chauncying, how to use the best possible means whereby to recover the place first assigned.
>
> JOHN DEE 1570

If you vouch for yourself being a 'sufficient vessel', I will explain the shortest good way and the aptest direction to attain the shortest time. In fact, it is easier to explain at Torbay than many other places, because this swim is not a particularly difficult or tricky one. Except for being eight miles distance in open sea!

Torbay is undoubtedly among the most sheltered bays in England. So far as any sea swim can be weatherproof, this one is; it is well protected by land on three sides, against 'storm and natural disturbances'. Even so, in 1959 the race had to be terminated at the half-way stage. And again, in 1962, weather conditions were about at maximum for the accompanying rowing-boats. Nevertheless to get 4½ swims completed in five years shows how fortunately nature has endowed this resort.

Tides, according to Admiralty Sailing Directions, are weak and irregular. Thinking that this generalisation was grossly inadequate for swimmers, I spent five years in research. After which I can only tell you that the tides *are* weak and irregular. In eight crossings of the Bay (four doubles) I have never discovered more than 350 yards total of tidal movement on any voyage. There are

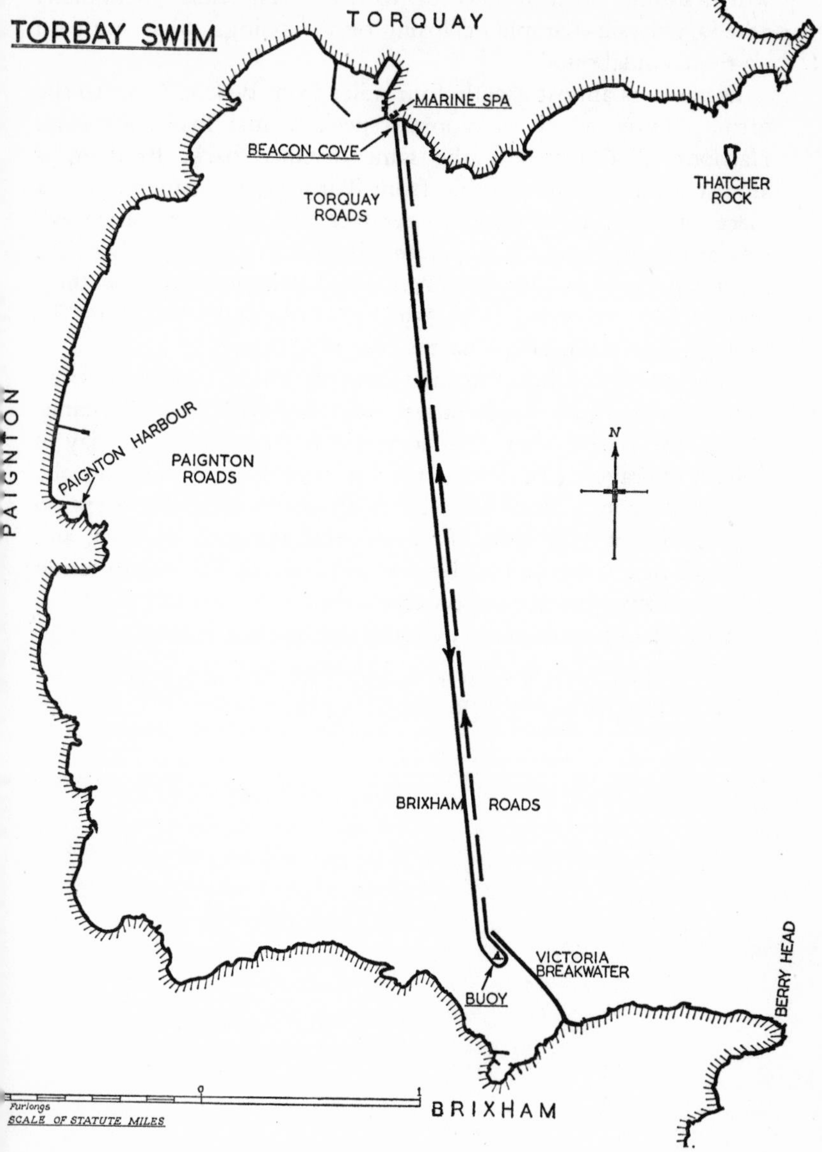
TORBAY SWIM
TORQUAY
MARINE SPA
BEACON COVE
TORQUAY ROADS
THATCHER ROCK
PAIGNTON
PAIGNTON HARBOUR
PAIGNTON ROADS
N
BRIXHAM ROADS
VICTORIA BREAKWATER
BUOY
BERRY HEAD
Furlongs
SCALE OF STATUTE MILES
BRIXHAM

certainly small eddies running hither and thither but they are not worth adding extra distance on to chase. The tidal phenomena here is a classic example of 'losing on the swings, what you gain on the roundabouts'.

Distance is almost exactly four miles from Beacon Cove to the turning buoy which is moored specially just inside Brixham Harbour. And naturally the same distance back. Brixham is almost always clearly visible from Torquay: so navigation is a piece of cake. In reverse 'to recover the place first assigned' similar remarks apply. Temperature is usually slightly higher than the main English Channel: over five Championships the thermometer has recorded 15° C (59° F) lowest, and 17·2° C (63° F) highest. Best Admiralty Chart is No. 26 (Torbay).

This championship was first held in 1958. It is sponsored jointly by Torquay Corporation and the British Long Distance Swimming Association. The normal date is the first Saturday in July. Coverage is by Press, television and radio. During the evening all competitors and officials are entertained at a reception by the Mayor. Hot baths, first-class refreshments, a dance, and car-park tickets are laid on by the Corporation. The organisation and the hospitality are impeccable.

A full list of successes is given in Appendix 4. Records are:

Michael Jennings (Gravesend) 3 hr. 39 min. 06 sec.
Pauline Goddard (Rotherham) 4 hr. 57 min.

20

The Morecambe Bay Championships

> The reason firm, the temperate will,
> Endurance, foresight, strength, and skill.
>
> WORDSWORTH

QUITE beyond doubt, Morecambe Bay is the most important single swim-venue in the country. The Inshore Championship described in a previous chapter, the Cross Bay Championship, the Twenty-Mile Championship, and the Fleetwood to Morecambe Championship. This selection of events is one to which quite a few swimmers are happy to devote their entire training throughout the year. The direct distance between Grange and Morecambe is only about nine miles, but devious routes through the sandbanks add considerably to the mileage. The Twenty-Mile Championship is from Morecambe to Grange and back. To marathon swimmers Morecambe is a Mecca to which it is essential to make a pilgrimage at least once or twice a year. What Henley means to oarsmen, Twickenham to Rugby fans, and Highbury Stadium to soccerites, Morecambe means to swimmers.

Other factors besides length make the Bay swims into unforgettably testing events. During the swimming season, the average sea-water temperature is slightly lower than the Channel. Much cold fresh water also flows in from the Lakes, especially after heavy rainfall in the Lake District. At high tide such cold fresh water is temporarily held in check, but as the ebb progresses, so increases the agonisingly painful cold-water patching. The swift-running ebb also kicks up a horridly rough little sea,

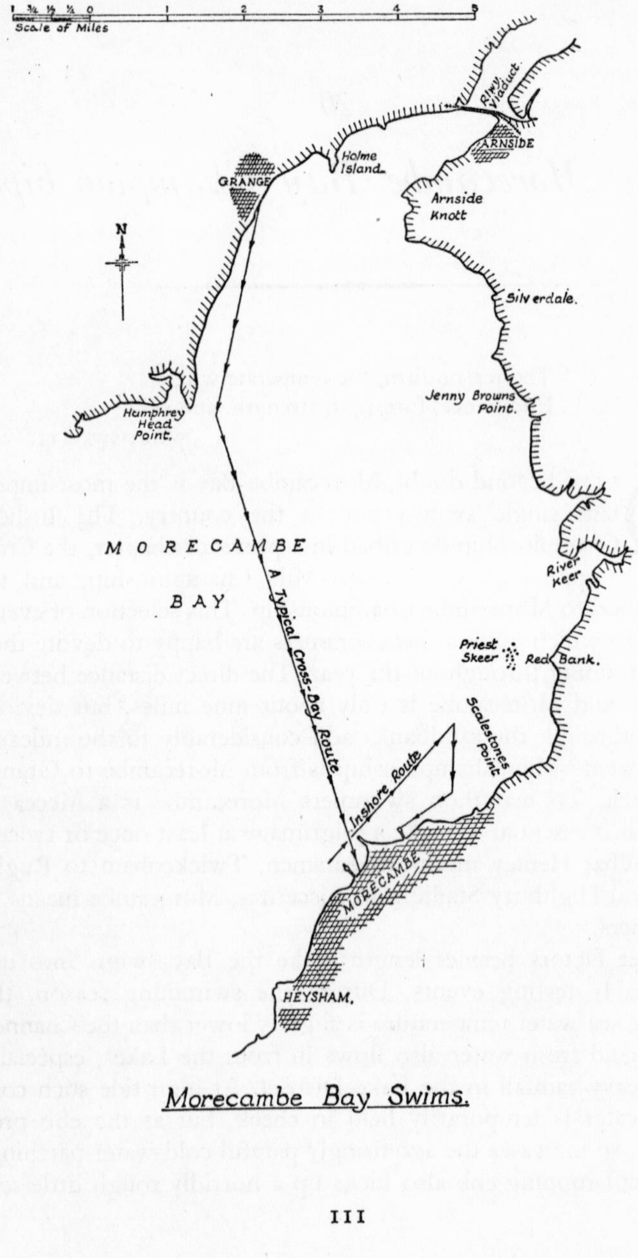

Morecambe Bay Swims.

when the wind blows against it. So there one has the précis. It is long, cold, rough—challenging.

That last word is vital, for wherever there is a challenge there is a swimmer anxious to meet it. In addition to would-be champions, scores of ordinary men and women come hastening to take up this particular gauntlet. Harold Bracewell of Blackpool is typical. He had a burning ambition just to complete the single course, but many years of endeavour elapsed before he did finally succeed. But the successful day is one he will remember throughout life. (He subsequently went on to do 16 hours in the Channel.) On my first occasion at Morecambe I had the good fortune to lead the field home in three hours six minutes, but at the other end of the field was a gamely determined twenty-three-years'-old girl who struggled to success in four hours fifty minutes. Septuagenarians have had a try and so have one-legged swimmers. In point of fact, this is perhaps the sport in which a one-legged athlete can compete more successfully than any other. One-legged action is almost as efficacious as two; in certain circumstances more so.

Many other ordinary men and women have tried the Bay crossing. They are examples of the obstinate persevering character which has brought us through two world wars, for those two wars were no more than marathon events of greater size, complexity and importance. Calm, collected, fit, strong-willed and stimulated by difficulty, such persons are the backbone of any country in sport and war. The Cross Bay Association therefore not only does a great service for swimming, it also does the same for Britain itself. The Cross Bay blazer badge is a mark of distinction second to none. It is the hallmark of the successful competitor and the stimulus to the unsuccessful. The right to wear it, more than compensates for all the hardship and endurance involved.

Navigational difficulties are also considerable. Luckily these particular worries are entirely out of the swimmers' hands; each contender is accompanied by a most capable pilot. The course is criss-crossed and spotted with channels and sandbanks which never remain exactly the same for two consecutive years. Acquaintance with both these features is essential in order to understand the pilots, otherwise mysterious, alterations of course. Tide runs fastest in the channels and slowest across the shallow spots; in some places it even runs slowly in the wrong direction. These points are catered for in the rules. 'Owing to changing conditions in the Bay', they state, 'it may be necessary for the pilot to bring swimmers over the course between Humphrey Head and Morecambe via the Flow Hole Channel'. And 'If, in the opinion of the judge, the competitor cannot complete the course and is in danger of being stranded, the judge shall be empowered to order him to leave the water.' Although one or two of the pilots are 'specialists', the majority do both the 'Inshore' and the 'Cross Bay'. They are real swimming enthusiasts and no one could ever be more knowledgeable about the changing moods of this locality. On non-swim days, they are professional trawlermen and their very livelihood depends on knowing every nook and cranny of their domain.

That tidal streams differ in closely adjacent areas is borne out by Police Constable Peter Cook. He relates how, while swimming at maximum speed himself, he was passed by a competitor treading water and eating biscuits!

After hearing all these difficulties, an aspirant must indeed have a few qualms. He is in thoroughly good company; for well over half a century very few first-timers have ever tackled the job without a most peculiar sinking feeling. Yet nearly five hundred persons have accomplished successful crossings; in addition to those at least that number again have had a jolly good try. Nearly a dozen have done the there-and-back feat, too. Aviators and mountaineers say they have exactly the same attacks of nerves on their own initiation trips, but subsequently go on to enjoy it. I have just mentioned two sports, but there are others just as demanding. This is no claim that swimming the Bay is the greatest thing in the world, but it is indeed *one* of the great achievements in Britain. It is a thousand times better, at least, than betting on somebody else's prowess, jiving at the Palais or drooling over a great Hollywood love epic. Marathon swimmers are doers and not just watchers. There is little of the insidious 'couldn't care less' frame of mind and much of 'I'll do it if I bust' mentality instead.

This Bay has been a breeding ground and rendezvous of celebrity swimmers almost since the inception of the championship. Miss Lucy Morton, breast-stroke Olympic winner, was one of the lady champions. Incomparable Tom Blower was champion in 1935, 1936, 1937 and 1938. He went on to swim the English Channel three times, the North Channel once, and to have an attempt at a two-way non-stop Channel swim. Other Morecambe Bay competitors who have gone on to swim the Channel are many—Bill Pickering, Eileen Fenton, Brenda Fisher, Philip Mickman, Margaret Feather, Kathleen Mayoh, Fred Oldman, Dorothy Perkins and myself. Anyone who can swim the Bay is—with the requisite extra training—fairly good bet for the Channel conquest. Gordon Hill took five years but did it well.

Olympic gold-medallist Henry Taylor (Chadderton) won this championship nine times in all. He also set up the rather perplexing record of two hours, two minutes, fifty-five seconds. Perplexing because swimming standards have since improved tremendously; yet no modern champions can approach anywhere near that time. To give that record full credit, it would be necessary to know the exact details of the starting position, course taken and state of tide. It is well known nowadays, that by starting the swim a considerable time after high-water, a much more powerful and advantageous tide is obtained. But at the time of writing a late start is not practicable because of the sandbank formation. In any case the Cross Bay Association, quite rightly, does not desire to shorten the duration; it wishes the race to remain one of the most arduous races in the country. But it cannot be ascertained whether the same views applied during the period that the record was established.

Brierly Law—the original champion—was one of England's outstanding swimmers during the first quarter of this century. He popped up again and again to win this event; by special training, indeed, he emerged as champion for the last time in 1932. On that occasion he was over fifty years old and a grandfather; his final score was six championships. Tom Blower was four times winner. In his heyday he was unbeatable in anything for which he trained. Charles Daly won the championship three times, but really hits the jackpot with another record. He successfully crossed from Grange to Morecambe no less than twenty-seven times. With thirteen crossings, I believe, I am the second most travelled swimmer in the locality! Those are the giants, but the popularity and success of this event depend on the support of the not so great.

On those enthusiasts who turn up every year to come second or third—or even, never to be placed at all. So long as they obtain their blazer badges and their crossing certificates they are happy without hitting the headlines. But one day, they may . . . perhaps . . . if the wind were exactly right . . . if there were a rail strike to keep the entry down . . . if, etc., etc . . . Hope springs eternal in every swimmer's breast.

So much for the stuff the swim is made of. The history, the legends, the personalities, and the records. Those things have given the event an indefinable 'something' which in turn gives character to the swim and makes for ever-increasing popularity. Recent entry lists have shown competitors from the Army, Navy and Air Force; from Wales and Scotland; from England, between the Scottish border and the Channel coast. In fact, as representative a cross-section of Britain as could possibly be found. On one occasion indeed when I posted my entry form during a trip abroad, I was later astonished to find myself representing Malta, G.C. That was, of course, purely a mistake; the Association has no need to exaggerate, for the entry is already interesting enough without embellishment. Most encouraging of all is the amount of new young blood which is yearly attracted.

The Cross Bay (single crossing) event really commences two and a half hours before the dive-in, for at that time competitors muster at Green Street Landing Stage for instructions. Pilots are allocated to swimmers and distinguishing flags are allocated to pilots. There is always much hustle, bustle, arrangement, and counter-arrangement; swimmers, trainers, pilots, officials, newspaper and cameramen all contribute requests, suggestions and information. The whole assembly sometimes embarks in two Morecambe trawlers for passage across to Grange. This trip is pleasant and valuable; it gives a preview of the whole course and affords a chance to take some mid-Bay temperatures. On other occasions transport to Grange is by chartered coach.

Weather is supremely important and is often unpleasantly deceptive. Through the years, many competitors have protested against abandonment of a swim when, from Morecambe promenade, the sea looked quite reasonable. But even with half a gale blowing, a deceptively mild appearance is possible if the wind is off-shore, and while the Bay is half-empty of water. Wolves in sheep's clothing have nothing on weather appearance in this locality. Once out of the shelter of the sea front—and seen from a lurching trawler—it unfolds a very different aspect. And on the opposite shore at Grange, it may be piling up breakers sufficient to stop a boat even approaching the beach. Wind, which—with the tide—looks harmless, can also become thoroughly vicious when the tide turns against it. Finally, although an accomplished swimmer—being low in the water—can make progress against quite strong head-winds and seas, it is much more difficult for a rowing-boat, no matter how skilfully handled. There is little point in expanding overmuch on the meteorology of the district, because first-class local information is always available from the pilots. When these keen sportsmen—as indeed they are—agree that a swim is 'off', it is no use arguing. They make their living on the 'Bay', and have 'seen it all before'; on their home ground there are no greater meteorological experts.

But overseas readers are not quite so interested in short-range forecasting as in long-range expectations during an average season. The 'season', which is June–September, has the following characteristics. For air temperatures mid-July is hottest; a typical daily temperature then ranges from 11½° C or 53° F (night minimum) to 19½° C or 67° F (day maximum) but, of course, some years will be hotter and some colder than this. August is similar, but September averages about two degrees centigrade lower at both extremes. Water temperatures—especially the top layers—are greatly influenced by air temperatures but do tend to lag a degree or so behind; they are also influenced by the inflow of fresh water effect. On the whole I would say that in mid-Bay, the water in late August should average 16° C (60° F) but dropping 1½° C for the month on either side. Hot weather, however, heats the exposed sandbanks at low water; this in turn heats the water slightly as the tide covers them. Winds from seawards (south-west, west, and north-west) are more uncomfortable than others for swimmers; unfortunately over half the recorded winds blow from those quarters.

The journey to Grange takes something over an hour. There is ample time left for final preparations. Through the courtesy of the bath-superintendent at Grange, a separate dressing-room is usually available for competitors and their attendant trainers. In this race, most competitors like to grease up fairly heavily and also to wear goggles. Personally, I find grease unnecessary, even for a seven-hour Bay swim; I now wear goggles though I used not to do so. Having no accoutrements to cause trouble has sometimes gained me many yards over elaborately-equipped opponents, but once again it must be an entirely personal decision. The way the waiting hour is spent is also a very personal decision. Some sleep, some eat a light meal, some gaze fixedly and apprehensively at the weather, some try to imbibe information which they should have learnt long ago. My general pre-race advice is to get to know the pilot. Besides getting up-to-date weather and tidal data, it is good to know one's partner in the hard work which lies ahead.

The 'dive-in' is a term now hallowed by tradition, but actually it is a walk-in. After cameramen and autograph hunters have had their due, the swimmers walk to a waist-deep position and await the starter's pistol. The starter must necessarily be a strict disciplinarian; he must start the race at precisely the correct time, despite appeals to 'wait just a moment or two'. This punctuality is not a personal whim, but is strict necessity to ensure that competitors catch the tide. Having a sufficient depth of water to swim in is a really important point! If fully understood by all, it would save swimmers and trainers much offence when their requests for more time had to be refused. If doubtful, ask Dorothy Perkins and Bryan Finlay! On one occasion they had to walk the last couple of miles!

From the start, swimmers strike out in *roughly* the right general direction. When they have sufficiently separated from each other there will be room for the pilot boats to ease in front of their respective swimmers. The boats' ideal position is about five yards ahead; the swimmer then feels he is neither 'on top' of the boat, nor being left behind. But—and this is another most important point—the boat cannot keep exact position, like a destroyer screening an aircraft carrier. For one thing it is propelled by oars, and oarsmen are human; they cannot help occasionally getting a little ahead or a little astern of station. For another thing, boats and swimmers have entirely different characteristics in the water. A swimmer is nearly 95 per cent submerged; he cannot therefore be blown about like a boat which is only 25 per cent submerged. As an apt illustration, throw a piece of wood and a football into a pond together; the wood will move very sedately down-wind, the football will scuttle off like a dingbat. That is very similar to a swimmer and a boat. It takes much good oarsmanship to maintain even approximate station for several hours, especially in cross-winds.

There are usually two oarsmen (one of whom is the pilot) and in the sternsheets is ample room for the trainer. Unnecessary conversation between the swimmer and the trainer is a sure-fire time waster. If the competitor is wearing ear-plugs, it is also exasperating and futile. For that reason it is better to have a single code of signals. To my mind the most useful information is one's placing and one's progress. Both these facts are easily conveyed from boat to swimmer by signal. Three fingers held up, for instance, means that one is in third place. A handkerchief waved until acknowledged, at the end of every half hour is a splendid method of communicating progress. More complicated messages can—but only if necessary—be communicated by easily seen capital letters chalked on a slate. Some mutually agreed signal is useful to signify 'ten minutes to go' as this will ensure against finishing with annoyingly untapped reserves of energy. Refreshment *en route* is still enjoyed by some weaker competitors. If required, the method (which is described in the Channel training chapter) should be rehearsed beforehand. I personally consider that refreshment in the middle of a three-hour swim is time-wasting, unnecessary and detrimental to rhythm. In the Twenty-Mile Championship, one is permitted to feed standing up at Grange before starting the return.

Finishing is an art in itself, too. The watch will be stopped as soon as the competitor can touch dry land with no sea-water beyond. It is thus important not to linger when first touching ground in shallow water. Get to your feet and gallop out. Or crawl if you feel more competent at that! Disregard of finishing technique has lost several races. For instance, I lost the 1955 championship by ten seconds only on account of feeling that—in such a long race—seconds were unimportant. If heavily greased, it is advisable at this stage to remove some of it on the beach before climbing into the boat; several pieces of old towelling should be in every swimmer's hold-all for this purpose. Removal of grease helps to keep the boat clean for the crew's clothing, and it also makes it easier to climb into the boat. Incidentally, a boat should always be entered over its stern, because an entry over one side can push the gunwale under water with uncomfortable results for all concerned. The 'current' walk-out finish in this race makes it necessary to retain a reserve of strength right until the last. In the old days, when it was only necessary to cross a finishing line, even exhausted 'floaters' could achieve the last bit by tide alone.

On completion, all swimmers are taken back to the Stone Jetty. Many spectators, sometimes thousands, watch the finish and they like to have a look at the competitors close-to. The commentator usually requests each new arrival to say a few words into the microphone. This is hardly an ordeal at all, for a high standard of oratory is not requested. The crowd will be quite sympathetic and satisfied even to hear merely that it was rough in the middle. More photographers, reporters, and autograph-seekers complete the set-up, for folk in the North take sport seriously. And who are we to blame them for that, when we ourselves think so highly of it? Nevertheless, on a cold day, a track-suit is a definite necessity to get through these formalities.

The Fleetwood–Morecambe swim finishes in the same place in the same manner. It begins by swimming out of the Fleetwood Channel on the last of the ebb. At slack water in the Lune Deeps turn right and follow the deep-ship channel to Heysham. Then by inshore boat-channel to the finish. Roughly thirteen miles.

Welcome hot baths, scrubbing brushes, and plenty of soap will be waiting at the Swimming Stadium. All Lancashire is hospitable, all Morecambe is friendly, but these qualities are present *in excelsis* at the Stadium. The Superintendent, Mr. G. C. Cooper, is untiring in his provisions for visiting swimmers and every possible facility is given to each athlete. In fact, this attitude of the Stadium authorities has a tremendous amount to do with Morecambe's popularity in the swimming world. As the Stadium is Corporation operated, much credit must also go naturally to the town councillors responsible for such amiable and able direction.

On one occasion six competitors arrived at the Stadium for hot baths without having swum a single stroke. For the beginning of that story it is necessary to go back to Grange. The competitors had disembarked, they had greased up, and their belongings had been put aboard their boats. Then a fierce onshore wind sprang up which threatened to swamp and wreck the boats. The two trawlers, by dint of good seamanship were able to get all the small boats in tow. But there was only one safe move—to make for shelter at Morecambe at full speed. The competitors were therefore left stranded at Grange, clad in little more than trunks, grease and the hair on their chests. Their only course was also to make for Morecambe—by train. It was a disconsolate little party that ultimately arrived at the Stadium after having had to travel *via* Lancaster. At that station, far inland, it is said that some main-line passengers seeing this unbelievable party swore solemnly never to touch another drop.

21

The Irish Channel Swim

There is a tide in the affairs of men,
Which taken at the flood, leads on to fortune;
Omitted, all the voyage of their life
Is bound in shallows and in miseries.
On such a full sea are we now afloat,
And we must take the current when it serves
Or lose our ventures.

SHAKESPEARE

IN 1947, Nottingham's magnificent Tom Blower swam from Donaghadee, Northern Ireland, to Portpatrick, Scotland. That distance is 21·7 land miles—or slightly more than from Griz Nez to Dover. Lionhearted Blower completed his swim in deteriorating weather in 15 hours 26 minutes. (This compares with an average of 15 hours 54 minutes for his three Channel successes.) Since that date, more than a few swimmers of top grade have tried their utmost to copy his example, but without success. Amongst the most illustrious have been Jack McClelland (1956 Butlin winner), Florence Chadwick and Jason Zirganos (both four times Channel conquerors). The last-named died on his attempt after seventeen hours in the water on 27th September 1959. It is evident that this particular sea passage is hard graft. Further north, a much narrower channel splits the north-eastern corner of Ireland from the Mull of Kintyre, Scotland. In the late 1920s that passage was attempted by Channel swimmer Mercedes Gleitz without success. Although the distance here is only 13·1 land miles, the crossing is more difficult than the wider southern route. I will discuss this aspect at length later.

Before assessing any sea swim, it is rewarding to study climatic conditions. There is, however, no weather recording station exactly where required—in mid-channel. Further, because of coastal effects and deflections, weather on the Irish and Scottish coasts can differ quite appreciably at exactly the same moment. Considering the two coasts are never much more than twenty-two miles apart

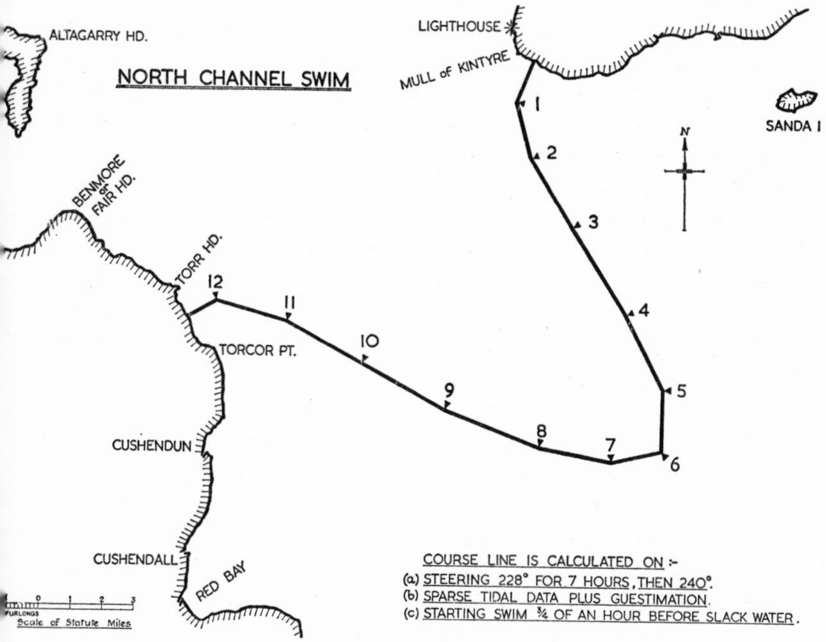

A 'short cut' route accross the Irish Channel planned by the author for himself in 1960 and 1961. But weather precluded starting.

that sounds odd. But it is true. So as to give maximum value to most people, I have taken a mean. My estimates are for a theoretical imaginary point in the geometrical centre of an area with Donaghadee, Portpatrick, Fair Head, and Mull of Kintyre at the corners. The date now given can be no more than a close approximation. But it may be regarded as a sound basis for planning.

The figures are for August, as that month covers the best swim period. Anyone wishing to consider a two-week period before or after that should subtract a couple of degrees from all the temperatures; the other data will remain very substantially the same. The average air temperature then is 17° C (63° F) in the afternoon and 11° C (52° F) before dawn. Average surface-water temperature is 13½° C (56½° F) but gets considerably less when bottom water is pushed up by turbulence. On one day a month there may be thick fog. The average wind strength is 13 miles per hour—which means that a swimmer must necessarily wait for weather better than average. Winds blow from these directions (in percentages)—north 10¼; north-east 6; east 6; south-east 7¾; south 17¾; south-west 16¾; west 17¾; north-west 16½. The remainder of the time (1¼ per cent) is calm! Probably that is the day it is foggy!

Tidal streams in the area have not been sufficiently observed and recorded for comfort and calculation. But they are certainly amongst the most formidable in the United Kingdom. I have visited Donaghadee, Portpatrick, Cushenden, and the Mull of Kintyre for obtaining personal notes on inshore streams and eddies. I have talked much with longshoremen, lifeboatmen, lighthouse-keepers, yachtsmen, packet-boat captains, and with half a dozen persons who have accompanied previous swim attempts. My notebook has also been afloat in the middle of both routes and overhead by low-flying aircraft. Superimposed on this practical stuff has been a couple of hundred hours of study of all the most authoritative charts and publications.

Resulting from these investigations, this is the tidal situation as I now see it. In the main channel (on both routes) the stream runs about 6¼ hours each way in a direction approximately parallel to the coastline. Very roughly, it runs southerly from the time of low water at Dover to the time of high water at Dover, and then turns to run northerly until the next low water, Dover. (To the layman, it may sound odd to relate tides here to times at Dover several hundred miles away. But seamen use Dover as a standard port to express the habits of tidal streams around the whole British coast. It serves very well for reasonable approximations although more complicated calculations are required for great accuracy.)

In addition to the main channel stream, however, there is a distinct inshore coastal stream on both coasts. The width of this may extend some $\frac{3}{4}$ mile to 2 miles off the coast; it is very slightly less strong and turns at different times to the main channel stream. Data for this inshore movement is extremely sparse and at times contradictory. It is based much on hearsay and isolated reports through the ages. In one place it is said to run north for 9 hours and south for only $3\frac{1}{2}$. But once again very roughly, it seems generally to turn in each direction about $1\frac{1}{2}$ hours before the main stream.

At times, it will thus be seen that the main and inshore streams run in exactly opposite directions, causing upset sea conditions on the dividing line. Off prominent headlands, strong tidal deflections inevitably inject a third directional disturbance. Shallow patches on the bottom, too, deflect the water vigorously upward just as headlands do it sideways. These several *directional* factors act to produce a most uneasy confused area of sea. Further, whenever the channel is constricted by narrowing or shoaling, it causes the *velocity* of stream to increase; i.e. the same amount of water has to go through a smaller hole in the same time. Wind—especially against or across the direction of stream—adds its own quota of turbulence. And, most particularly on the northern route, an ocean swell rolling in from the Atlantic does likewise.

In certain places, this confusion is extremely marked. Off the Mull of Kintyre, for instance, the 'overfalls' are said to be 'especially violent and (in certain circumstances) dangerous to small craft'. When steering a motor yacht through these 'boilings' in no more than a gentle breeze, I certainly felt that all control over the boat was temporarily gone. There is no doubt that even in the finest weather, these patches are quite impassable for swimmers at certain states of tide. In addition, the local fishermen speak darkly about swirls and whirlpools. For my own peace of mind when swimming, I felt impelled to try and check this point. Selecting the Mull of Kintyre, a prominent headland with the most vicious tides in the whole swim area, as an observation point, I settled down with a notebook and binnoculars.

Without doubt, a number of whirlpools did form. But they appeared to be slow moving with small vortices. They looked unpleasant and quite capable of temporarily reversing the direction of a swimmer willy-nilly. On the whole, however, they did not look dangerous. It needs emphasis that my observations covered only eight hours in fine weather at neap tides. In breezy weather at spring tides another story might well have unfolded. Nevertheless, I personally felt willing—it would be an overstatement to say happy—to undertake a swim in this vicinity if necessary. But very strictly at a time and date of my own choosing. Since the Mull of Kintyre sponsors the most violent conglomeration of tides, no worse whirlpool conditions should occur elsewhere in the swim area. It seems a reasonable bet to say that although whirlpools around here are unpleasant, their dangers have been overstated in the past. That is if swimmers do not attempt to force their way across in the wrong kind of weather.

On the whole, perhaps, that is not a very encouraging picture. But no sea swim ever is. Chances can be much improved by careful planning. By swimming only on a calm day. When turbulence due to wind is excluded. By swimming at slackest neap tides, when the velocity of tidal streams is halved. By avoiding, if possible, headlands and charted overfalls, so that directional disturbances are out. By going south to the Donaghadee–Portpatrick route, where the channel widens and the tidal velocity correspondingly cut.

Just one final piece of general information in connection with that last suggestion will be of interest. The time taken by a hypothetical successful swimmer on the short northern route would not significantly better that of the same successful swimmer on the longer southern route. The distance advantage of 13·1 miles against 21·7 miles is very greatly negatived by severer conditions. As an indication, my own personal estimate was that if the northern route could be successfully negotiated, it would take 93 per cent of the southern crossing time. For many, that will seem hardly a significant return for the added disadvantages and uncertainties. No doubt Mr. Superman of the future will make a nonsense of this calculation in due course. But he is certainly not around at the moment.

As a result of all that reasoning, my ranking of the four alternative courses of action has evolved. They are given below.

Donaghadee to Portpatrick. Chances of success (for a good class cold-water marathon swimmer) are reasonably good. Attempts on this route go in same direction as prevailing weather. The tidal stream is—except in isolated places—approximately the same strength as in the English Channel. The surface temperature about half a degree higher than the mean given in a previous paragraph. A long stretch of coast is available for landing; this is particularly useful for overcoming the effects of unavoidable guesswork in navigation. Boatmen are available at Donaghadee. As a result of one successful swim and a score of other attempts from here, an amount of knowledge and experience is building up in local boating circles. The best Admiralty Chart is 2198. North Channel. Southern part.

Portpatrick to Donaghadee. Chances of success are fair. There is less (but adequate) straight coast for landing and the swim-direction is against the prevailing weather. The last factor is reduced in importance by the fact that prevailing weather may possibly not be prevailing at the time of attempt! Nevertheless, it must reduce the chances of success mathematically. Remarks on tides and temperatures are the same as for the last paragraph. Boatmen are available at Portpatrick; one or two have been on previous attempts. The best Admiralty chart is 45—Clogher Head to Burrow Head.

Mull of Kintyre to Ireland. Chances of success—poor. There is a degree less water temperature on the surface compared with the southern route; and the areas of very cold patching are more extensive. Swim direction is against prevailing weather. The vicinity is more exposed to oceanic swell and has less settled weather conditions. Tidal streams are 1½ times as strong as the southern passage and contains numerous whirlpools and tide races. Slight navigational miscalculation may mean terminating a swim in severe overfalls or being swept away in a direction differing greatly to that desired. Because of these many unstabilising factors, the sea whips up into roughness more rapidly than elsewhere. Campbeltown, 17 miles away by sea, is the nearest practicable base. This factor entailing a 2½ hour boat trip is an extra complication to planning. Despite the larger size of port, boatmen are almost non-existent; it is pre-eminently a fishing port and August is a peak fishing month. The best Admiralty Chart is 2199—North Channel. Northern part.

Ireland to Mull of Kintyre. Chances of success, very poor indeed. The only advantages attaching to this direction of attempt is the prevailing weather and the fact that boatmen are (or were when I last visited) available at Cushenden. The remarks in the last paragraph about tide, temperatures, weather, swell, and quick-changing conditions apply equally. Further the Mull is a narrow target to aim for; in the strong tidal conditions here a swimmer would be extremely fortunate not to be swept to one side or the other. Especially as he would arrive necessarily in the most confused, coldest, and most difficult area at an uncertain time and when partially exhausted. Of course this route will be conquered one day. But to my mind that day is not yet nigh. The best Admiralty Chart is as given above for the reverse route—No. 2199.

My possibility-ratings although not over optimistic, are considerably higher than that of local residents. For instance, I have never met one single pundit who considers the Mull of Kintyre route possible in either direction. But neither—until Tom Blower did it—did the locals consider Donaghadee to Portpatrick possible. In this connection, it is interesting to read a contemporary account of Captain Webb's preparation for his pioneer Channel swim. One passage reads thus—'It was the preconceived notion of its being impossible that had been taken up by many persons, whose strength of opinion is too often proportionate to their ignorance of the subject, that had a great detracting effect on his efforts.' Cautiously indeed, I would say that from 1875 until today human natures have changed little. And the fault is now confined to one section of the community. It is a fact that few swimmers understand navigation and few navigators understand swimming. But given a first-class boat, and a crew enthusiastic for the task, it is possible to minimise risks and to improve the chance of success on any route. Even more important is that the swimmer should be of top class and of top sense. As one example of that last, any obstinacy in abandoning the swim when ordered by the boatman could lead to extreme risk for all engaged on the venture.

In this connection, some guidance will obviously be useful. I advise not starting any Irish Channel swim unless the forecast for the following 24 hours is settled and promises winds not more than Force 3. Of course forecasts *have* been wrong. But it is hardly a good bet to start the swim of a lifetime by assuming that the best meteorological brains in the country are going to be wrong! Finally, I believe a swim in this area ought to be discontinued if a wind Force 5 is encountered. Unless the skipper of the accompanying boat is confident that it is no more than a very temporary condition. Or if one is within half an hour or so of finishing.

Incidentally, the greatest part of the foreshore adjacent to both routes is rocky and rises quite abruptly out of deep water. One or two shelving beaches do exist, but a landing on rock is a virtual certainty. For this reason, it is preferable to arrange a swim to terminate in daylight. Even a three- or four-foot swell complicates landing. And a push on to rocks, which might mean no more than abrasions in daylight, could well provide a cracked rib in the dark.

This discussion opened with an appropriate quotation and may equally appropriately be closed with another. The 'Observations' of Sir Richard Hawkins state in one place—'One of the principal parts required in a Mariner that frequenteth our coastes of England is to cast his Tydes, and to know how they set from poynt to poynt, with the difference of those in the Channell from those of the shore.'

None of the above departure or arrival points are on the coast of England. Nevertheless aspiring Irish Channel swimmers would do well to note the advice. And to ally themselves as early as possible with such a Mariner.

22

The Channel. Special Training

Wise men gain experience from the misfortune of others, fools only from their own.

ROBERT BLAND

CONQUEST of the English Channel is an ever-pressing, but sometimes secret, ambition of most marathoneers. That is true not only in Britain, but in many far corners of the earth. There are countless equally swimmable patches of sea scattered round the world, but none appear even to approach the abiding magic of the Straits of Dover. As some men yearn for the sun, others for snow and mountains, we swimmers crave fine weather and the sight of Gris Nez in the background.

If ordinary marathon swimming is demanding, Channel-swimming is all demanding. There is no leisure time from the beginning of serious training to the end. Spare time—which is wholly different from leisure time—will abound. But it will be at all the wrong times, sandwiched between one training period and another. Or before a swim or after a swim. For over four months swimming must be the be-all and end-all of existence. Like every other exacting and rewarding experience in life, many are called and few are chosen. The record book shows that clearly.

For a successful Channel crossing there are two real essentials. They are—as in any marathon swimming—the ability to swim the distance in any reasonable weather, and ability to withstand the cold. Acclimatisation to cold was dealt with earlier in the book; every point then made remains valid for this longer distance. Preparation for marathon swimming was dealt with similarly.

Every point in that chapter is also applicable to the Channel. But now, instead of being the ultimate end, those instructions are only solid bedrock on which to build further.

Much sterner measures are now necessary; we will deal with the temperature aspect first. One must get accustomed to living at a temperature fifteen degrees below the ordinary man. The Channel attempt will probably be made in an approximate temperature of 16° C (61° F). It is thus obviously advantageous to live at that temperature, as much as possible, from the beginning of training to the end. It means doing without fires and central heating, and keeping warm by exercise instead. Dr. Bannister, the first four-minute miler, said that, in winter, the only thing which made him comfortably warm was running; for us it must be swimming. The warmth that comes from inside the body is many times as effective and comfortable as that which emanates from outside.

Open windows are a must in winter and summer. Hot baths are forbidden; cold or tepid showers at the swimming-pool must take their place. Overcoats, even in mid-winter, are also out. Unfortunately the English climate does demand a raincoat, but even that should be a light one. Scarves, gloves, and thick socks are softeners; so are 'long-handled' underpants. As the thermometer rises through spring and summer there should be a progressive shedding of day and night clothing. Bare comfort without luxury is the keynote of this conditioning.

There will always be a fool who overdoes the conditioning, or carries it out in jerks instead of gradually. These matters cannot be rushed; as in snakes and ladders the over-impatient competitor will find himself right back at the start. For health purposes, it is better to lag behind with the shedding of clothes than to be ahead of schedule. But good common sense and a good thermometer will almost always solve the problem. Once again each individual must be the arbiter of his own fate.

During a swim nothing can equal a healthy circulation for maintaining body-heat. Because nicotinic acid tablets are an aid to circulation, they may be used—with medical permission—for a few days before the big swim itself. A reasonable amount of flesh on one's bones is a great help, too. On the other hand, grossness is no more of an asset in Channel swimming than in other sports.

Extra fat certainly insulates against cold, but it detracts from speed and adds considerably to exertion. Artificially-induced heat is generally non-profitable; it is in the form of speculation with one's resources in place of sound investment. Chilli-paste irritates the skin and temporarily makes it feel hot. Hot whisky and water is a nice drink, and that also produces temporary heat; so does camphor. But the basic fact remains that any body has only a certain amount of heat to give away. It is better to spend that heat gradually, evenly, and naturally, than erratically and artificially. The artificial way sets the stage for collapse instead of natural fatigue.

Warm, sweet drinks are not artificial heaters. They put natural fuel into the body in easily and quickly usable form. They therefore warm and invigorate naturally. One word of warning here. The drinks should be little more than warm; too great and sudden a difference between inside and outside temperatures produces stomach upsets and sickness. On one occasion, after swimming Windermere, a kindly offered steaming cup of tea made me feel much worse than had the swim itself. Grease is, of course, no heater; but it does slow down the rate at which body heat leaks out into the sea. To what exact extent it slows down the leakage is not known, but most Channel swimmers use it on the 'every little helps' principle. (The best discussion on the subject that I have so far encountered was a special article in *The Lancet*. This was in the issue of 8th October 1955—'The Physiology of Channel Swimmers', by Doctors L. G. C. Pugh and O. G. Edholm.)

Most of the experienced swimmers I know favour lanoline as the basis of this covering. When warmed, it spreads evenly, and is nicely adhesive. Unfortunately, cold water contracts, hardens and coagulates it during a swim. It then drops off in lumps or, at best, gives most uneven protection. To stop that happening it is necessary to thin it down with an oil or lighter grease to an easy consistency. Thinning down also has the incidental benefit of easier removal at the end. And anyone who has tried to remove neat lanoline from a hairy chest will be unreservedly grateful for that benefit.

Application of grease—like so many other things in this sport—is a matter for individual ideas. Each swimmer feels the cold most in certain parts of his body; but the offending parts differ in different swimmers. For instance, my calf muscles and chest are most vulnerable; other swimmers have trouble in back, shoulders, or stomach. Each man must therefore apply extra grease to his own personal weak points. Portions that are constantly alternating between air and water need extra attention, too. That is the neck, shoulders, and upper arms.

The lower arms are tougher and more weathered; they can well do without grease. That has a secondary advantage, too. Grease on the lower arms and hands always somehow transfers itself to the goggles. And that is a major disaster to any swimmer. (Grease makes goggles difficult to see through; it makes them non-watertight and quite unfastenable.) In conjunction with grease the thorough oiling of every chafing surface is essential, and the necessity for the closest possible shave cannot be over-emphasised. Heat is certainly generated by friction, but the type of friction produced by a bristly chin is extremely local. It is also extremely painful.

Food, it has been mentioned before, is a fuel and a natural heat producer. It follows that a reasonable meal about an hour before starting is valuable. That time interval balances the need for part-digestion with the heat-producing advantages of a recent meal. The composition of the meal requires the wisdom of Solomon in advising. It requires to be of high calory value; to be easily digestible, and appetising enough to tempt a necessarily rather strung-up athlete. It should also be not too far different from the normal meal for that time of day. All those aspects are important, but emphasis, if any, should be on the last two. Getting to the start warm and contented is not quite 'half the battle', but it is a not insignificant factor.

During the swim, it is possible partially to recharge the body with very light meals taken 'on the run'. Solid foods are time-wasters and a strain on the digestion. Even chocolate, easiest of the solid foods, is strangely reluctant to go down the throat; when it does, it seems to take an extraordinarily large amount of sea-water with it. For that reason, highly nutritious drinks are quite the best form of meal. (I speak with feeling, having done my first very long swim on chicken sandwiches.) Beef-tea and soups cannot be bettered—especially the latter. Unfortunately, one cannot help swallowing much salt water on passage, and an after-effect of that is sometimes to make soup and beef-tea repugnant to the palate. In that case, a great and palatable freshener-cum-stimulant is sweet coffee. No doubt sweet tea would be equally good for those who normally like it that way.

My own favourite refreshment is a proprietary brand of glucose drink. Without doubt, it puts a clean new taste in the mouth. To my mind (imagination perhaps), it also sends new energy coursing into every part of the body. Glucose is universally recognised as a quick worker, but to work at the speed of my imagination it would have to be a miracle medicine. Individual fads again come to the fore. Bill Pickering likes a raw peach, but the thought may not attract others. Some swimmers like coffee sweetened with lashings of glucose. Ugh! That's all I can say about that. But that is the way it goes.

The matter may, in fact, be summed up in Dr. Hill's previously quoted words, 'A little of what you fancy does you good.' So long as the refreshment is liquid, palatable, and nutritious, it will be satisfactory. The most important point to be stressed is prior planning. Give it a good deal of thought beforehand, and try one or two alternatives to test their worth. Channel attempts cost much money and it is not sensible to embark on one without knowing the most suitable foods. Certainly in wartime the R.A.F. used to declare—when things went wrong—that 'it'll be all right on the night'. That, however, was mere modesty over operations that were as faultlessly planned as possible. Good planning applies to Channel swimming too.

Keeping warm is an art in itself. And knowledge of any art is not picked up overnight. Indoctrination must start from earliest training days so as to absorb it gently and naturally. I hope that constant reference to this book will help, but that is not all, for there is never a 'best' idea at anything. Somehow or other, there is always a better one germinating. It may be in your brain. The theory sounds complicated but the practice is not. There is, in this connection, a well-known story about a worried little bear who thought he would never learn to walk. He debated desperately which leg to start with. Should the legs work singly, in pairs, or some more complicated style? When he was almost sick with worry, his mother solved his problem with a thump over the ear. 'Get out and *walk*,' she said. He did.

The moral, therefore, is to get out and do something somehow. Refinements, advancements, and more detailed additions can be thought up weekly. Every mistake made is a lesson learned. Every new idea is a bonus, even if sometimes not payable till next year. So much for the theory and practice of keeping warm and comfortable in the water; the other half of a Channel success must come from sheer ability to swim. The foregoing remarks apply to that aspect with equal force. The ability must be fostered and improved slowly, steadily, and regularly.

Advancement of Channel training cannot be carried out too slowly, however. There is a big gap to bridge in a short time. Most marathoneers swim about half a mile a day in winter. From that starting point one must work up to twenty-one miles by mid-July. It is thus quite obvious that progress in training can never lag. There are two major alternatives in the method of training. One is to aim at a fast crossing, in which case the training accent is on speed. The other is to aim at a reasonably certain success, and in that case the accent is on stamina.

The fast, record-breaking method I intend only to sketch lightly. By the time swimmers reach that stage, they should have evolved their own ideas; they will probably also be taking a full-time trainer's advice. So here, for general information only, is the outline method. About three hundred miles swimming should be a sufficient groundwork. That swimming should be liberally punctuated with time-trials over relatively short distances. There should be a mile time-trial at least once a week; there should be several three-mile timed swims and several of four miles. Towards the end, the training should be topped off in the last three weeks with two fast six-hour swims and one eight-hour 'flat out' swim. This method gambles on the great occasion being able to squeeze extra reserves into play; in fine weather it is likely to produce conspicuous successes. That, in fact, is the crux of the whole matter; even quite moderate weather can 'kill' a swimmer trained by these methods. But for those who like to aim at the stars-or-nothing, it is ideal.

The slow but almost sure method is much more likely to be useful to readers, and it deserves discussion at greater length. The training period must be long enough to prepare the body, but not long enough to revolt the mind. Once the mind finds the prospect distateful, the battle is almost lost. For that reason the intensive training should be kept to about twenty weeks' duration. Of course, before starting on the twenty-week syllabus, much preliminary mileage should have been achieved. But that is pleasant recreation; it is the horse-work which comes later that could blunt the spirit. And let no one underestimate the horse-work; during the last part of the training, there are nearly twenty hours of swimming to be done each week.

That is not quite the whole picture. Few people are fortunate enough to live alongside their training ground. So travelling time, sometimes in annoying conditions, must be added. Undressing and dressing will also count for half an hour. All in all, the Channel aspirant must expect four hours hard voluntary daily toil on top of his normal—presumably eight-hour—working day. When meal-times have bee taken away, 'the rest of the time', as they say satirically in the Service, 'is his own'. No wonder staleness overcome even the sturdiest of spirits. In 1955, for instance, an Indian lawyer gave up his attempt when he had reached quite a favourable position in the Channel. He said he had 'lost interest in Channel swimming'. *The Times* fourth leader remarked that after coming thousands of miles and enduring much training, it seemed an odd time and place to lose interest. It was indeed, but the gentleman in question has my entire sympathy. Staleness strikes harshly and quickly, just like that.

Since Channel training is so much more arduous than ordinary marathon training, I recommend two rest days a week. For business reasons, it may not be possible to split the week evenly between rest days; the main thing is not to have those two non-swimming days consecutively. One of them should be after the weekly long swim. All my advice, it must be qualified, is directed at part-time amateurs; full-time professionals can stand a much more rigorous routine. The latter can arrange their life and their recuperation periods so as to absorb much more swimming work without exhaustion or staleness. But even professionals are vulnerable in the end. In highly professionalised League football a falling-off in form is often noticeable in the last few weeks of the season.

It is for that particular reason that a twenty-week programme and a mid-July peak has been selected. Nothing can ever be perfect, but that combination is as good a compromise as possible. The peak is timed for the first reasonable Channel swim period; indeed sometimes the *only* reasonable weather occurs during that month. Under-training and over-training are both undesirable, but in endurance events the latter is slightly preferable. So a mid-July peak can—with care—be maintained for a month into the alleged ideal part of the season. But whichever way one looks at it, there is obvious sense in being ready too early rather than too late. English weather—like time and tide—waits for no man.

Date	*No. of weeks*	*Four days a week Normal daily swim*	*Once per week Weekly special swim*	*Weekly total*
7 Jan.	1			
14 Jan.	2			
21 Jan.	3	PRELIMINARY TRAINING		
28 Jan.	4	'GO AS YOU PLEASE'		20 (4 weeks)
4 Feb.	5	MILEAGE		
11 Feb.	6	SHOULD BE ABOUT 45.		
18 Feb.	7			
26 Feb.	8			25 (4 weeks)
3 Mar.	9	1¼	2	7
10 Mar.	10	1½	2½	8½
17 Mar.	11	1¾	3	10
24 Mar.	12	2	3½	11½
31 Mar.	13	2¼	4	13
7 Apr.	14	2½	4½	14½
14 Apr.	15	2½	5	15
21 Apr.	16	2½	5½	15½
28 Apr.	17	2½	6	16
5 May	18	2½	6½	16½
12 May	19	2½	7	17
19 May	20	2½	7½	17½
26 May	21	2½	8	18
2 June	22	2½	9	19
9 June	23	2½	10	20
16 June	24	2½	12	22
23 June	25	2½	14	24
30 June	26	2½	16	26
7 July	27	2½	18	28
14 July	28	2½	20	30

Now for the details of the training plan. It visualises an already competent marathon swimmer commencing after his winter stand-easy. It also assumes a France–England swim in mid-July. For an England–France swim the weekly trials must lead up to distances 30 per cent greater than those tabulated. For a later date (if you disagree with the arguments in the last paragraph), just slide the whole routine back. The plan is carefully devised to cater for those whose swimming time is limited. The distance swims are pushed up gently and gradually each week.

Schedules, I have found, can never be rigidly adhered to. Business, Service, or health reasons always intervene. So long as the swimmer feels in his heart that he has done his best, all is well. It is the spirit and not the strict letter of the schedule that counts. After all, the Channel attempt is certainly voluntary, so no benefit comes from cheating oneself. One last word. Use the rest days to best advantage. Do something completely different involving no physical effort at all. Have a picnic, see a play, attend a lecture or write your letters. So long as it is a complete change it is good.

23

Every Little Helps

For want of a nail the shoe was lost,
For want of a shoe the horse was lost,
For want of a horse the rider was lost,
For want of a rider the battle was lost.
OLD FRENCH MILITARY PROVERB

IF you can swim well enough and stand the cold long enough, this chapter could be redundant. It deals with all those minor matters which retard every swimmer, and undoubtedly dismay some of them. Individually, each mentioned point is worth only a minute or so. Collectively, they may put an hour or more on a Channel swim. For a tidal swim, in which every moment is planned and precious, they are all nails which could ultimately lose the battle.

Night swimming is one case in point. Hardly one swimmer in a hundred ever practises at night. Yet it may well happen—quite unexpectedly—for part of a Channel attempt to extend far into the dark hours. It is wise, therefore, not to neglect this matter entirely during training. The point requires no tremendous emphasis because, between day and night swimming there is no tremendous difference. But even hard case Bill Pickering confessed that he found night swimming a little eerie at first. And where some mental disquiet exists, there can never be full physical efficiency. Practice can be obtained by hiring a boat once or twice, and having a trial spin after dark. Less ideally but more economically, one should obtain permission to swim in a darkened bath after everyone else has left.

As an aid to realism, a bright light must shine directly into the face. That is to simulate the floodlight which most Channel boats use for keeping their swimmers in sight. Lights shining into the face can be sheer torture as many ex-prisoners-of-war will confirm. But this light really is for one's own benefit. To dodge out of it is foolish unless one fancies being lost at sea. It is just one more thing to endure, and is best not left till the actual attempt before making its acquaintance. It's mighty lonely on a dark rough night in mid-Channel.

Treading water is another knack worth a brush-up. Every competent swimmer fondly imagines himself to be an expert at this without practice. But when tried simultaneously while using both hands to adjust goggles, it is sometimes more difficult than expected. It is therefore good value from earliest days to carry out all goggle adjusting in the deep-end of the training pool. The shallow-end is certainly more convenient but equally certainly there is no convenient shallow-end in mid-Channel. The knack is soon acquired, but—once again—is best not left until the big day for first experiment.

Into a similar category comes the matter of feeding in the water. This requires a threefold ability. First, to tread water effortlessly, second, to hold a drink container well clear of the sea, and third, to drink from that container. The procedure is by no means easy at first, but soon becomes so. One or two trial runs are all that are necessary. Receiving the container from the boat is difficult only if the method has received no prior thought. Boats are relatively clumsy to manœuvre but swimmers can do very much to help themselves with a deft stroke or two.

The different behaviour of boats and swimmers has already been noted in a previous chapter. Because of these differences any boat must necessarily lose time in approaching to transfer food. That is quite unavoidable, but delay can easily be halved by use of cardboard containers. These can be thrown away after drinking and the boat does not have to return to the swimmer to collect the empties. A six-foot-long stick can also cut down the necessity for a good deal of boat manœuvring. Fastened to the end of the stick should be a ring into which a cardboard cup can be inserted. (Such things are easily obtainable. They are standard bathroom equipment for holding tooth-mugs.) Knowledge of the capabilities of boats, and provision of this elementary piece of apparatus will save minutes at every feeding stop. Many swimmers prefer to drink from medicine (or similar) bottles because it is easier to exclude salt water from getting in. If considered as expendable these are, of course, just as convenient as cardboard cups.

On a twelve-hour swim, the swimmer-trainer code of signals assumes much additional importance. On an average, there will be one or two communications desirable in each hour. Above everything else, the swimmer will wish to know his progress. For this purpose, two sets of diving judges cards will be invaluable. One set in black may indicate 'hours from the start'; the other set in red may indicate—when it becomes known—'hours to go'. Alternatively, or additionally, short messages can be chalked distinctly on a slate in block letters. No attempt should be made to pass verbal messages; if the ears are plugged it can only lead to misunderstanding, or annoyance.

Even chalked messages must be concise, helpful, and infrequent. Woolly remarks like 'You're doing fine', 'or 'Keep it up', are neither informative or particularly encouraging. No one knows better than the swimmer himself how he is doing, and a chalked-up message on a slate will not restore his energy if he is feeling bad. Much more useful is definite information which he has no means of knowing otherwise. 'On schedule', or '15 minutes ahead', are good examples of encouragement. Messages in reverse (from swimmer to attendant) can be shouted. These also should be confined strictly to requirements and must never become conversational. Talkativeness is one of the most fruitful sources of wasted time. If one minute can be saved on each of twenty occasions the total benefit is obvious.

Checked and tested equipment is of paramount importance. Defective equipment is responsible for more delay and more heartbreak than any factor except the weather. For lesser marathon swimming I have sometimes advocated not using goggles, earplugs and helmets. But Channel swimming belongs to the supermarathon category and such aids now become advisable for the majority. The number of Channel crossings completed without some or all of these aids can be counted on the fingers of one hand.

Some ear protection is essential, and here is a suggested method. First dip a little finger into the vaseline-pot to get a light covering.

Then transfer that *light* covering to the inside of the ear passage. Great lumps of vaseline are definitely not required; vaseline on the ear-drum is as unwanted as wax, and equally difficult to remove. The light covering of vaseline is merely to give a smoothly treated surface to the cotton wool that follows. (The skin may otherwise become irritable after several hours' contact with cotton wool.) Next comes the small wad of cotton wool. That should be flattened out, some vaseline applied, and then rolled into a plug with the vaseline *inside* the roll. This gives the plug a pliable consistency, which will keep it in place for many hours. On top of that should be fitted a much larger wad into the outer ear. If the whole is now covered with the flap of a helmet or cap, nothing short of a depth-charge will ever shift it.

I particularly advise cotton wool, because practically nothing will keep the ear entirely watertight. (Plasticine is one exception, but many ears are allergic to it.) The main object therefore becomes to prevent painful onslaught on the ear drums by constantly repeated douches of cold salt water. Cotton wool, by maintaining an insulating wall between body-heat and water-heat, does this admirably. It has the advantage over rubber plugs of being adjustable to size and depth of ear. It is also, of course, easily replaceable.

Helmets are like fancy waistcoats; everyone has his own idea of what is most suitable. White ones have the merit of being easily visible from the boat on most occasions. Black ones, on the other hand, are almost invisible in the sea, but they do attract any heat which is present in the sea. (For confirmation of that point, put a black helmet and a white one side by side in the sun for half an hour, and then feel the difference.) Water-polo caps have the merit of ear-flaps, which are perfect for keeping the cotton wool plugging in position. Some types of rubber helmets have the same advantages. Skin-tight rubber helmets are much more of a hindrance than a help, however. They rapidly become uncomfortable, and also efficiently retard circulation. Notwithstanding all advice, nothing is more certain than that everyone will continue to please themselves. They will continue to wear their 'lucky' cap, their favourite colour, or just the cap they found in the dressing-room five seasons back.

Of all items of swimmers' equipment, goggles are quite the touchiest. More time and temper has been wasted with them than with any other cause. One must swim regularly in goggles from the very start of training; by the time of the Channel attempt wearing them will then be as natural as swimming itself. By that time, too, the particular idiosyncracies of one's own pair should be entirely understood. Some goggles react so temperamentally to the strap being only an inch out of position on the back of the head, that they flood-up every two or three minutes. It is extremely wise to buy two pairs and to use them alternately. Then an accident to one pair is merely a minor annoyance and not a major tragedy. I am a 'belt and braces' man myself; I keep four pairs!

Misted-up goggles are constant and inevitable frustrations. Alleged methods of prevention are as numerous as pigeons in Trafalgar Square. Glass cleaning with methylated spirits, using gas respirator anti-dim ointment, and rubbing with a piece of raw potato are amongst the favourite remedies. To my own idea the best method is to keep a small amount of water *inside* the goggles; then, by putting the head down and shaking the captive water, it is always possible to clear the lens without difficulty.

For that reason, it is undesirable to empty the goggles of water automatically. Every few moments spent in adjustment is a few moments wasted. Goggles can become nearly a quarter-full before becoming really unusable. Whenever emptying appears to me imminent, and necessary, I resolve to swim another thirty strokes. Then, if possible, another thirty, and so on. Very often the goggles seem partially to empty of their own accord. Sometimes, of course, that does not happen, but at least the frequency of stoppages is cut down and the end-total reduced.

Swimming for the first time in goggles, ear-plugs, and helmet is a thoroughly peculiar experience. The world outside seems quite remote; one swims in an incredibly silent and comfortable world of one's own. It is like flying in a closed aircraft after the exhilaration of an open one. But both forms of closed-in activity have their advantages; chiefly it is that one can withstand the elements for a very much longer period of time. I am sure that the additional warmth and comfort has made just the required difference which enabled several border-line aspirants to win through.

Pre-swim accessories are also important. Thrillers, playing-cards, writing materials, hobbies. Their nature is unimportant so long as they absorb every moment of spare time. Much spare time will undoubtedly ensue; unless it is fully occupied the nagging doubts and worries begin to creep in. One great relief I have found personally is to realise how many quite ordinary people have performed even greater physical feats than crossing the Channel.

In 1888, George Littlewood ran six hundred and twenty-three miles, in six days' non-stop running. In 1897 George Haroo and Frank Samuelson *rowed* across the wide Atlantic. For sheer guts and endurance, without much physical exertion, Poon Lim's record is awe-inspiring. He was one hundred and thirty-two days alone on a raft in a North Atlantic winter. On reflection, swimming the Channel on a selected day seems rather small beer compared with the strong ale of those incredible achievements.

By the way, one last tip. If, during an attempt you realise some planning aspect has been overlooked, don't worry. Bash on for the other side regardless. Despite what I have written, everybody forgets *something*. After five minutes' swimming on my successful England–France record attempt something occurred to my mind. My ear-plugs were still at the bottom of a bag in the attendant boat—instead of in my ears! As author of this chapter on 'how never to forget things', I was too proud to stop and admit an oversight! So I swam on for another 13½ hours without them!

24

Introduction to the Channel

To strive, to seek, to find, and not to yield.
TENNYSON

THE first, the most important, and the most anxiously argued point is the distance from Dover to Cape Gris Nez. In a straight line it is seventeen and three-quarter sea miles, or twenty and a half land miles. Recently, after making that point in a lecture, a not-so-bright young thing immediately asked me how much was the reverse distance from Gris Nez to Dover. I hope and believe that most readers will be able to work that one out for themselves.

The difference between land miles and sea miles immediately spotlights a difficulty. Because of it many swimmers, throughout the century, have been hopelessly confused. They, being used to land measurement, have naturally used statute miles for the basis of all calculations. Boatmen and pilots, being men of the sea, equally naturally use nautical miles. So, on very many occasions there has been misunderstanding right from the start. For convenience, and the general benefit, I shall try to relate everything in this chapter to the land, or statute mile.

Nevertheless, it may well be necessary to consult other publications which are not geared to land miles. For that reason three short explanations follow. A land mile is five thousand, two hundred and eighty feet. A sea mile is six thousand and eighty feet. A '*knot' is a speed of one sea mile an hour*. Very roughly, then, for the purpose of comparison, six land miles are just a trifle more than five sea miles. And because of that five knots bears the same proportion to six land miles per hour. These few simple details should clear confusion once and for all. (For those abroad who normally use the metric system, it should be noted that a kilometre is 3,282 feet—or very roughly half a sea mile.)

I have carefully analysed Tom Blower's 1951 two-way Channel attempt. It certainly appears that failure was most tremendously bound up in that misunderstanding of measurement. Tom told his navigators that he could swim for over a day at *two knots* constant speed. The navigators then scientifically and methodically worked out the best courses related to that speed. Tom, I believe, meant that he could swim two land miles an hour for that period, but unwittingly gave the navigators the wrong basis for calculation. Because of that, the cumulative error gradually wrecked the navigators' schedule. My reason for the conclusion is firstly that a speed of two knots requires each land mile to be swum in twenty-six minutes. And secondly that at a Nottingham bath he once swam 55 miles at an average of 32½ minutes apiece; over 21 miles he would doubtless have been faster but never a two-knotter.

Those who have swum even one single straight mile in twenty-six minutes know that pace to be pretty fast. It is the equivalent of a twenty-four-minute mile in an enclosed bath. Further, by the use of graphs and several experiments, it can be proved that a swimmer able to reel off twenty-six-minute miles indefinitely, should be capable of sprinting a single twenty-one-minute mile when required. Tom Blower, although the supreme distance swimmer of his day, was *not* quite so fast as that. Not even in a swimming-bath, let alone on the turbulent Channel waters. So, although other factors intervened (a conflict of opinion at the start, a patch of adverse wind and sea, and later a strained shoulder), that misunderstanding seems to stand out as the real cause of failure.

So much for the distance; now for the courses. As a matter of precision, the nearest points on the opposing coasts are joined by a line running from 145° to 325°. (North is 0°, east is 90°, south is 180°, west is 270°, and North—to complete the circle—is also 360°). As a more readily understandable generalisation the compass courses are north-north-west and south-south-east according to which coast is the destination. It would be economical in energy and record-breaking in time, if a swimmer's track could exactly follow those directions. Unfortunately, the tides sometimes flow at twice as fast a rate as the swimmer; as a result the track usually takes the form of a lean but recognisable letter S.

The question next uppermost in people's minds is to know the best direction for swimming. For two reasons the easiest direction is quite certainly from France to England, rather than vice versa. The first reason is largely self-evident and is easily demonstrated. Take a pair of dividers and lay out a chart or map of the area (incidentally, Admiralty Chart No. 1895—Dover Strait—is excellent). With one divider point fixed on the extreme tip of Cape Gris Nez, swing the other one across to the English coast. It will be seen that—with the same span of distance—the moving divider point runs along the English coast from South Foreland to Shakespeare Cliff, a distance of four and a half miles. Therefore a France–England swimmer can miscalculate, or be swept off course, by several miles without much inconvenience. He will still be able to land, albeit on a different part of the coast, without having to swim any further. Now look at the route in reverse. It is quite evident that a swimmer who misses landing precisely on the isolated tip of Gris Nez will be faced with an extra swim of a mile or so.

The second reason is easier to state but harder to prove. The tidal stream flows through the Strait from the Channel to the North Sea and vice versa. But because of configurations of the coast, the stream never runs exactly true through the Strait. Although the bias is averagely only a few degrees towards the English coast, it does give a measurable advantage to an England-bound swimmer. Conversely, there is a measurable disadvantage to a France-bound swimmer. So the conjunction of advantage to one and disadvantage to the other does open up quite a time-gap between, say, two equally competent swimmers attempting opposite directions in equal conditions.

The distance factor plus the tidal stream factor does therefore make a France–England swim a considerably easier proposition than the reverse. To cement the proof I had intended to average out the times of all successful southbound swimmers and plot them against those of all successful northbound swimmers. On reflection, however, it was obvious that a misleading picture would be presented. For one thing, no one can now judge the relative speeds of the various pre-war swimmers in undisturbed conditions. For another, the England–France total would be heavily outweighed with the earlier and slower breast-stroke conquerors. It is better, therefore, to consider two swims by the same swimmer. Even that method is affected by certain factors, but if known they can be taken into account.

Tom Blower was a wonderfully consistent swimmer over the years. It is indicative therefore that he took five hours longer from England to France than vice versa. As previously observed, I consider that he lost quite considerably on the navigational score; he may also have been swimming a trifle slower in order to save something for the return trip. The effect of these factors would be to close the difference to about three hours. Abilio Couto, a mature non-temperamental swimmer, crossed both ways during a period of one month in 1959. He was 1 hour 16 minutes faster on the France to England route. It is necessary to make one important point here. The France–England advantage—although ever-present—will become less pronounced as swimmers get faster. For statistical analysis the Mickman swims must be entirely disregarded. He had appallingly bad luck with tides on his France–England swim and was anyway an improved and more experienced swimmer on his later reversed course swim. That is an example of what was said in the last paragraph about known factors being taken into account.

The degree of extra difficulty varies with the speed of swimming. This point is important. For instance, in the case of the earlier swimmers, the England–France crossing appears to be 50 per cent more difficult than the reverse way. But in the case, say, of a 30-knot destroyer there would be only a few minutes of difference—and a very small percentage. The greater speed largely, but not of course altogether, over-rides tidal effects. Most of we modern swimmers are between the slow swimmers of yesteryear and the destroyers and suffer proportionate tidal effects. In my opinion, for a reasonable crawl performer, the extra difficulty might be assessed at approximately 15 per cent.

Whichever way one swims, tidal effect is of extreme importance. As previously stated the stream sometimes runs at a rate of more than double that of a swimmer. Although the swimmer himself—being far from any landmarks—never notices any difference, the tidal conditions are the constant care of pilots and boatmen. From their higher and better vantage point it should be generally possible to keep an exact tab on sets and drifts, and to allow for them. Patently, it is quite useless to swim *into* the tide, one would merely become exhausted—and go backwards into the bargain. Neither is it useful to swim directly with the tide. Although a speed of six miles an hour could be achieved on occasions, progress would unfortunately not be in the correct direction. The only solution is to calculate the timing of swims, so that each successive tide cancels out—as far as possible—the disadvantages of its predecessor.

Here is the theory: the practice is slightly more difficult. There are two complete tidal cycles daily in the Straits of Dover (many people may think that mentioning two tides daily is stating the obvious, but that is not so; at close-by Southampton there are four tides daily). Anyway, a twice-daily tide means roughly that the tidal stream runs six hours in one direction before turning to run six hours in the other. That further means that a piece of wood thrown into mid-Channel at slack water might travel several miles towards the North Sea and then back on the return tide. After one complete tidal cycle it would be in much the same place as when it started.

Bearing that principle in mind, a swimmer should start at such a time as to have a fairly equal amount of tide in each direction. All that then remains for him to do is to swim on the right course for twenty-one miles. After approximately six hours he may be swept alarmingly far from his correct line of progress, but after twelve hours the tide will have returned him to it.

Let us carry that a stage further. Consider a swimmer who cannot complete a crossing in such a tidy time as twelve hours. For an estimated fourteen-hour crossing he will require roughly seven hours stream in each direction; for a fifteen-hour swim, seven and a half hours stream in each direction, and so on. Since the tide never runs more than six hours either way, the balance must be made up with odd bits and pieces. For simplicity the movement towards the North Sea will be called north-east stream; that travelling towards the main English Channel, south-west stream.

Take the case of the fourteen-hour swimmer. He can use one hour's south-west stream, six hours' north-east stream, six hours' south-west, and finish with one hours' north-east. That will approximately balance our fourteen hours of tides and—since the tidal cycle occurs twice daily—give him the option of two starting times every day. Alternatively, he can start with one hour's north-east stream, and reverse the whole sequence. That provides two more alternative starting times. Obviously the same type of 'tidal share-out' can be made for fifteen hours, sixteen hours, or any other length of swim. Ultimately, with a twenty-four-hour swim, one again achieves a tidy answer with two whole tides in each direction. There is obviously a great deal to be said for the ultra slow swimmer.

If it is so easy in theory, why is it so difficult in practice? Unfortunately, the sea can never be relied upon to work to rule. Contours of shallow patches and configurations of coastlines divert the stream from true. The tide does not move neatly and tidily in one mass; the direction changes in different places at different times and rarely—as might be expected—does change occur at high and low water. In places where the stream runs parallel to the coast, there is usually a slight indraught into bays and indentations. The twelve-hour tidal cycles are not quite exact; successive high waters follow each other at intervals of about twelve hours, twenty-five minutes. In addition to the tidal stream, there is a regular current which flows slowly from the English Channel to the North Sea. Winds affect the rate and direction of that current. These are all unpredictables which make calculation and planning so difficult.

There are two main ways of cutting down errors. The first is to swim in settled meteorological conditions; that is almost always done, but occasionally it is not possible. For instance, a swimmer who has been waiting for weeks is sometimes forced to have at least a try between patches of bad weather. The other error remover is to swim at 'neap tides'. Twice a month the sun and moon pull in the same direction and produce big tides which are known as 'spring-tides'; exactly in between those spring-tides the sun and moon pull at right-angles to one another and much reduce the size of tide. This last effect is called 'neap-tides' and because the resultant streams run much slower, any errors in calculation are correspondingly smaller.

Swimming at neaps is particularly desirable on the England–

France direction. As previously shown, the net result of all tidal factors is to produce a definite (albeit slight) tendency towards England. A swimmer going in the reverse direction will therefore wish to cut that effect down as much as possible. By swimming at neaps that is achieved together with greater precision of navigation. On the other hand, a France–England swimmer can land anywhere between South Foreland and Shakespeare Cliff and precise navigation is not so essential to him. A swimmer in that direction will wish also to augment the tidal advantage to maximum. Since spring-tides produce maximum rates it is obviously useful to him to utilise them. Thus the advantage lies with the neap-tides from England to France, and spring-tides from France to England. There are always exceptions to every rule, and several good times have been done without these conditions. Spring tides also make the final landing more difficult.

It is for those reasons that Channel swimmers are heard to speak about the 'first August tides' or the 'second July tides'. At the best those terms are generalisations, at worst—as it all depends on the direction of swim—they are complete misnomers. For a France-bound swimmer, about one and a half days either side of exact neaps is considered very suitable; for an England-bound swimmer one and a half days either side of springs is held in equally high regard, provided one can finish at slack water to facilitate landing. Overseas readers who wish to forecast ahead but who have no access to Dover tide-tables are not lost—there is a good enough guide. Full moons and new moons are shown in most diaries; add a day to those dates for the rough dates of spring tides. And naturally, having ascertained the date of a spring tide, neaps can be calculated by adding or subtracting one week. Adjustments may have to be made later when the tide tables become available, but for long-term forward thinking the diary method is adequate.

Therefore, from the theoretical maximum of four starting times daily from either side, one is now brought to a more practical figure of *four possibilities daily for two periods of three days in each month*. There is also a further restriction. Since day air temperatures are several degrees warmer than night temperatures, it is foolish—if any choice exists—to swim by night rather than day. So that again halves the number of ideal starting times. Inevitably, however, pilots will be forced by circumstances to abandon idealism for opportunism. Bill Pickering's 1955 record swim was a case in point. He had waited for several weeks, and was forced to swim or go home. 'Pop' Burwill, his pilot, calculated correctly and got his man to victory, although the tide certainly was not ideal. Pickering did his part in the improvisation by agreeing to swim through the night.

By now it must be evident to all what tremendous faith it is necessary to place in the pilot. I hope those unused to the sea can see that pilotage is a big and tricky job. It is not just a question of —as one Channel aspirant put it to me—starting up the boat and steering for the other side. I get rather tired of six-knot yachtsman friends telling me, 'You thirty-knot destroyer captains can never know the first thing about tides.' A good deal of my spare time is spent navigating at one quarter of their admittedly modest speeds and without their instruments. I would like to assure everyone that navigation at one and a half knots is a real work of art—and that the local pilots are great artists.

The pilots' method of calculation is practical and instinctive. They look at the swimmer to note his speed, look at the weather to see how it is settling, look at how the sea is running; then they make their decision. Furthermore they are able constantly to adjust the answer as new or changed conditions complicate the problem. The ordinary swimmer, therefore, wisely and safely leaves all these matters to his pilot.

Occasionally however competent navigators come to the Channel lacking only specialised knowledge of swimmers' capabilities. For these I believe a paper of mine—'Navigation in Channel Swimming' in *J. Inst. Nav.* vol. XIII, No. 1—will help. But it must be emphasised that *this* chapter is not intended to make 'every man his own navigator'. It is primarily meant to sow the seeds of understanding in swimmers' minds. And to show that a crossing is a partnership between the pilot's experience and his own physical fitness; neither could be successful without the other. 'Know-it-all' swimmers are doomed to constant friction and 'go-it-alone' experts bound for tragedy. Edward James May was a case in point. He was strong as an ox, could swim like an otter, and bristled with confidence. Pulling his necessities behind him on a raft, he set off by himself and regrettably never again seen alive.

Other things feature in an introduction to the Channel besides study of navigation and tides. Such mundane things, for instance, as expenses, rules and official observers. The first is of outstanding interest for intending competitors. Hotel bills, fares, pocket-money, boats and pilots' fees all swell the total. Without skimping, about £250 would cover, for one person, an attempt preceded by four weeks' waiting at Dover. *With* skimping, that might cover the trainer's expenses as well.

The rules are all laid out in the handbook of the Channel Swimming Association, to which every aspirant is advised to belong. Use of an official C.S.A. observer is a benefit of membership, which rules out the necessity for filing attested affidavits. One must walk into the sea from the point of departure and swim until able to touch dry land on the other side with no seawater beyond. Only one tug or motor-boat is permitted plus a small boat for feeding purposes. It goes without saying that buoyant apparatus and webbed gloves are definitely not *de rigeur*. Committees and competitors frequently generate new ideas at Annual General Meetings. It will be wise therefore, in due course, to consult official C.S.A. literature rather than to rely implicitly on this paragraph.

25

Channel Weather

Dirty British coaster with a salt-caked smoke stack
Butting through the Channel in the mad March days.
JOHN MASEFIELD

CHANNEL aspirants are fortunate that they need never select the month of March for their endeavours. But even the largest Channel swimmer is considerably smaller than a dirty British coaster. Because of that relative size the swimmer could feel much discomfort in August if he tried to 'butt' through the Channel. Weather study is as important to the swimmer as it is to the captain of a ship.

Readers of *1066 and All That* know that history is divided into *good* things and *bad* things. So, too, is meteorology. Generally speaking, anti-cyclones—despite a forbidding name—are good things. Depressions are bad. Such generalisation may cause a wagging of sage heads at the Meteorological Office, but for the swimmer it is true. The ordinary marathoneer cannot spare time to explore the fascinating byways of physics and advanced meteorology; he wants only to know the bare bones of the matter as they affect him. Should any reader be inspired by this chapter into desiring more knowledge, that is an unplanned bonus. His local librarian will reveal a score of excellent and interesting books to carry the study further. Right here I intend to keep to the minimum of essentials.

Critics will rush to the cliché. 'A little knowledge,' these do-nothing little men shout tediously, 'is a dangerous thing.' There is certain truth in the allegation. But I hope to convey only enough information to ease the sometimes strained relationship between swimmer and pilot. There is much difference in the outlook between a stolid weather-wise seaman and a tensed-up, inexperienced anxious channel aspirant. Bridging that gap is a service to both sides. It will also provide enough knowledge to recognise the quite impossible swimming periods, and even that negative knowledge will save much worry. This chapter will certainly not turn out a meteorologist, but it will turn out a swimmer with that 'little extra something the others haven't got', as a petrol advertisement so succinctly observes. That extra something cannot fail to be an asset. So tell the critics that 'In the kingdom of the blind, the one-eyed man is king.' And then read on.

A depression is a circular or oval 'dent' of low pressure in an area of higher pressure. Naturally the high pressure pushed towards the low, and this sets up an air movement known as wind. Wind does not blow directly towards the centre but spirals inwards. Like the celebrated 'never-never bird' it flies in ever-decreasing circles until it collides with itself in the centre of the low pressure area. Besides spiral movement there is also vertical movement, but, since the swimmer is unconcerned with conditions at twenty-thousand feet, that aspect is unimportant here. The spiral action is due to the earth's rotation and is thus—in the Northern Hemisphere—always anti-clockwise. A homely analogy which will clarify the description is that of bath-water spiralling around the low pressure area of the plug-hole as it runs out. (Whether bath-water, under undisturbed conditions, always spirals anti-clockwise is a research in which I have spent many bath-robbed hours which could have been better employed.)

Depressions have tidy habits. Besides rotating anti-clockwise, they usually move towards the north and east, and they usually

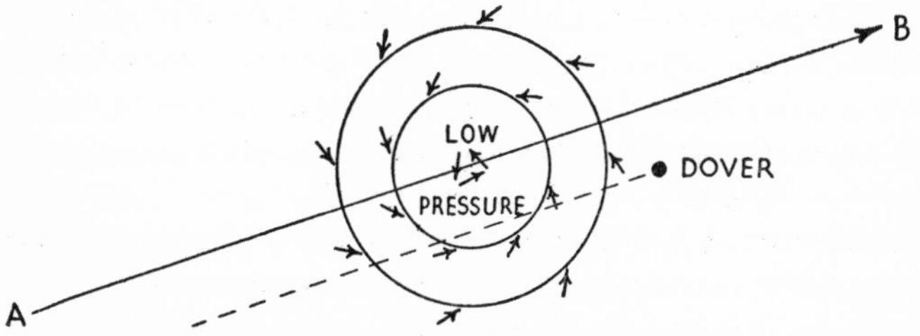

pass north of Dover. That is quite convenient, because it brings a more or less stereotyped train of circumstances. An illustration of a depression is at the foot of the previous page. It is approaching and passing north of Dover. At the moment of illustration that town is experiencing light south-east breezes as can be seen by the nearest wind arrow. But as the depression gets nearer, the wind strengthens and changes. If you can imagine the whole system, spiralling away along the long arrowed line AB you will see that Dover will go in one side of the system and come out the other. As I cannot show the system passing *forwards* over Dover, the dotted line shows Dover imaginarily moving *backwards* through the depression to gain the same relative effect. So by moving a pencil back along the dotted line you can see, by the wind arrows, what the changes will be. From south-east the wind will veer to south and increase as the centre approaches. Then south-west, west, and dying out in the north-west as the depression recedes into the distance. That cycle of events, or part of that cycle, will occur every time a depression passes to the north of you.

That knowledge should help a swimmer to understand the boatman who advises against starting a swim, even though the wind seems favourable. He knows that, under shelter of the coast, the sea can look deceptively calm. Every mile offshore builds the sea higher, and a shift of wind will turn it into a series of angry frothing pyramids which make swimming impossible. Starting in those conditions only wastes his time. More important, it wastes your energy and money. During the time you are recovering from the abortive swim—and most swimmers require three days or more—you may miss a good and suitable spell of weather. Better therefore to do what the pilot advises. After all, even very qualified and experienced ship-captains have been doing just that thing for many years.

The foregoing sketch shows one depression only. It would be excellent if they always operated singly and that fine weather followed automatically. Unfortunately they sometimes follow each other like customers at a cafeteria counter; in that case it may be weeks before settled weather arrives. But why should a pilot sometimes vote against a weather forecast compiled by specialist scientists? That question is frequently asked and is easy to answer. At best you will be lucky to get even a wireless forecast compiled from data which is only about two hours stale. At worst, with newspaper charts, the information may be half a day stale. For that reason, the pilot with bang up-to-date observation allied to local knowledge can often produce a much superior forecast. To simplify still further, the scientists know what *ought* to happen; the seaman knows what *is* happening.

Nevertheless, the newspaper or television chart is useful if correctly used. It shows, better than anything else can, what *type* of weather to expect. It shows whereabouts the centre of the low pressure is situated. The spacing of the oval lines (isobars) shows the approximate strength of wind. Spaced widely apart is an indication that pressures are not very different and therefore the wind will be light. Closely spaced isobars indicate steep differences of pressure which in turn indicate violent air movements. So with the weather map to give the general picture, the last diagram to recall the theory, and your own eyes to make up-to-the-minute observations, amateur forecasting should not be too difficult. There is one other important point about wind direction. In the Straits, winds are often deflected by the coast-line and may not represent, say, the mid-Channel wind. For that reason I prefer to watch the lowest clouds possible as direction markers; they do need to be fairly low because high clouds frequently move in quite a different direction.

It is not necessary to be able to box the compass; nor indeed is it necessary to have a compass to box. Eight directions will be sufficient for our use in elementary calculations. Everyone knows north, south, east and west; almost everyone knows that mid-way between north and east is north-east, between south and east is south-east, and so on. It is also well to know that, when reading a map, north is almost always at the top. (Perhaps this is too elementary for some readers, but others are treading this seaman-like path for the first time. And having lectured to young seamen over several years, I well know the folly of trying to start from too advanced a point.) Noting direction comes automatically after a time. Here are one or two tips on how to go about it. Wind blowing from Dover to the nearest French coast is north-west; from the nearest French coast towards Dover is south-east. From the North Star, north; towards it, south. The sun rises nearly east and sets nearly west; at one o'clock in the afternoon (1200 G.M.T.)

it is due south. There are direction vanes on flagstaffs. One of these aids to direction-finding will always be present until a sense of direction becomes entirely natural.

So much for day-to-day study of the weather. Swimmers from abroad will be keen to know what they may reasonably anticipate. During the Channel swimming season, over half the winds blow from south-west, west, and north-west, in accordance with the habits of depressions. Nearly a quarter blow from exactly opposite, i.e., north-east, east, and south-east. The other directions are also-rans. According to statistics, flat calm weather and gales should be equally non-existent, and in fact the average wind is in the region of fifteen miles an hour. Such a wind speed should not stop swimming but does make it difficult. One's wish should therefore be for something better than average. Again according to statistics, open-sea swimming should be possible on at least one day in two. But, and this is the point, the suitable weather may not always last long enough for a ten–fourteen hour crossing. That sounds rather discouraging but should not be so. Long spells of better-than-average weather sometimes persist for weeks; they are often results of anti-cyclonic systems. I have left discussion of these systems until now on the principle of keeping the best things until last.

Anti-cyclonic (high-pressure) systems do bring settled weather. They are less frequent visitors to the U.K. than depressions, but when they do arrive they are usually stickers. Nothing will shift them until—in their own good time—they dissipate their pressure and die naturally. Depressions either bounce off or travel round the outside. This is good news for the swimmer because many of the best Channel crossings have been done in such conditions. High pressure systems are larger than depressions and spiral clockwise and outwards, an exact reverse to depressions. Armed with the diagram below, general weather conditions can be forecast fairly accurately.

Once again Dover is shown on the eastern edge of the system and is encountering northerly winds. I have pictured this particular position because local authorities contend that this is exceptionally good augury. If these light northerly winds persist for a few days, settled weather is an excellent bet. Sometimes the situation remains unchanged for two or three weeks. Anti-cyclones

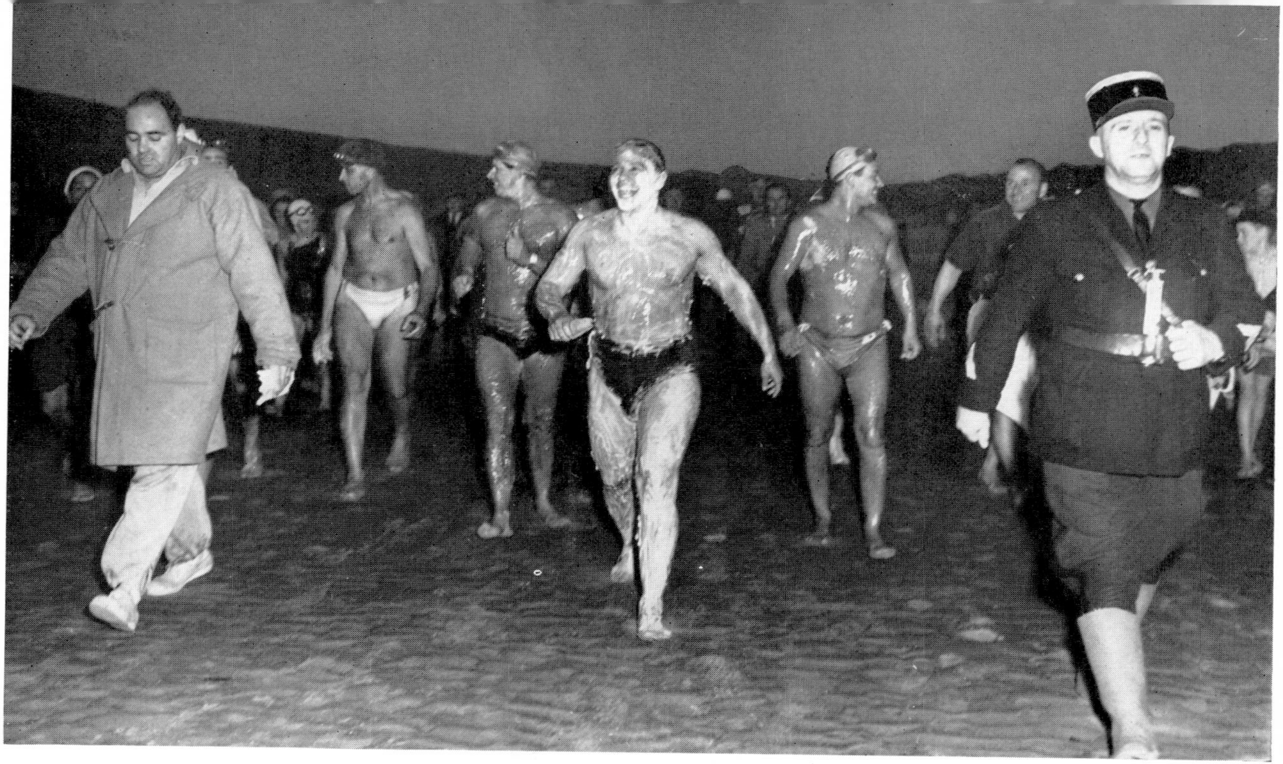

Fast Channel swimmers are not grossly overweight, the photograph shows four well-developed physiques.

Author is served with breakfast in Loch Lomond by Jack Brown and George Owen.

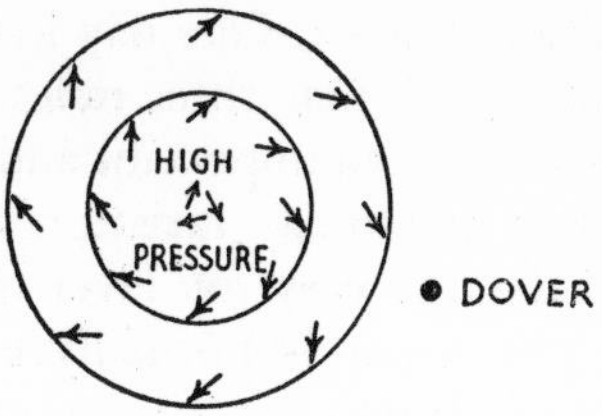

may move in any direction and sometimes even reverse their courses—without much warning. But by comparing yesterday's chart with the day before yesterday's it is usually possible to get a good idea.

Even the best of friends have defects and anti-cyclones are no exception. The calm conditions they produce are favourable to fog, that other enemy to the Channel aspirant. Off Dover, true sea-fog is not the main offender; land radiation fog is more common. Since the swimmer cannot see to swim in either variety, that appears to be rather an academic point but, in reality, is not. Land radiation fog is usually thick at sunrise, but gradually clears up as the sun heats the land. Smoke pollution does aggravate these conditions but it is nevertheless comparatively rare for a whole day to be unsuitable. This type of weather is therefore greatly preferable to sea-fog which persist for days.

In my opinion a Channel crossing ought never to be attempted when the visibility is less than three miles. There are two main reasons for that; one is safety, the other is wastage of effort. There is much shipping in the Channel, and some of it is very fast traffic indeed. A twenty-knot ship covers three miles in nine minutes and that does not allow much time for action. A ship cannot brake like a car; it goes sliding on for miles after the engine is stopped. Turning to one side or the other is easy, but only if other ships and the proximity of shallow water permit it. Altogether, a swimmer in low visibility is a menace to the Channel traffic and to himself. Near the end of a swim and off the shipping lanes, it may be permissible to carry on. The pilot must be the sole arbiter in every case. The other aspect is navigational; unless there is sufficient means of directing the course a swimmer is only wasting time and energy. Being slightly off-course may put hours on the crossing; being badly off-course means actually going backwards at about two miles an hour. One day in four is likely to contain a period of visibility less than three miles.

Water temperature is an important and most interesting factor. Luckily it has little day-to-day variation with one exception; on a particularly hot day the very top layer of water may warm up a degree or so. The water is normally coldest in February and warmest in August; during the latter month it *averages* about 16° C (61° F). Very roughly one can expect 1½ degrees Centigrade colder for each month backwards or forwards from late August. Once more I must emphasise that these are only *typical* temperatures. During one abominable year the thermometer never measured above 11 °C (52° F). On a brief moment of glory, it once touched 20½° C (69° F). English climate is so variable that only one thing is moderately certain; the Channel has never yet frozen over, even in February.

Air temperatures are not quite so important, but do make some appreciable difference to a swimmer's comfort. August is once again hottest with an average of 16½° C (62° F). July and September about one degree Centigrade colder. Add 2½ degrees Centigrade for afternoon temperatures and subtract 2½ degrees Centigrade for those in the night. That is the rule-of-thumb that cannot always be right but it will give a good indication. Because of cool sea breezes the air temperature has hardly ever exceeded 32¼° C (90° F). If you get a chance I advise settling for that.

Wind, sea temperature, air temperature and fog. All these affect the swimmer intimately, but the greatest of these is wind. That, as they say in Australia, 'is daddy of them all'. It can overrule all other conditions, and can do so to advantage or disadvantage. The Greek god Æolus once tied all the adverse winds neatly up in bags and presented them to Ulysses for safe keeping. Because of the curiosity and ill-discipline of Ulysses' crew we are back where we started. Since they opened the bags for a 'look-see' those released adverse winds have plagued sailor and swimmer alike through the centuries. Early in my sea-going career I remember having this emphasised. A candidate was being examined in seamanship by a veritable tiger of an examiner.

'You are at anchor and it suddenly comes on to blow a gale. What do you do?'

'Pay out another shackle of cable, sir,' suggested the candidate rather timidly.

'That's right,' agreed the examiner. Then, wishing to know what other precautions a prudent officer would take, he put another question. 'Now it's come on to blow harder still. What do you do?'

The candidate had run out of ideas, however, and decided to stick to his previous success. 'Pay out another shackle of cable, sir,' he said firmly.

Three times the examiner increased the wind and repeated the question. Three times he got the same answer, and could contain himself no longer. 'Good grief man! You've paid out an extra shackle of cable five times. Is your perishing ship full of cable?'

Goaded by desperation, stage-fright, and sarcasm, the candidate lost his control—and also his pass-mark in seamanship.

'No, sir!' he replied. 'But I'm beginning to wonder if you're full of wind.'

I hope the reader is not beginning to think the same thing about me. Let's change the subject. But just before doing so, you may be interested in further study of the subject later. Probably *much* later! In *The Marine Observer* of July 1961 I wrote an article called 'Weather Aspects of Channel Swimming'. As it was for a Meteorological Office periodical, it is somewhat fuller and more technical than this chapter.

26

Professionals in the Channel

It is the hope of reward that sweetens labour.

OLD SAW

PRIOR to 1950, there was little competitive scope for professional swimmers in Great Britain. They coached, taught, gave exhibitions and performed in aqua shows, but they had no race of real standing. The *Daily Mail*—as it has so often done with twentieth-century history—changed all that. That enterprising newspaper thought the public would be thrilled by the startling conception of a cross-Channel race. Events were to prove exactly how right it was.

Right from the project's first announcement, enthusiasm and an interest was kindled; by the actual date of the race enthusiasm and interest was ablaze. All the sporting world was agog to know the result of the experiment; sceptics and believers were in nearly equal proportions. Today, it is well-known history that the believers won out—the race was a really outstanding success.

As an amateur, I wished desperately that the *Daily Mail* had given such a grand chance to amateurs, I wrote forthwith to the organiser to ask if a separate section could possibly be held under A.S.A. laws. A polite—if rather terse—note came back from Mr. Truby. He said plainly that it was difficult enough to organise one race without embarking on another. His point was obvious and I therefore worried him no more. After all, a boost for swimming is welcome fare, be it for amateurs or professionals.

Without delay, the A.S.A. clarified their end of the situation; they declared all those who posted entry forms to the *Daily Mail* to be professionals. Swimmers were thus left in no woolly predicament about the matter; their decision had to be clear cut between professionalism and amateurism. The A.S.A. by one bold decision ensured that no encroachment of 'shamateurism' occurred in Britain.

At that time I was playing water-polo for my ship and for Portsmouth Command, and was also swimming for the Navy in the Inter-Service competition. Those pleasures and privileges outweighed all other considerations with me, and I remained an amateur. That so many of my swimming friends decided otherwise is a tribute to sturdy British independence of thought. That point is really worth making, because few people ever realised what intense soul-searching went on all over the U.K. in spring and summer of 1950.

From the outset, the Egyptians entered wholeheartedly into preparation. Out of fifty-seven nominations, they trained, seeded, and eliminated, until only the very pick of Egypt was selected to come to England. How well that forethought fared can easily be seen from results. Egyptian swimmers gained two out of three 'places' in each of the *Daily Mail* swims. Other countries had neither the official encouragement for the high-efficiency methods, but nevertheless they sent excellent individual athletes. The Frenchman, de Morvan, was one example; he was runner-up in both races and only minutes behind the champion on each occasion.

This book has hammered frequently at a special theme; now the hammer strikes again. Human will-power allied to discipline, knowledge, experience, and organised planning will permit very few things to beat the human body. The *Daily Mail* contest proved that once more.

Will-power was little bother, for each contender's most dominant desire was to cross the Channel. Weaklings, waverers, and mountebanks had already been weeded out by stringent medical and swimming tests. The result was a Service Commander's dream conception—a corps d'elite whose sole ambition was to excel at the job in hand. With such a corps d'elite, inflexible square-bashing discipline is not necessary; each member's effort requires merely to be directed into the correct channel. By establishing a headquarters at Folkestone, and superimposing a loose corporative discipline above individual training methods, the *Daily Mail* achieved that object ideally.

Knowledge and experience were also harnessed as never before. Chosen pilots, a special weather service, and Britain's most experienced (at that time) Channel swimmer E. H. Temme were all enlisted to assist. Organisation and planning was supplied by the Special Service Department of the paper. Comment is hardly necessary on that last score; the title itself suggests ability to organise anything from a tea-party to a Test Match.

The proof of any pudding is well known to lie in the eating. The success of the Channel races indicated this to be one of the matters in which the Special Service Department could hardly be faulted. In 1950, no less than nine out of twenty-four competitors crossed the Strait. In 1951 the result—to borrow Hollywood idiom—was stupendous. This time eighteen out of twenty starters completed the course. However, there is no need to gild any lily. Credit goes to the sponsors without stint, but it must be pointed out that, in 1951, only the very top-notchers even got as far as the starting line. There were originally one hundred and twenty-five volunteers, and by the day of the race they had been whittled down to twenty. The starters were—by that token—a very exclusive selection of athletes.

In 1950 the long-standing record of ten hours fifty minutes was set up by Hassan Abd-el-Rheim. Next year the winner's time was over twelve hours and blasé bar-room pundits shook their heads

	1950	1951
Abd-el-Rheim	10 h. 50 m.	12 h. 25 m.
Abertondo	16 h. 25 m.	14 h. 14 m.
Barnie	14 h. 50 m.	15 h. 01 m.
de Morvan	11 h. 02 m.	12 h. 13 m.
Hamad	12 h. 10 m.	12 h. 12 m.
Kammersgurd	16 h. 30 m.	15 h. 38 m.
Zirganos	16 h. 19 m.	14 h. 10 m.
Total	98 h. 06 m.	95 h. 53 m.
Average for competitor	14 h. 01 m.	13 h. 42 m.

over a slow race. More informed opinion disagreed; it merely spotlighted the unpredictability of sea conditions—even when prediction is attempted by a veritable brains trust. Take a look at the times of these swimmers who crossed successfully both years.

Fact and opinion both emerge from that simple investigation. That 1951 was a faster, not slower, race than 1950 is indisputable fact. Similarly, it is certain that although the leaders lost time, the rearguard picked it up. Opinions differ inevitably as to the cause of such an odd occurrence. I have given much consideration to the problem but nevertheless somewhat diffidently present my own idea of what happened.

Firstly, the average times show that tides and conditions did not—in general—differ greatly. Secondly, it is probable that, during the intervening year, much intense training had been undertaken by all competitors. As a result the 'slow section' must necessarily have effected greater relative improvement than the speedsters. That is no supposition, it is a well-known fact; in any sport long handicap men improve by leaps and bounds, whereas the scratch men—already near the zenith of efficiency—can only hope to edge his performance up by a fraction. That goes some way towards explaining the closing up of the field. But the slow time of the leaders remains to be explained.

It is most unlikely that the leaders actually swam more slowly in the second race. On the contrary, after their hard training and previous experience, they should almost certainly have been capable of fractionally better performances. Did they, perhaps, through misjudgement of pace, take the race too easily? That, too, is unlikely. At the finish only thirteen minutes separated the third man home from the champion—and they swam almost neck-and-neck throughout. Such competitive stimulus would certainly tend to increase the pace rather than to decrease it. Could there have been a loss of form in the competitors? That is possible, but again not very probable. It is rarely that three top-class athletes are struck by loss of form on the same day.

It is my opinion that none of those causes was responsible for slow times. The leaders were most probably hoist by the petard of their own fitness and efficiency. By swimming a little *too* fast, they got ahead of the best of the tide. The slower swimmers, coming along later, caught the peak tidal conditions and were so given extra help to close the gap. Mr. Aesop's tale of the hare and the tortoise seems almost equally applicable out of its purely pedestrian setting.

A full list of successes follows. There are two good reasons for including such a list; the first is that such accomplishments should self-evidently be included in a book like this. The second—not so obvious—is its value for comparison. Many countries are repre-

1950 Race

(1)	Hassan Abd-el-Rheim (Egypt)	10 h. 50 m.
(2)	Roger de Morvan (France)	11 h. 02 m.
(3)	M. H. Hamad (Egypt)	12 h. 10 m.
(4)	Sam Rockett (Britain)	14 h. 20 m.
(5)	Ned Barnie (Britain)	14 h. 50 m.
(6)	Eileen Fenton (Britain)	15 h. 31 m.
(7)	Jason Zirganos (Greece)	16 h. 19 m.
(8)	Antonio Abertondo (Argentine)	16 h. 25 m.
(9)	Jenny Kammersgurd (Denmark)	16 h. 30 m.

1951 Race

(1)	M. H. Hamad (Egypt)	12 h. 12 m.
(2)	Roger de Morvan (France)	12 h. 13 m.
(3)	Hassan Abd-el-Rheim (Egypt)	12 h. 25 m.
(4)	Said el Arabi (Egypt)	12 h. 42 m.
(5)	Brenda Fisher (Britain)	12 h. 42 m. (Women's record)
(6)	G. Chapman (Britain)	12 h. 56 m.
(7)	Winnie Roach (Canada)	13 h. 25 m.
(8)	Enriqueta Duarte (Argentine)	13 h. 26 m.
(9)	Lars B. Warle (Sweden)	13 h. 28 m.
(10)	Raphael Morand (France)	13 h. 45 m.
(11)	Daniel Carpio (Peru)	13 h. 50 m.
(12)	Jenny James (Britain)	13 h. 55 m.
(13)	Jason Zirganos (Greece)	14 h. 10 m.
(14)	Antonio Abertondo (Argentine)	14 h. 14 m.
(15)	J. van Hemsburgen (Holland)	14 h. 20 m.
(16)	Sally Bauer (Sweden)	14 h. 40 m.
(17)	Ned Barnie (Britain)	15 h. 01 m.
(18)	Jenny Kammersgurd (Denmark)	15 h. 38 m.

sented in the lists, so that the successful competitors are widely spread through the world. Many people will therefore have a chance to check their own (or their protégés') performances against one of the experts over a similar distance. Then, by consulting the list, rough guide to one's own chances in such events can be obtained. That has much psychological value during the bleak spots of training.

That—in synopsis—is the story of the *Daily Mail* races. A complete story would fill a book—and the book would be absorbing. High endeavour, setbacks, humour, improvisation, national touchiness, personal successes. All those qualities pulsated through the event from early spring to late summer. It was only a pity that the great venture had to end on a note of discord with the Egyptian swimmers refusing their prizes because the *Daily Mail* had remarked adversely on King Farouk. At the time, it appeared as a real storm over the Channel; in retrospect, it was clearly a storm in a teacup. And as it turned out—what the British newspaper thought in 1951, all Egypt thought only a year later.

In 1952, the Channel race lapsed for lack of a sponsor. The *Daily Mail* had inaugurated the 1950 race as an epoch-making event and had—in response to public wishes—staged it a second time as a special Festival of Britain attraction. After that, they laid down the burden. And, make no mistake, it *is* a burden to plan, organise, and carry out successfully such a project. Perhaps the Egyptian monarchists ingratitude was to the *Daily Mail*, as the biblical straw was to the Egyptians' own national beast of burden.

However, the two races had thoroughly whetted the appetite of public and swimmers alike. Many enquiries were made and several feelers put out. Ultimately the challenge and the burden were shouldered by Billy Butlin. If there were more Britons of that calibre, Britain and Commonwealth would benefit immeasurably. One feels that, to him, life without challenges and burdens would be intolerable. Born in South Africa, brought up in Canada and working in Britain, he has much of our own forefather's pioneering—perhaps even buccaneering—spirit.

His organisation is finely geared to knowing the wishes of the people of Britain, and—of course—catering efficiently for those wishes. Butlin, fortunately for professional swimmers, has a heart as well as a head. If he considers something really worth while he never hesitates to put more into the project than he takes out. It is quite certain that the Channel race was a good advertisement for the Butlin holiday organisation. But whether it entirely repaid the hard work and financial input is at least open to conjecture. And especially so when weather caused long and expensive delays.

That is very slightly a digression, but it is a point I am anxious to make. The older one gets, the crosser one becomes at thoughtless individuals who take so many things for granted. Professional swimmers must count themselves lucky; they could hardly have found a better sponsor.

Under the new régime, the Channel race organisation remained substantially as before. The headquarters was at Folkestone Seawater Bathing Pool; the pre-race tests and elimination heats continued, the influx of foreign competitors went on. And organisation and planning were carried out in an up-to-date fashion. In 1955, for instance, a helicopter was used for the first time, in addition to the sea-borne armada.

The race results are given below. These will be useful, not only for the personal comparisons, but also for assessing the merits of the different races in the varying conditions. Luckily, certain competitors succeed year after year and supply the necessary thread of continuity. Assuming that their swimming ability varies no more than a small percentage, their average crossing times give an excellent yardstick by which to measure one race against another

1953 Race

No competitor was successful.

1954 Race

(1) B. Periera (Portugal)	12 h. 25 m.
(2) M. H. Hamad (Egypt)	12 h. 49 m.
(3) Brenda Fisher (Britain)	14 h. 36 m.
(4) J. Zirganos (Greece)	16 h. 23 m.
(5) Margaret Feather (Britain)	16 h. 52 m.
(6) A. Abertondo (Argentine)	16 h. 53 m.
(7) M. El Soussi (Syria)	17 h. 55 m.

1955 Race

This race was delayed several days by weather. Because of that, the tidal conditions necessarily deteriorated from their best. The point is worth remarking, because certain of the previous races—notably 1950—were held in near ideal conditions.

(1) Abd-el Latif Abou Heif (Egypt)	11 h. 44 m.
(2) T. Park (United States)	12 h. 02 m.

(3) S. Guiscardo (Argentine)	14 h. 33 m.
(4) D. P. Beltran (Mexico)	15 h. 08 m.

It is interesting to note the Guiscardo was originally disqualified for inadvertently touching the Goodwin Sands. Guiscardo's appeal was allowed, because although the official observer's boat lost touch, the organisers were satisfied that he swam right over the bank without grounding.

1956 Race

Because of an encouraging forecast, the event was started in borderline conditions. Unfortunately the weather worsened instead of improving. As a result, no competitor was able to finish the course and there were many protests from disappointed swimmers.

Such dissatisfaction emphasises that organising a swim is a thoroughly thankless task. Had the race been postponed there would have been an equal number of protests from equally disappointed athletes; some of them would have been forced to leave Folkestone without waiting for a rearrangement. At least, in this event, there was a swim reasonably close to the advertised date and the prize money went to those who survived longest, and got furthest across. First prize was awarded jointly to Jack McClelland of Belfast and Tom Park of U.S.A. The ladies championship was split similarly between Diane Cleverly of New Zealand and Maria Meesters of Holland.

The fact that two swimmers persevered for about eleven hours shows that conditions were not impossibly bad. It is even more certain that no better weather presented itself over a period of several weeks. Organisers of big events must necessarily press on when the slightest opportunity offers. General Eisenhower, who also once organised an international Channel event, would vouch for that. He was equally bedevilled by weather forecasts and he, too, had to take a chance in borderline conditions. Luckily, his calculated risk came out the right way and resulted in a successful crossing. It also made British and American participants Channel champions for 1944.

1957 Race

There were 24 entrants and two finishers. I was immersed in the Channel myself this day (going the other way) and confirm that the conditions were far from ideal. And in the dark hours that was something of an understatement!

Lady.	(1) Greta Andersen (U.S.A.)	13 h. 53 m.
Man.	(1) Ken Wray (Southport)	16 h. 00 m. 25 s.

1958 Race

Lady.	(1)	Greta Andersen (U.S.A.)	11 h. 01 m.
Men.	(1)	Brojen Das (Pakistan)	14 h. 52 m.
	(2)	Ronald Tarr (London)	15 h. 12 m.
	(3)	Raphael Morand (France)	16 h. 22 m.
	(4)	Ramon Ocana (Mexico)	17 h. 05 m.

One other competitor—Haldun Ismen (Turkey)—crossed in 15 hours 25 minutes. But he was disqualified for landing on a breakwater!

1959 Race

This year's race again started in borderline weather. Probably the worst weather of an otherwise good season. Some competitors were unable to start or to contact their boats in the surf on the French coast.

Men.	(1)	Alfredo Camerero (Argentine)	11 h. 43 m.
	(2)	Herman Willemse (Holland)	12 h. 49 m.
	(3)	Baptista Periera (Portugal)	13 h. 12 m.
	(4)	Helge Jensen (Denmark)	13 h. 17 m.
	(5)	Brojen Das (Pakistan)	13 h. 53 m.
	(6)	El Nawab (Iraq)	15 h. 12 m.
	(7)	William Bristowe (London)	18 h. 01 m.
Ladies.	(1)	Greta Andersen (U.S.A.)	15 h. 25 m.
	(2)	Myra Thompson (U.S.A.)	15 h. 35 m.

Mr. Butlin offered a consolation prize of £200 for any disappointed competitor for a completed swim within the next ten days. It was not claimed.

1960 Race

It was cancelled and no others have since been held.

27

The Two-Way Channel Swim

Double, double, toil and trouble.
SHAKESPEARE

ADMITTEDLY a two-way swim does *not* exactly double the mental and physical toil required for a one-way passage. It does, however, need courage, determination, patience, and physical powers high above the ordinary. Curiously, there is a certain breed of human being which flutters compulsively to the flame of challenge as a moth to an ordinary candle-flame. So it is not unnatural that one of the most urgent and constant topics amongst top-class swimmers is that of a there-and-back Channel swim. A double-Channel is a physical possibility; this has been proved by Abertondo's 1961 epic feat of endurance. Navigationally I vouch for his record being extremely vulnerable. But the feat requires precision pre-planning, perfect operational organisation, and near-perfect weather. The first two aspects I can help with. Only benign Providence can assist you on the weather aspect, but I will analyse past records.

Before starting particularised consideration, it will be beneficial to look at the project broadly, and then to make some broad general decisions. What is the exact task? Is it personally possible? What is the best date to start? Which way should the swim be orientated? I will deal with these aspects in that order.

The task. The minimum crow-flight distance is 20·8 statute miles each way. A total of 41·6. But boat navigation can never be entirely accurate. Nor can one rely on crossing at the very narrowest part. In addition, present weather and past weather can both

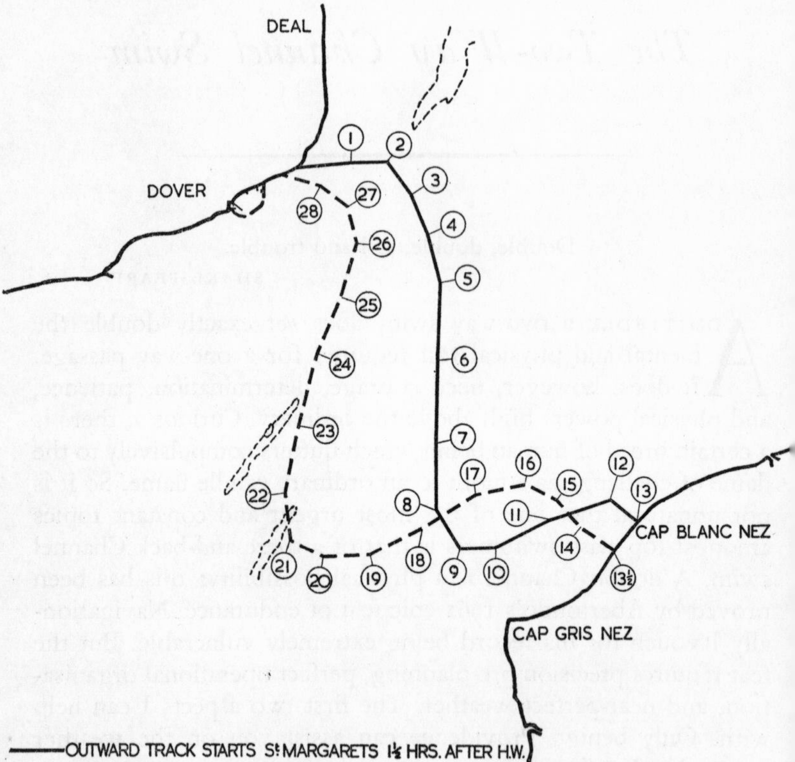

Two-way Channel swim planned at author's speed. Figures in circles indicate 'hours on passage'.

influence currents and thus add much to a swimmer's task. Allowance for an extra ten per cent would therefore be wise. That makes the distance 46 statute miles, 40 sea miles, or 74 kilometres.

Personal possibility factors. Even to *train* for this distance is a most formidable undertaking. Over a nine-months' preparatory period, it will be necessary to *average* four hours a day of waterwork. Towards the end of training, that average will be very much exceeded. This fact alone will undoubtedly place the project beyond the reach of most amateurs with a normal job to do. Extreme single-mindedness and prodigious mental and physical guts is an absolute essential. Complete freedom from eye, ear, nose afflictions, too; a physical defect of any kind augments itself unbearably during such a length of immersion and exertion. Excellent bodily health plus a contentedly stolid temperament must therefore be the twin pillars to support success.

Best swim dates. For a super-marathon such as this, it is obviously wise to set off in conditions which cause the minimum hindrance. considerations include water temperature, air temperature, length of daylight, absence or presence of jellyfish, strength variations of tidal streams, and possibility of settled weather. Whether one is a right-side or a left-side breather, it is evident that 'breathing into the weather' will be necessary on either outward or homeward leg. Different swimmers have different ideas about the relative importance of most of these factors. But every one knows that the settled weather requirement towers over the others like a giant among pygmies. To my way of thinking, optimum conditions are found during the slackest neap tides in early August. With similar tides in late August running a reasonably close second.

Orientation of swim. A two-way success is navigationally possible starting from either side. But, as this is being read in the English language, it is probable that aspirants will base themselves in England. In that case it will be advantageous to start from home base. This choice of starting points eliminates the discomfort of the initial boat passage to Gris Nez and the inconvenience of a four-hour return trip on completion. Altogether, then, a start from this side cuts about eight hours off the total; consequently, it makes the planning somewhat easier. Further, an initial leg from England to France gets over the most difficult hurdle first.

So much for general preparatory thoughts. Now, for the precision of pre-planning. This consists of three sections. Arrangement and completion of a suitable training programme by the selected date. Arrangement and completion of a navigational plan by that date. Arrangement and completion of all administrative details concerning accommodation, boats, services required, signals, etc. I take the points in that order.

Training Programme. This matter does not require a great deal of emphasis; it is so exceedingly and obviously vital. Further, by the time a swimmer has got to the point of considering a double-swim, he must already be a marathon athlete of some standing. As an established performer, he or his trainer will doubtless have strong views on training methods. It will be best therefore if I merely state the way I would go about the job and then leave the matter to individual taste.

In an early chapter of this book there is a specimen routine for working up to a one-way attempt. That routine takes 28 weeks. I would now add on to the end of that another 8 weeks—each week increasing the distance of the trial swim by three miles until the final trial was over 44 miles. That sounds terrific. And it is. But it is quite useless to start this swim without the basic ability to swim the whole distance. Add another four weeks for reserve—it is rare for an athlete to go nine months without a cold interfering with training—and the total is 40 weeks. That figure is important to note. It makes clear that training must commence in early November for a swim the following August. By Christmas one would not have reached any peaks of training but should certainly be frolicking amongst the higher foothills. There is one exceptional class of swimmer, however, who will not need such a prolonged programme as this. That is the international champion for whom life is all summer time, with competitions in the appropriate hemisphere. Superimposed on perfect water-fitness, such a person could at any time manage the additional training effort in two months' hard labour.

Navigational Plan. I believe that most swimmers will wish to leave navigation entirely to their pilots. They will be extremely wise to do so; for navigation can no more be mastered in a few months than any other trade or profession. After twelve years at sea, I qualified as a Master Mariner and then believed that I knew everything. Now, twenty-one years later, I know that a horse and

Happy at Dover after record-breaking England-France swim.

Unexpected records: The Channel swim in 45·2 minutes.

cart could be driven through the gaps in my knowledge. However, no intelligent person can ever fail to be interested in the theoretical aspects of the matter he is testing practically. I shall therefore discuss some general principles without going into detail (Navigators requiring such detail will find it in my notes in the *Journal of the Institute of Navigation* dated 1st January 1960). It will be useful to obtain two charts for interest and reference. Admiralty Chart No. 1895 gives the largest obtainable picture of the Straits of Dover. Chart No. 5059 shows, in pictorial form, the tidal streams for every hour of the day.

In planning my own individual swims, I act strictly on the principle that every little helps. For instance, although water temperature does not significantly vary throughout the day, one can certainly choose periods with better air temperatures. And those parts of the swim more difficult than others, it is advantageous to do in daylight. Further, I like to start a swim in the morning after a good night's rest. With those objectives in mind, this then is how I would wish my own attempt to go.

Start from St. Margaret's Bay 1½ hours after early morning high water. A course of 144 degrees True—that is, south 29 degrees east magnetic—takes one comfortably close to the South Goodwin Light Vessel after two hours. That same course takes one on a shallow reverse-S curve and arrives at the French coast after 13 hours. The landing point cannot be accurately foretold, but it should be between Gris Nez and Blanc Nez. After the permitted 30 minutes' rest, start the return journey on a course of 310° True—that is north 43 degrees west magnetic. This homeward course takes one quite close to the two mid-channel sandbanks, but this is an advantage rather than otherwise. Although it will be low water at the time of passing, there is plenty of swimming depth over the top of the banks and the tidal stream will be small; most important, it gives a chance to fix an exact navigational position by the buoys moored adjacent to the bank. This is particularly useful for ascertaining whether the schedule is working correctly. With the rather primitive navigational equipment in an average boat, passing close to some such sea-mark is quite the surest way of position finding. Altering course to 330 degrees (N. 23 W.) after 7 hours should ultimately arrive one on the English coast some 29 hours after starting out. Once again it would be prudent merely to say 'between St. Margaret's Bay and Folkestone' rather than to attempt greater accuracy of forecast.

It may sound inordinately timid and grossly inaccurate to forecast a landing in France 'between Gris Nez and Blanc Nez' or in England 'between St. Margaret's Bay and Folkestone'. But there are several reasons why greater precision is not possible. The hydrographic data is certainly magnificent but unfortunately the survey periods have not been prolonged enough to guarantee the data for 365 days a year. A prolonged enough period of gales may cause a 'through current' to be superimposed on the normal tidal movement; such a through current may persist for days after the gales themselves have vanished. A fresh breeze during the swim may well induce a 'wind drift' in the top strata of water; this naturally affects a swimmer. Finally, if a swimmer—through cramp, longer feed-stops than anticipated or adverse weather—does not maintain his estimated speed, he will arrive late. Lateness in arrival means being exposed to vigorous cross-tides for longer periods. Even one extra hour *could* sweep a wearying man four miles to one side or the other. And just that sort of time-lag might very possibly happen at the end of a day and a half of swimming.

Discomfort and hard labour on a swim like this, is a *sine qua non*. But you will see how my plan has minimised them. Take off at a reasonable time, after a night's rest; clearance of the Goodwin Sands in daylight; approach to the French coast in daylight. On the return journey there is the psychological benefit of exactly checking one's progress by buoy marks on the middle banks. And the last few miles will be swum during the hottest, brightest part of the day; this last is a factor which might possibly just turn the scale for an exhausted swimmer. The only poor point is that the actual landing on the French coast is in darkness. But in a tidal swim one cannot arrange *everything* just right. Once again I must emphasise that this routine was arranged to suit my own speed and my own inclinations; every swimmer is different and every swim must therefore be individually arranged. There are traditionally more ways of killing a cat than by choking it with butter!

Administrative details. The most elementary administrative matters are those pertaining to accommodation, transport, food and equipment. Given prior thought, most of these difficulties are molehill size. Without prior thought, they become most oppressive mountains. But I do not propose to offer advice on that score. No marathon novices will be embarking on this swim. And those who are not beginners will (or should) have learned the lessons on previous ventures.

Quite the most vital component of this swim or any other is a seaworthy boat with an efficient pilot or boatman. A few words on this subject may be a considerable help. First, it is important to know that the peak Channel-swim season is also a peak fishing season and a peak pleasure boating season. There is thus much competition for boats. Boatmen being in the business to earn a living naturally take the best terms. One cannot eat, or bank, the prestige of being on a double-Channel swim. Understanding of this point will put any approach on a firmer basis. So I counsel getting the best pilot possible through personal introduction or Channel Swimming Association. Plainly state the task—i.e. that it may mean a two-day stint. State categorically the days on which you will be available to start; this leaves him free to book up other days for other tasks. Discuss and firmly agree the financial terms. Unfortunately there have been in the past some 'moonlight flitters' amongst Channel aspirants; so to prove oneself not in this category, and to seal the bargain, I advise a small deposit payment.

Having obtained a reliable boatman, he should be taken thoroughly into one's confidence. He should be generally regarded as a vital member of the team, be given all information available and asked tactfully whether he has all equipment for a two-day expedition. Lights, fuel, food, etc. This query is necessary because this would be a much longer absence than they are accustomed to. And, by the way, it is over-optimistic to expect a large rebate in fee if the swim is eventually abandoned part way across. The boatman will already have expended a considerable amount in getting extra crew for a 'deep sea' trip; he will also have paid for extra fuel, extra provisions, and extra insurance premiums for his boats. The foregoing remarks have the appearance of being pro-boatman and anti-swimmer. But it is no more than hard fact. There are still swimmers who feel that boatmen should give their services freely in the cause of sport. These are, alas, by coincidence, the swimmers who will find themselves without a boat on the big day! Goodwill on both sides is not only an essential for success; it is also an essential for getting started at all.

One last point on the subject of boats. It is most advisable to have a training swim of reasonable length in the dark. There is nothing like a night swim to bowl out defects in the organisation. Lights and steering arrangements will rarely be thoroughly effective first time, either in the main boat or the rowing-boat. Failure of equipment on trial leads to productive discussion and rectification of faults. Failure on an actual swim could lead to abandonment and many recriminations. A night trial is also the most effective juncture to test the boat's cooking facilities. Lastly, it gives the oarsmen practice in keeping station on the swimmer—a chore which inefficiently performed can also break a swimmer's heart.

So much for the varied major planning aspects which have to go into such a gigantic project. There are naturally other minor ones. But they are matters of common knowledge and common sense rather than of specialised knowledge and experience. As such they would be space wasting to tally up here.

Operational Organisation. The combination of an experienced boatman and an experienced swimmer should solve most operational problems. I shall therefore again merely put forward a few points which I should observe personally if carrying out the swim.

Extra care is necessary with swimming equipment, greasing-up, and especially with underarm, shoulder, chin, neck and crutch lubrication. Thirty hours is a long time to endure a painful chafe. Or a dangling strap. Or a leaking goggle. To my mind another essential is to keep strictly to the agreed schedule. Delays at the start due to photographers, and, later, the insertion of extra food stops all put on extra time and wrecks tidal computations. Will-power and common sense will deal with these situations.

The last point on which I have strong views is that of the stop at the half-way stage. I should prefer to leave the water for only the very minimum time required for re-greasing and readjusting equipment. At night I should hastily re-enter the water and take a reasonable meal in the shallows. In the middle watch it is warmer immersed in the Channel than exposed to the night air. In addition there is to my mind a psychological advantage in remaining 'on the job' and not relaxing.

Earlier I said that a two-way Channel swim demanded precision pre-planning, perfect operational organisation and near-perfect weather. The first two points have been discussed. Here, then, are a few remarks on the weather aspect.

Neither the swimmer nor myself can do more than just note what is likely to happen. And in the unpredictable climate of England even 'likely' is an overstatement. But here is what *might* happen based on past meteorological office records! Sea temperature 16° C (61° F). Mean air temperatures between 20½° C (69° F) (day) and 13° C (56° F) (night). Winds blow from directions in approx. percentages: north 6, north-east 8, east 12, south-east 2, south 8, south-west 43, west 11, north-west 9, calm 1. The average wind speed is about 15 m.p.h. One day in the month will have fog.

It will not be a good bet to start a swim if the forecast for the following 24 hours anticipates more than force 3 (or force 4 at the very utmost). Much as I dislike fog, it may be necessary to take a calculated risk and swim through it. The danger is of being run down by one of the many ships constantly passing through the Straits; the risk is small but ever present. Perhaps, however, not more so than the possibility of being run over by a car in the street.

Finally, in the words of Longfellow:

> Let us then be up and doing,
> With a heart for any fate;
> Still achieving, still pursuing,
> Learn to labour and wait.

Particularly—if I know Channel weather—to wait!

28

The Scan Bag

Anything wot's scullin' abaht goes straight into the scran bag.
ANY OLD-TIME CHIEF BOSUN'S MATE

In the Royal Navy untidiness is abhorrent. Everything must be squared off. Halyards triced tight, ropes coiled, 'Irish pendants' eliminated. All spare gear stowed in its proper stowage. Any items which get left lying about on the mess decks or the upper deck get relentlessly thrown into the scran bag by the chief bosun's mate or the coxswain. In similar tradition, I am putting all my remaining material into this concluding chapter, instead of leaving them 'sculling'. I hope you will think the end-product is 'shipshape and Bristol fashion'.

The residual subjects vary in size and importance. Some are only a few words of anecdote. Some are snippets of news. Others are almost—but not quite—worthy of a chapter of their own. Some are even incomplete in their information. I apologise for this last-named defect, but the greatest enthusiasm, the greatest expenditure on stamps, and the most voluminous reading cannot produce all the answers out of a hat. Anyway, as a long distance swimmer, all the items have interested me. And for that reason I believe they will in turn interest you.

Many of the items have come from my own knowledge and research. These I am prepared to vouch for as accurate. Others have come from correspondents and have not always been possible to recheck. These must therefore stand on the statement of the correspondent. To distinguish them from my own material, they are marked (c) immediately after the title.

AGE. Some people think Long Distance Swimming is an old man's sport. In fact, it can be *any* fit person's sport. Guts, ability to stand cold water, and willingness to train are the requirements.

It is true that Egyptian Abdel Rheim set up the England–France record at the age of 40; that I set up an England–France record at 45. And that Ned Barnie swam the Channel at 54. That is one side of the record. On the other side the age scale descends.

One year, Joe Smith, aged 25, won the Morecambe Inshore, Morecambe Cross Bay and Windermere Championships. Joyce Bricknell, a good looker of 19, won the ladies' section of all those races. Rodney Johnston, 13, became the youngest competitor to complete the 10-mile Morecambe Cross Bay swim. Ann Johnston went one better and swam it both ways non-stop; she was 16. Frank Robson, 14, did Ullswater in good time. Michael Davies, aged 15, and recovering from polio effects, swam five miles across the Solent. So did Anthony Moorey and Peter Gorvin, 18 and 17 respectively. In the past the Channel itself has been crossed by Philip Mickman, 18, Marilyn Bell and Margaret White, 17. Susan Lynch was A.S.A. Long Distance Champion at 17.

ALDERNEY–FRANCE. Jon Kay-Mouat of Alderney and Otter S.C. is a barrister. By grit and perseverance he jumped almost to the front rank of marathon swimmers in one season. At the New Year 1958 he was a swimming pool 'potterer about' but by September he had swum Windermere and from Alderney to the French mainland; this last through the cresting overfalls and vicious tides of the notorious Alderney Race. Time 5 hours 17 minutes. Just beforehand I timed him in a pool. He reeled off hour after hour of 25½-minute miles.

ANTONIO ABERTONDO (C). This immensely popular Argentinian has done what so many talked about. On 20th, 21st and 22nd September 1961 (and that sounds good in itself!), he accomplished a 'there and back' swim in the English Channel. Time, 43 hours 05 minutes. Splits—England to France 18–50. Return 24–10. Everyone knew that, given the weather, he could succeed. Whereas you and I do an eight-hour swim once weekly and think it something, he does it once a day and thinks it nothing. And besides having once swum 262 miles down the Mississippi in three days and eighteen minutes, he also had swims of 62 and

69 hours to his credit. This book—on behalf of all its readers—salutes Senor Abertondo as the 1961 *maestro* of *maestros*.

ARGENTINE MARATHON (C). A professional race with prizes ranging from 3,000 dollars to 100. Held periodically and results do not always reach me. Result of 1960 race—1. Guiscardo (Argentine); 2. Greta Andersen (U.S.A.), 14 hours 47 minutes; 3. Camerero (Argentine) 14–59; 4. Willemse (Holland); 5. Mary Kok (Holland); 6. Kasenoy (Mexico). There were 17 starters. In 1961 Helge Jensen (Canada) won—no other details available.

Course along the coastline from Miramar to Mar Del Plata. Distance 28 statute miles. Water temperature about 20° C (68° F). Director General de la Competencia was (in 1960) Eugenio Mario Guiscardo, Entre Rios 3146, Mar Del Plata, Argentina.

ATLANTIC CITY 25-mile PROFESSIONAL CHAMPIONSHIP (C). In 1953 two lifeguards, Ed Solitaire and Ed Stetser, swam the course in an experimental challenge; they were encouraged by Jim Toomey who is now Race Director. For the record, Solitaire won by an hour. The course is one complete circuit of Abesecon Island, entailing roughly 11 miles of ocean and 14 miles of Inland Waterway. Water is salt and tidal; temperature approximates 20 degrees Centigrade (70° F). Open to men and women of the whole world on payment of 35 dollars entry fee. A boat and two boatmen are provided by the Committee; one's own trainer is also allowed in the boat. Trunks or costume to be worn for starting. Winners—1954 and 55, Tom Park (U.S.A.); 1956, Cliff Lumsden (Canada); 1957, Alfredo Camerero (Argentine); 1958, Tom Park; 1959, Cliff Lumsden; 1960 and 61, Herman Willemse (Holland). First Women—1954, Marilyn Bell (Canada); 1955, Lies Put Jamnicky (Canada); 1956, 57, 58, 59, Greta Andersen (Denmark, later U.S.A.); 1960, Mary Kok (Holland); 1961, Greta Andersen. Times are dictated by weather and tidal conditions; the race has been won in times between 9 hours 21 minutes and 12 hours 17 minutes. Greta Andersen on one occasion only missed first place by 21 minutes and actually beat Cliff Lumsden by 54 seconds for second place.

BARE LEGISLATION. At the 1962 Channel Swimming Association A.G.M. several rules were given a buff. My dictionary states that *to* buff is to polish; and that *the* buff is the bare skin. Both meanings are appropriate. Embarrassingly, it was found that the Association's rules permitted grease, goggles and a cap. But nothing else. The word 'costume' has now been inserted into the rule book with only one dissentient voice. Mr. Secretary Wood—a man who is always 'with-it'—suggested that the term costume was too olde-worlde. He advocated that, as the majority of modern swimmers use six- or eight-beat crawl, the term 'beat-knicks' would be more felicitous.

BARROW–BLACKPOOL ATTEMPT (C). Edward James May in 1951 swam across the strong tides of Morecambe Bay. He was troubled by jellyfish and finally landed ¾-mile short of the Blackpool boundary—at Cleveleys. He was quite fit on finishing. Time, 13 hours 10 minutes.

BRIGHTON PIER-TO-PIER. The race is a mere three-quarters of a mile in length, and thus cannot qualify as a marathon in itself. Nevertheless, it is a sea race, in sea temperatures, and in sea conditions; on occasions it can be quite arduous. It is an initiation ceremony which is the perfect prelude to tougher degrees ahead. Many marathon swimmers have had their interest first whetted in just such events as this, and have gone on to great successes later. The inducements to swim in this particular race are really tangible and solid. Besides the enormous *Palace Pier Challenge Trophy* there are six prizes; three for the first men home, and three for the first Sussex men home. For the delectation and earnest consideration of possible competitors, I believe the first, second, and third prizes to be valued at £8, £4 and £3 respectively.

Swimming this race is entirely straightforward. In fact, it can be won or lost by just how straightforward the competitor can steer. My tip is to locate the finishing point on the Palace Pier before starting, and subsequently to glance at it every thirty strokes or so; it is quite prominent and easy to keep in view. Because thirty or forty competitors dive from a confined space, the first moments are as jostled as when the traffic lights turn green at Hyde Park Corner. Some swimmers prefer, and are allowed to start in the water; they can then line up for the start clear of the crowd. Others put their trust in a fierce sprint at the beginning, so as to achieve the clear water in front. Yet others again—and this includes me—prefer to rely on their 'water-polo elbows', and to maintain their previously calculated pace.

There is many a laugh at these functions. I remember one swimmer being told he was ineligible to swim because his entry form had not arrived in time; much expostulation ensued but he was finally ruled out. He stood on the starting platform and ruefully watched us all dive in. Then realising that the sea was public property anyway, he dived in too, and followed. By the half-way mark he was up with the main body, and by the finishing point annoyance and frustration had driven him ahead of the whole field. He was a magnificent swimmer (no names—no mastheading) and as he climbed out at the finish he gave the officials one triumphant glance before walking away to dress. If ever a look spoke that one did. And if it could have been interpreted into English it would certainly have said 'So there!'

BRISTOL CHANNEL. The traditional route is from Weston-super-Mare to Penarth. Or vice versa. It is considered cheating to cross farther east. Strictly speaking the Bristol Channel changes into the Severn Estuary on a line Sand Head–Lavernock Point. Minimum distance 8½ land miles. More likely distance 10 land miles. Four-knot cross-tide at spring tides; 2·1 at neaps. Successes: 1933, E. H. Temme (Plaistow United), 7 hours 05 minutes; 1949, Jenny James, 10 hours 05 minutes; 1950, Jenny James—reverse direction, England to Wales, 8 hours 23 minutes; 1957, Florence Chadwick, 6 hours 07 minutes.

CANADIAN NATIONAL EXHIBITION 15-mile PROFESSIONAL CHAMPIONSHIP (C). In the past this event has been held over varying courses. Recently, it has been swum in Lake Ontario opposite Exhibition Park, Toronto. Open to anyone in the world without entry fee. Both sexes compete in the same race. Thirteen triangular laps of a mile are swum; half in shelter behind the breakwater and half outside in exposed conditions. The final two miles are swum up and down inside the breakwater. For starting, trunks or costume must be worn. Competitors must provide two 'handlers' to look after them during the swim. This lap repetition is not such enjoyable exercise as striking offshore and getting somewhere. But it has the advantage that swimmers are able—without relying on trainers—to gauge their progress and fatigue-rate. Free board and lodging for ten days goes to competitors from overseas, but they have to pay all other expenses. Winner in 1961 was our old Channeling friend from Holland, Herman Willemse. Time not available.

CAPRI CHAMPIONSHIP (C). Professional swim sponsored by International Long Distance Swimming Federation. Course Capri to Naples. Distance approx. 30 kilometres. Warm, non-tidal water.

CATALINA CHANNEL. Greta Andersen, former Olympic and professional Channel champion, scored an outstanding success on her own Californian front doorstep. In Autumn 1958 she became the first person ever to swim the Catalina Channel there and back.

The shortest crow-flight distance from Catalina Island to the Californian mainland is 19·7 land miles. But swimming between these two nearest points requires an absolutely perfectly balancing of tides. This is difficult with a one-way swim but almost impossible with a two-way attempt. In this case, the most probable workable distance is 21·4 land miles. So Miss Andersen swam 42·8 miles and most probably slightly more. And I want to emphasise that *swam* is the operative word—and not drifted. The time was 26 hours 25 minutes. Reasonable weather on the first leg, poor on the second. Split times—10 hours 49 minutes and 15 hours 36 minutes. She had a 27-minute rest at the turn. Deepest point is 2,964 feet!

Besides setting a grand inaugural record for the two-way event, almost every other one-way record toppled in passing. One of these was Florence Chadwick's woman's mark. It seems worthy of reporting that one of Greta's first messages of congratulations was a telegram from Florence. I was thus reminded of when I managed to break her Channel record. My *very* first message of congratulations was signed Chadwick. Not all athletes salute their victors so promptly. The gesture shows magnificent sportsmanship—and a magnificently widespread 'intelligence network'. I have no access to a full list of successes. But these certainly include Tom Park and George Young. There was once a Wrigley Championship worth 25,000 dollars won by the latter.

CHANNEL RECORD: A COMMENT. Most spectacular 1960 achievement was that of professional Helge Jensen. With a time of 10 hours 23 minutes he smashed the long-standing Hassan Abdel Rheim mark of 10 hours 50 minutes. Going the difficult way, this was a thoroughly top-class performance; it indicates a 9¾-hour potential for the reverse route. As a week previously he had surpassed my Windermere amateur record of 5 hours 19 minutes by 21 minutes (approx. 2 minutes per mile) his calibre was accurately known and a good Channel time expected. But it is interesting to analyse the reasons for a success more thumping than the form-book suggested. It is difficult to explain in a few lines, but the main factor is this. Generations of France-bound swimmers have been tantalisingly close to Gris Nez at slack low water (I was only 4·1 miles short after nine hours' swimming). At that juncture, the north-east going stream starts to fan out from the Cape, giving average speed swimmers a long tough finish. With his extra speed, however, Jensen was some 1¾ miles ahead of any predecessor on this route. He thus broke through the vital area of maximum offshore stream before it had actually started. From that advanced position he was able to conclude his swim through moderate cross-tides which were neither favourable nor retarding. A year or two back I wrote in *Journal of the Institute of Navigation*—'Even a difference of 0·1 m.p.h. can arrive a swimmer in a place where a very different train of tidal circumstances would have ensued 30 minutes earlier or later.' The Danish-Canadian's magnificent feat is proof of that statement. Jensen ranks with the fastest marathon men of all time.

COLD. In a recent issue of *Which* there was a graph of survival chances in waters of various temperatures. I cannot, at the moment, trace the original source which is presumably a medical research unit. Take one example, at temperature 55° F. One enters the marginal zone (50:50 chance of survival) after 80 minutes; and the lethal ('you've had your chips') zone after 5 hours 30 minutes. Since Dorothy Perkins swam 20 hours 26 minutes across the Channel in just this temperature, one of two things is evident. Either Dorothy should stop looking so ridiculously healthy and alive. Or the researchists ought to check their sums again.

On this same subject, Gus Brickner, a former Channel aspirant, bathes regularly in the harsh North American winter. In that of 1960–1, he broke the ice 46 days running; his thermometer showed a minimum of minus nine degrees F. And at home, I personally know several regular Serpentine ice-breakers. But these dippers are not menaced much by the graph. It shows that, at 30° F, there is twelve minutes of 'safe time' before entering the marginal zone.

Tailpiece. In 1961 J. Thorne and D. H. Johnson swam beneath eight feet of Antarctic ice for 28 minutes in $27\frac{3}{4}$° F. Despite frogman clothing, they were so chilled on emerging as to be unable to lift a coffee cup. Anybody know the feeling?

CHANNEL SECRETARY. The secretarial appointment has brought letters of acclamation from countries all over the world. Mr. J. U. Wood's conviction is that the swimmer's interests take precedence over all other considerations. As a result, he has gained the respect and esteem of swimmers to a most extraordinary degree. In (tell it not in Gath) forty years of personal experience of competitive swimming, I know of no official who has left so immense a trail of international goodwill and gratitude in so short a time. The job is an exhausting one. Whether at home or outside, he is constantly assailed by telephone or personal contact. 'Can you get me a boat?' 'When's high water?' 'This is Associated Press . . .' 'Is it a record?' 'What's your opinion on . . .' 'Can I have my certificate tomorrow?' 'This is the Brazilian Embassy . . . India House . . . Pakistan High Commissioner . . . etc.'

Being Channel Swim Secretary is the most demanding honorary task I have encountered in many a long year. For three months or so, indeed, it is more than a full-time occupation. Tides do not keep neatly to ordinary office hours. Overseas telephone callers do not realise that a call during their working day shrills its message in the middle of the English night. Newspapers—although usually respecting the sanctity of the middle watch—consider him fair game from 6 a.m. to midnight.

COOK STRAIT separates New Zealand's South Island from the North Island.

Three things make this passage easier than the English Channel;

one or two things make it harder. On the good side it is only 13·9 land miles across and is on average 1½°C or 3°F warmer than at Dover. Current velocities are normally less too; although the tidal stream occasionally approaches 7 knots one would not swim in such circumstances. On the other hand the sea bed, although deep, is uneven and this produces swirls, eddies. Also, because land suddenly emerges from a vast expanse of ocean, temperature and pressure changes make for unsettled weather. Even in summer short but violent storms occur.

Several persons have tried the Strait without success. In 1959 after four years of intensive training A. W. Clark (Auckland) gave battle for several hours before retiring; he hopes to try again. In 1961 Bill Penny failed by only a mile. He got into a tide-rip which was going the wrong way and had to withdraw. Legend has it that only one person has crossed—a Maori woman fleeing from pursuit. No record admissible, however. She infringed A.S.A. and B.L.D.S.A. rules by carrying her small child on her back. (20 November 1962, Barrie Devenport succeeded in 11 hrs. 20 mins.)

CUTS. When starting or finishing a swim, keep walking to a minimum. Broken glass has cut many swimmers' feet.

DEAD SEA (C). How low can one get? Two Americans swam the Dead Sea on 22 June 1959. This inland sea is shown on my atlas as 1,295 feet below sea level. Although several rivers run in, there is no outlet. As a result the level is maintained by evaporation and very high water density results. It is said that *anyone* can swim here and it is quite impossible to sink. In two world wars thousands of Commonwealth soldiers put theory to the test without upsetting it.

The heat, excessive salt and stickiness renders swimming far from pleasant. Messrs. Griffin and Johnson therefore deserve all credit, especially for their good pioneering spirit. The time was seven hours flat for nine and a third miles. By Windermere comparison this is good without being outstanding. By the way they swam *across* so there is still time for a British lengthways record. Only 52½ miles!

DOUGLAS BAY SWIM (C). This Isle of Man Championship

commences at the beach at Port Jack and finishes at Peveril steps. Approx. distance 1½ miles. Information about this race rarely reaches me. But the *Isle of Man Times* would doubtless put an inquirer on the right track.

EDDYSTONE LIGHTHOUSE TO PLYMOUTH PIER. On 1st July 1914 'Jappy' Wolffe completed this course in 10 hours 45 minutes 02 seconds. Crowflight distance 15 land miles, but cross-tides inevitably make it more. This was 'Jappy's' last major swim. War broke out next month and he joined the Middlesex Regiment.

EYES. Have you tried Optone? It is a kind of Optrex in a plastic squeezer which one can carry about, and a few drops in the eye after swimming are a great relief. I hope this together with goggles may stop any worry with chlorinated water.

FLEETWOOD TO MORECAMBE CHAMPIONSHIP SWIM. This goes with the prevailing weather and is thus, statistically, less susceptible to weather cancellations. The idea is to start down the Wyre Estuary before the last of the ebb from Fleetwood; this gets competitors into the Lune Deeps at slack water, ready for a dash to Morecambe when the tide turns. It is easy in theory but very slightly different in practice. The first task is to make enough getaway to ensure not being swept back to Fleetwood on the turn of the tide. The second task is to avoid being sucked into the River Lune when crossing its mouth. The third task is the ordinary routine one of maintaining a reasonable pace for about six hours. The distance is around 13½ miles.

GALILEE SWIM (C). Although few British swimmers can afford a special trip to Israel some may be going that way for private or business reasons. We have many overseas readers, too, and the matter is of considerable interest to distance swimmers everywhere. The Galilee event is of established international stature and well maintains its attraction and strength. In successive events, 23, 35, 42, 28 and 33 competitors have taken part; they have come from Britain, South Africa, New Zealand and Sweden, as well as from Middle East countries.

The route is from Kibbutz Ein-Gev (eastern shore of the sea) to Tiberia's western shore. I have swum here and enthusiastically commend it as one of the most picturesquely beautiful swim-venues possible. The water temperature in autumn after a long hot summer will be up to indoor pool standard.

The last but one race—in 1953—was won by Manfred Salomon of South Africa in 2 hours 21 minutes 39 seconds, and the woman's champion, Malka Teenanbaum, took 3 hours 16 minutes 10·6 seconds. The course is said to be 6·2 miles but intending competitors should check this on a good, large map. The only reason for my slight note of doubt is the fantastically fast time of the male champion. He appears to have swum 6·2 consecutive miles at 22 minutes 35 seconds a mile, and there is no distance swimmer in Britain with that time already to his credit. Even the Michael Jennings, Raymond Holmes, Gordon Hill and John Slater types of British champion would take two minutes per mile longer than this. But the woman's standard is lower. Our British ladies would have a good chance. The results of the 1958 race were not sent to me.

GIBRALTAR STRAIT. On 20th September 1961, Jack McClelland of Belfast swam the Straits in 7 hours 5 minutes. This crossing was neither an inaugural one or a record, but it is the best documented: the *Gibraltar Chronicle* does not have a complete list of successes and the Tarifa pilot could not supply one either. From my own scrutiny of the Press, I know that Jaime Cortazar, Baptista Periera (5 hours 4 minutes), Daniel Carpio and Florence Chadwick have got across. But other crossings have faded from local knowledge.

McClelland's swim, however, was witnessed by a *Daily Mail* representative, a Press Association representative, and several independents. He has a certificate from the Tarifa pilot and the swim is entered in the marine history of the Port of Tarifa. The minimum distance is 9 miles, but tidal streams inevitably add another couple of miles. His route was from La Isla de las Palomas to near Ceuta. The average temperature was 24° C (75° F). He was bitten (stung ?) by an electric eel which left a crown-size cavity in his body; he also encountered sharks—fortunately non-belligerent. The best Admiralty Chart is No. 142. Strait of Gibraltar: this gives the best tidal information available.

GIVING UP. This phrase impels me to air a grievance voiced by very many swimmers. That is the use, by the Press, of the terms 'failed' and 'gave up'. This terminology is only correct when the swimmer (or trainer) decides that—because of muscular fatigue, mental fatigue, or cold-exhaustion—no further useful progress is possible. 'Abandoning a swim' through adverse weather is very different. That is good sound common sense and the best swimmers have no hesitation in doing it. Couto and Chadwick are examples of good troupers who come out when told and preserve energy for a future occasion. A personal example may further illustrate the point. In 1958 I came out of the English Channel after two hours—and I hope nobody will say I had shot my bolt after that short immersion! In fact, it was a record attempt and I withdrew after careful thought; the densest of fogs was making a nonsense of navigation and there was no point in going blindly on. Termination at that stage saved me £30 in hard cash and enough energy to break the double Windermere record three days later. In such cases, I suggest the following phraseology—'dropped (withdrew, halted, suspended, discontinued, terminated) the attempt'. But not 'gave up'.

GOGGLES. My correspondence on the subject of goggles has been, at times, overwhelming. Obviously it is an especially important subject for many swimmers. For that reason another few words seem necessary.

Goggles are kept watertight partly by suction and partly by tight straps. There is no such thing as complete comfort in goggles—so have you got your straps tight enough? Have you shifted the goggles up—or down—your nose a bit? Have you tried a different angle of pull on the strap by cutting it higher at the back of the head—or lower? Have you persevered long enough to let the rubber mould itself to your face with body heat and use? It is little use to try someone else's equipment; that will have moulded to *his* face. Give any goggles a good prolonged trial over two or three weeks; often a pair which is not good enough at first becomes a winner later on.

Three-quarters of British long distance swimmers use either the O'Flanagan Patent Water Goggle or the Hurricane No. 2. Anyway, beginners can do no better than try these well-proved types. If you are stuck for a local dealer, write to George Grose,

Ltd., New Bridge Street, London, E.C.4. Over lunch recently, I was talking to Mr. Ron Grose of that firm and he promised to help. The Groses are, of course, a swimming family long connected with the Amateur Swimming Club.

HELLESPONT: Leander's legendary nightly swim from Europe to Asia to visit Hero. Probably it was next swum by Lieutenant Ekenhead, United States Navy, together with Lord Byron, on 3rd May 1810. Times 65 and 70 minutes respectively. Shortest possible crossing is 1¼ miles but cross-stream makes it longer. Several others have since repeated the feat including Florence Chadwick and Jason Zirganos.

JUAN DE FUCA STRAIT (C). Between Vancouver Island and U.S.A. About 18½ miles across cold and strongly tidal water. Attempted nearly eighty times to date. Successes—1957, Bert Thomas, 11 hours 17 minutes; 1958, Cliff Lumsden, 11 hours 35 minutes; 1960, Helge Jensen—exact time not available, but a record.

LEG WORK. Two letters from abroad ask about leg work. One from Washington queries advantages of six-, eight- or ten-beat, etc. The other from Crete craves personal advice: he says 'one leg is almost immovable and the other is not continually beating'. Same answer to both. Intensive effort on a kicking-board is required. After that the legs automatically pick up the most advantageous beat. Over long distances comfort overwhelms many other considerations. 'Doin' what comes naturally' is a winner. The legs' main task is to position the body for minimising skin-friction, eddy-resistance, and wave-making resistance. Propulsion is a very secondary matter indeed.

LAKE MICHIGAN. Ted Erikson, chemical engineer, swam 36¾ miles in fresh breeze and choppy water from Chicago to Michigan in 1961. Time 36¾ hours. A man dearly after my own heart; he felt slightly cold and said that next time he would consider using grease.

LANCASTER–MORECAMBE SWIM. From Lancaster on the warmish river ebb, round far projecting Middleton Sands at slack low water and thence past Heysham to Morecambe on the cold sea flood. Distance by water about 22 miles and by road 4 miles. There must be a moral here somewhere, if we swim enthusiasts could see it! An invitation race was held on 30th June 1962, with four first-class swimmers competing. But the cold rough passage proved too much for all except Kendall Mellor of Keighley. He set up an inaugural record of 7 hours 45 minutes. Great credit is due to organiser Arthur Shipley. He mentioned this dream to me four years previously. Slowly but surely, he brought it to most successful fruition. This swim deserves greater mention than this but it took place after the book manuscript was in final form. It just shows how useful a Scran Bag can be!

MALTA TO GOZO. Three miles separates these two islands in the Mediterranean. Warm water and non-tidal. A challenge match between J. E. Guast—a former Solent champion—and myself took place in 1954. It was a remarkably close race in the conditions obtaining. A twenty-knot, south-westerly wind drove a rough cross-sea and swell through the channel throughout; near the end it was almost impossible for the control boat to keep the swimmers in sight. My time 1 hour 46 minutes. Guast 1 hour 50 minutes. To the best of my knowledge I still hold the record with a crossing of 1 hour 24 minutes 11 seconds in 1953.

MANHATTAN ISLAND (C). Said to be the most expensive piece of real estate in the world. 13½ miles long, maximum width 2 miles. Almost 29½ miles round. Mrs. Diane Struble circumnavigated it on 16th August 1959 in 11 hours 16 minutes by astutely working the tides. First said to have been swum in 1926: lady swimmer's name not available.

MISTAKEN IDENTITY. The B.L.D.S.A. 1959 dinner and A.G.M. 'went off like a bomb'. Particularly the latter (cryptic remark!). Most noteworthy incident concerned Coventry's Deputy Mayor posing with swimmers for a Press photograph. The harassed photographer tried hard to get the correct names and details for his picture caption. 'And what year did you swim the Channel, chum?' he asked the City's No. 2 dignitary.

MOLOKAI CHANNEL, HAWAII (C). Approx. 29 statute miles, water temperature good, tidal streams not too bad. But there are things with teeth that go snap in the night! No one has succeeded so far. Greta Andersen has tried twice.

NIGHT SWIMMING. American distance swimmer Don Jonz gives a tip which I have not encountered before; it sounds useful as a night-swimming aid. In a threepenny chemical test-tube he inserted a battery and a bulb. This attached to his cap without weight or impediment being noticeable. The contrivance much helped the night vigilance of his crew.

ODD SPOT (C). Charles Burton, American merchant seaman, fell overboard and swam for 22 hours in shark-infested water. But Susan Baddeley need not worry about her endurance record; Mr. Burton had no official timekeeper!

ONTARIO (C). Fresh-water lake quickly affected by weather. Distance approx. 30 miles. It has been swum by Marilyn Bell and Johnny Jaremy of Toronto. Also in 1956 by Brenda Fisher of Great Britain. Brenda's time was 18 hours 51 minutes.

PHILOSOPHY. Many persons spend £100 on an organised summer holiday. We hard-bitten swim addicts never have a formal holiday but make an informal one every summer week-end in a different part of the country. And if we do spend £100 on our sport, we break even with the conventional tourist. And because of unfailing good company, unfailing battles with the elements, and occasional flashes of glory, we enjoy ourselves more than they do.

POOLE HARBOUR SWIM. Three miles with tide. Duration about 1 hour. Harbour entrance to Poole Bridge.

PRESIDENT WITHOUT PEER. Without exception, successful organisations owe their success to two main factors. One is efficient and enthusiastic teamwork. The other is a perceptive and sage leader. The British Long Distance Swimming Association is extremely fortunate in both these necessities. The team consists of general secretary, treasurer, committee, life-saving organiser, swim secretaries, and area representatives. For enthusiasm and efficiency, it is difficult to fault them. The President is quite outstanding in calibre. It is considered pretty un-British to pay any office-holder a compliment—except in an obituary notice! But sometimes the immensity of accomplishments breaks through the barrier. In particular, the B.L.D.S.A. President deserves more than that one terse commendatory phrase.

Philip Rising proved himself practically by swimming the Channel in both directions, by setting up a two-way Windermere record which lasted six years, and by blazing a way across Torbay. He has proved his administrative ability by five years of most productive B.L.D.S.A. presidency backed by still longer periods of club and area A.S.A. committee work. But that is not all of a president's task; I have listened to more than a score of his first-class speeches at public functions—each requiring enormous diligence in preparation and equally enormous tact in utterance. I have seen him greeting—and entertaining from his own pocket—at least a hundred parliamentary, civic, and sporting V.I.P.s. Add to this formidable total of attainments, the donation of a trophy or two and a cheque or two. And there you have a President very *comme-il-faut*. A champion in his own right.

RECORD BREAKING . . . In a note to me, Couto, four times unsuccessful before striking a winning vein, put things in a nutshell. 'Swimming the Channel is like playing cards. The swimmer to be successful must hold the four aces—physical fitness, mental fitness, good pilot, and good weather. But for record breaking, he must hold the joker, too—good luck.'

RECOVERY RATE. One vital question is often asked by long distance competitors and Channel aspirants. How fast does one recover from the effects of a long swim? They are anxious to know whether racing on two successive Saturdays or trying the Channel on two successive neap tides is too much for the human body.

To seek an answer it is first necessary to define a 'long swim'. If some definitive precision is sacrificed to some degree of common sense I believe this is fairly easy. It is in fact 'a swim somewhere near the limit of a swimmer's capability having regard to his state of training and water fitness'. Thus in February a ten-mile swim would be long for a Channel swimmer, whereas in August the same distance would be 'a piece of cake'. Five miles in January might similarly be termed long.

With that definition an answer to the 64,000-dollar question becomes possible—at least in theory. Just take a number of swimmers of varying ages and make them swim distances which to them are 'long': then measure their fatigue daily until it totally disappears. Unfortunately in practice the numbers of guinea-pigs are not forthcoming. And just how does one go about measuring fatigue? Without a medical research organisation and a battery of instruments I could only think of one way. That was to be the guinea-pig myself; to do a long swim and then time-test myself daily over a mile until the stop-watch showed me again to be doing normal times. The results are tabulated below.

Saturday	Long swim. Fatiguing at time of performance but only after effect was a feeling of nicely exercised well-being.
Sunday	Rest day. No swim. Lazy 'yawny' feeling only perceptible after-effect.
Monday	Yawny feeling persists. Swam one mile at 96 per cent normal pace.
Tuesday	Slightly tired feeling until mid-morning. Swam one mile at 97 per cent normal pace.
Wednesday	No noticeable effects remain. Swam mile at 98 per cent normal pace.
Thursday	Swam mile at normal pace.
Friday	Ditto.

The experiment thus indicates that all trace of fatigue had disappeared in five days. Since this was carried out by an elderly subject while maintaining an ordinary working life it is likely to be a maximum figure. A younger man or one given special facilities for rest, massage, and relaxation would obviously recuperate more quickly. The five days' period might be exceeded only where the swimmer had forced himself beyond his physical limits on the long swim.

A very interesting point is that although on the Wednesday one *felt* a hundred per cent fit the stop-watch showed conclusively that the figure was only ninety-eight. This undetectable element of fatigue may well be the thing which is normally called 'loss of form' or staleness and plays havoc with championship swimmers —and water-polo teams, too.

REMARK FROM MORECAMBE. A day visitor, gazing at the tide rapidly disappearing from the Bay exploded in exasperation. 'You'd think that on special occasions the Corporation would arrange high tide at a more convenient time for visitors.'

SARK TO GUERNSEY. Distance roughly 6 to 7 statute miles. Warmish water but strong tides complications. Swum, in 1961, by Ruth Oldham of Grange-over-Sands, Lancashire. Time—5 hours 21 minutes.

SCHELDE SWIM (C). From Breskens to Flushing. An invitation championship for amateurs. Both sexes. Very strong cross-tides but swim is timed to obtain least tidal effects. The aim is twenty minutes weak flood tide, twenty minutes slack, and twenty minutes weak ebb tide. But neither tides nor swimmers are always predictable or punctual! So the finish especially for slow swimmers is always a hard tidal slog. Distance approx. 2½ land miles. Swimmers give glowing reports of generosity by Muller's steamships and by individual Dutch hosts. With a new record set up the most successful British year was 1936. Cecil Deane (Penguin) won in 1 hour 1 minute. F. G. Godwin (Brighton) was second in 1 hour 4 minutes. E. H. Temme (Plaistow) won in 1933 from F. G. Milton (Otter) by four-fifths of a second! Joe Smith (Rochdale) and Joyce Bricknell (Coventry) were third in their respective section in 1959. In 1962, Malcolm Humphreys and Peter Hatfield were respectively second and fifth men home.

SEASIDE SWIMS. A WARNING. Practically every notable seaside town stages a 'pier-to-pier' or some very similar event. It is one of these free entertainments which do so much to stamp a town's name into people's minds, besides providing their visitors with a most interesting sporting event. Usually sponsored by the local swimming club. Every so often, however, a nigger creeps into the woodpile, and some new organisation—probably through lack of knowledge—endeavours to run a swim without being properly affiliated. It is therefore entirely wise to inquire into the antecedents of any competitions in which one is interested. It was just such an inquiry which saved me a year or two back from entering a most attractive newly arranged marathon, the sponsors of which were happily intending to dispense large cash prizes. Thus does one's amateur status perish if not alert.

SELECTION OF EVENTS. It is essential for ambitious

swimmers to nominate their target-events, or target-distances right. In our specialised modern sport, it is no longer sufficient to 'travel hopefully'; it is 100 per cent necessary to travel purposefully.

Distance-selection is an intensely personal decision. Into the personal computing machine go estimates of (*a*) physical ability (*b*) temperament (*c*) past performances over various courses (*d*) time available for swimming (*e*) finances available. Great conflicts between these factors will undoubtedly ensue but a common-sense answer should emerge. And although circumstances may later force deviations, that is a thousand times preferable to starting your preparation aimlessly.

SHARKS. U.K. readers forgive me while I deal with the most frequently repeated query from overseas. Shark repellants? Here is the nutshell synopsis. Seven species of shark are known to be dangerous to man. (These do not include the type encountered in the Torbay Championship!) Estuaries and coastal waters are worst because sharks are here 'blooded' on offal. In clear water, danger is much reduced; numerous cases are on record of men accidentally immersed in shark-infested waters for long periods. Only last year a first-tripper fell overboard from his ship and swam for seven hours—in the Coral Sea. Sharks locate their food by sight, touch, smell, hearing, and echo-detection. It is most difficult to foil all those methods. Chemical repellants, until recently thought to be efficacious, are now under suspicion by scientists. Noise repellants—such as explosive charges—are also now believed to attract inquiring sharks to the area. The only completely trustworthy repellant is therefore the physical barrier of a net. And that does not rule out—as one might think—tropical channel swimming. At least one Australian championship that I know has an answer; every competitor swims in an individual buoyant 'cage' towed by his escort boat. Incidentally no attacks have been recorded in water under 21·2° C (70° F). So if it is 21·1° C you may be O.K.!

SOUTHSEA PIER-TO-PIER SWIM. This is a first-class 'lead-in' event for prospective distance swimmers. And an enjoyable stimulating sprint for those already established. Distance 1¼ miles from Clarence Pier to South Parade Pier. Tidal streams are fairly unpredictable because of inshore eddies. Temperature slightly warmer (in summer) than the main English Channel. There is a ladies' and men's championship under A.S.A. laws. Course is shown on Ryde–Southsea swim chartlet.

STALENESS. Despite all sensible precautions, there is a crisis point in training at which swimmers are apt to become disenchanted. Hard work, prolonged training hours, crowded pools, complicated travel arrangements, weather and finance worries; all these combine towards a joint boiling over. Later, with an achievement or two in the bag, all will seem worthwhile. But at the time it is sometimes difficult not to rebel against the restrictive routines, and equally difficult not to feel a revulsion against swimming. No matter how dedicated the athlete, a black mood comes to all in due course. At least—despite the contrary statements made about Wardrop and Breen—I have never met a swimmer who was exempt. One of our most indefatigable marathoneers wrote me a little while ago in distress. No names, no mastheading. But the advice I offered may be useful to others when so afflicted.

'In my experience there are only three ways of defeating staleness and boredom. Method 1 is to bash on regardless and beat the feeling by sheer will-power. This way is only applicable when self-analysis shows no valid reason for the lapse. Method 2 is to go completely off swimming for a couple of weeks. Make a point of doing all the things you have particularly wanted to do but have missed by swimming. You may not know it but you may be grudging the time and looking forward to the end of the swim instead of to the swim itself. Take late nights, lay abed in the mornings, eat all your fancy foods, watch television and cinema shows, go shopping. These are only examples of what athletes go without and (occasionally) secretly resent. Your trouble may be something else but pursue this line of thought and you may find the answer. Method 3 is to progress your training by other than orthodox measures. Come out and have a good lunch and rest in the middle of your long swim. Or divide your weekly long swim between two days instead of doing it straight off. Or increase your weekly total by cutting out your day's rest and swimming, say, four miles a day instead of having a long weekly swim. So long as you honestly think that you are somehow improving on the previous week, you will benefit mentally and physically. Even spend a couple of weeks on nothing but mile sprints.

'If you decide on the second method do not worry. You are a fit and experienced marathon swimmer. The short abstention will only affect your speed and not endurance. If racing is not your top priority, this is immaterial. I had 24 days off at the beginning of 1959 and came back to do Morecambe Bay Two-Way, Lough Neagh, and Loch Lomond; it was not until I took an hour longer in the Windermere Championship than the previous year that anyone twigged anything amiss.' Readers who have suffered thus may be glad to hear of a fellow sufferer; those who have not suffered should spike this item for future reference. One day they will need it!

STATE OF SEA CARD issued and sold by H.M. Stationery Office. On this card, photographs illustrate the appearance of the sea corresponding to each force of Beaufort Wind Scale. Range of wind-speeds and means are printed for each force. Description of sea is given according to World Meteorological Organisation values. As a hanging wall-card (M.O. 688) 21½ in. by 14½ in. it costs five shillings; as a foldable card (M.O. 688A) 10¾ in. by 14½ in. it is six and sixpence. A magnificent present for those of one's friends who habitually over-state their swim conditions. And stop thinking of me. I've got one!

SWIM OFFICIALS. The devoted people who give so much time and energy, deserve the grateful thanks of every competitor —but naturally never get them. For when a score of competitors arrive with a score of time-keeper-trainers, and a staggering number of 'mums', 'dads', and other supporters, there is also inevitably a protest or two to be found somewhere amongst them. These officials undoubtedly get many more 'kicks than ha'pence'; why they never resign *en masse* is a mystery to those who do not understand the calibre and enthusiasm of the sport's amateur officials.

Rained on, sprayed on, and occasionally even reviled by the competitors, these excellent sportsmen marvelllously seem to turn up smiling for more. Similarly with official Channel observers. Sitting in small boats facing forwards and looking backwards for 15–20 hours is no joke. All these pillars of the sport perform endurance feats almost equal to the swimmers. Thanks a lot, chaps!

TAY SWIM. Up North 'over the wall' Ye Amphibious Ancients sponsor the Tay two-way swim. Typical average time is one hour; although it has been done in three-quarters by Scottish champion Bob Sreenan. Typical temperature 51 degrees. Human sacrifices. (Sassenachs welcome!)

TIDAL CONSIDERATION IN RACES. Note the time of the start; then note the time of high-water, from newspaper, information bureau, or tide-table. From that information it will be evident the race will commence a certain time 'before or after high-water'. That form of words is the key to getting tidal information from any boatmen. Old salts can rarely anticipate what the tide will do at 3 p.m. on Saturday 26th July, but they generally do know what happens, at, for example, 'two and a half hours after high-water'. Armed with such further information from the local boatmen, a race duration can be estimated again with much greater accuracy. From that estimated race duration stems the swimmers own judgement of his most efficient pace.

Personally, I like to rely entirely on my own calculations and thus have another method. Tides happen roughly twice daily; in actual fact, they usually get fifty minutes later each day. It follows, therefore, that if one can be on the course twenty-four hours and fifty minutes before the start (or twelve hours and twenty-five minutes) there will be tidal conditions exactly similar to those of the forthcoming race. That state of affairs is an 'open sesame' to further knowledge for any race.

But for short inshore swims, with two pieces of heavyish wood it is possible to obtain invaluable tidal data, because they will float fairly low in the water—like a swimmer—and not be blown about by the wind. One piece of wood should be dropped offshore from the starting point and its *direction* of drift watched carefully. No intricate calculations are required, but this experiment will immediately show whether the current is favourable or adverse, and whether it is off shore or on shore. The next experiment requires a pier and does require calculation, but not a very difficult one. Take the second piece of wood to the upstream side of the pier; then drop it overboard at the same instant noting the time of the nearest second. As it drifts into sight on the downstream side of the pier note the time again. From those observations it is easy to work out the rate of drift, i.e. if the pier is one hundred feet wide and the wood takes one hundred seconds the rate is one foot in the second. By further simple calculation it is evident that in twenty minutes there will be twelve hundred feet of tidal movement (or four hundred yards). One further mental calculation will turn that into about five minutes' worth of swimming, and thus a thoroughly accurate adjustment to the race-duration has been produced.

The tide will rarely run conveniently at one foot per second but anyone—like myself—who has ever achieved the dizzy heights of any school's fourth form will be able to work it out. The method has been used by mariners for a good many centuries and is well known at sea as 'the Dutchman's log'. Here are three other tips which may help in its use. Firstly, the 'fifty-minutes-later-each-day' rule for tides is an approximation only, and inspection of the official tide tables will give very much more accuracy. Secondly, to get tidal results which will approximate to the average during the race, it is obviously best to conduct the experiment in an imaginary middle-of-the-race time. This method is only useful in races up to a couple of miles along the shore. The principle remains the same for longer races but one requires too much time and too many pieces of wood. And a boat and a slide-rule!

TIDES. Rattling through my letterbox comes a regular stream of enquiries about tides and tidal effects. It is evident that a much simplified and much concentrated *précis* is necessary to ease swimmers' hearts and minds. Here then—from the swimmer's angle—are the basic facts.

Gravitational effects of moon and sun attract a 'hump' of water directly underneath those bodies. But nature detests excessive lopsidedness. Therefore, to restore balance, centrifugal force throws up a similar hump on exactly the other side of the world. Naturally, the water for these two humps must be obtained from other areas. Thus there is *high water* (high tide) on the humps and *low water* (low tide) in other areas. Then, as the earth revolves on its axis once in 24 hours, various parts of the world receive their high and low tides in ordered daily sequence.

Twice monthly moon and sun get themselves into a straight line with the earth. The result is a unified gravity pull—and a larger water hump than at any other period. Centrifugal force—the old equaliser—responds by throwing a similarly large hump on the other side of the world. So tides at this time are bigger than others; they are known as *spring tides*. Note that they occur fortnightly and not only in springtime! Between those spring tides come much smaller jobs known as *neap tides*. The decrease in size is because sun and moon have worked themselves into a position of pulling at right-angles to one another.

All the foregoing refers to up-and-down water moves. That is important when organising a comparatively shallow swim such as Morecambe Bay. It may mean the difference between completing a swimming race or walking home across the sandbanks. But generally speaking the 'to-and-fro' water movements are more important to swimmers. These horizontal movements are known as *tidal streams* and they directly result from the things already discussed. Like this. If a gravitational (or centrifugal) water-hump is due in the North Sea, then the water for it has got to get there. So it flows in through Dover Straits (and round the north of Scotland). At spring tides, it flows very fast to make a big hump; at neaps, it flows more slowly to form a smaller hump. That is why swimmers usually like to swim *across* channels at neap tides; the to-and-fro movement is approximately halved.

TRAINING FACILITIES. A correspondent, resident in London, asked for details of lakes in which to carry out long distance training. Since the dictionary seems to set no definite limit between a small lake and a large pond, one was able to mention—on or near his home territory—Hampstead Ponds, the Serpentine, Ruislip reservoir, and Welsh Harp. Further afield, selected places in the Norfolk Broads and various large stretches in the Lake District are a delight to swimmers. Additionally there are many smaller pieces of water on moorland up North and disused sand, gravel, and chalk pits in the other parts of the country. There is no 'Baedeker Guide' in existence for these, and one just has to explore, look and ask.

It is my experience, however, that for 90 per cent of long distance training a carefully chosen pool is better than a lake; one has all the equal pleasures and benefits of sun, fresh air, pleasant surroundings and the necessary low temperature water. Equally important to any one of those attributes is to swim in precisely measured laps. The day and age when long distance men merely swam interminably not caring greatly about mileage is as departed as the dodo. In order to register success nowadays it is imperative to swim against the clock rather than the calendar.

In long distance swimming, training an hour of fast calculated pace is worth a day's aimless lazy lolloping. To the value of lap swimming also add the benefit of the occasional companion for a half mile or so; even the ultra-slow breast-stroker who one can lap every six lengths is of use to break monotony. The occasional bumps against other swimmers are also useful to stir one out of placidity. Pampered 'glasshouse' swimmers who avoid all difficulties in training are ill prepared to meet the shocks, annoyances and emergencies which always occur on 'the day'.

VETERANS. First, Dr. G. B. Brewster, aged 68 in 1959. On 3rd October he swam from Dover Harbour to Deal Pier in 2 hours 45 minutes. Wind was fresh at the start, dying to a calm off Deal. Distance, 8·6 land miles by shortest inshore route—probably more as swum. Naturally there was tidal assistance, but it is nevertheless a good performance. Two years later Doctor Brewster swam 17 miles tidally from Dover to abeam of Ramsgate in 4 hours 30 minutes; this *must* be the best ever for a 70-year-old.

Another swim that made me want to stand up and cheer in 1961 was in the Solent. President and chairman of Solent S.C. swam briskly together from Southsea to Isle of Wight. Time—2 hours 32 minutes for a 4½ tide-ripped miles. At age 57, Mr. Jim Bland's fitness is quite superb—even for a former long distance swimmer of repute. But John Moorey's *first* major swim, at 48, was even more remarkable. With relentless determination—and he is good enough to say with my former book—he started swimming at 45.

WASH SWIM (C). From Hunstanton Lighthouse to Skegness lifeboat station is 15·7 land miles. In 1962 local businessmen organised a professional race but weather caused it to be abandoned after a few hours. The only known person to have swum the course is Mercedes Gleitz. On 29th June 1929 at 5.08 a.m., she set off from Butterwick; at 6.25 p.m. she landed at Heacham Beach. She had dull, still, weather at first; towards the end there was a fresh breeze and a choppy sea.

WEATHER. For day-to-day prediction, there are a number of most useful seamanlike sayings; these will help arrange anything from a Channel swim to a Moray Firth duckshooting party. I learned the first when I was sixteen and the last about 25 years later. Acknowledgements to any author seems quite impossible; I believe that—like Topsy—they 'just growed'. You may smile cynically, but they have assisted seamen through the ages. And there is a scientific basis for most of them.

BAROMETER READINGS

When the glass falls low, prepare for a blow.
When it rises light, you can fly a kite.

Long foretold, long last; short notice, quickly past.

First rise after very low—indicates a stronger blow.

GENERAL INDICATIONS

Red sky in the morning is the sailor's warning.
Red sky at night is the sailor's delight.

or Evening red and morning grey, indicates a decent day.

When it rains before the wind,
You'll get some beastly weather mind.
If the wind before the rain,
Soon shall matters ease again.

Sound that travels far and wide, a stormy day doth soon detide.

The forecast's cold and it's turned out hot,
Blame Forsberg's rhymes—the clueless clot.

WHITBY SWIM (C). Course Sandsend to Whitby—about 2½ miles. Organised by Whitby Seals Swimming Club usually on a Sunday in August. Sheltered from prevailing strong winds. But in the event of weather interference, can be swum in River Esk, ending in the harbour. Shallowish coastal water makes for comparatively comfortable water temperatures. Brian Winn (Lancaster) holds record in 58 minutes 30 seconds.

WICKHAM, ALECK. Introducer of crawl stroke to Australia.

Lives on the Roviana Lagoon, New Georgia. Still swims, 1963, at the age of 77.

WONDER SWIMMER. On 26th November 1959, Michael Jennings wrote me a 'how-does-one-go-about-marathon-swimming' letter. On 19th July 1960 he knocked the Torbay record into smithereens—my record. What progress; what gratitude!

Since then he has gone from strength to strength. In 1960 his Torbay time was 3 hours 50 minutes; in 1961 it was 3 hours 46 minutes; in 1962 it was 3 hours 39 minutes 25 seconds. This last swim means that he swam eight consecutive miles averaging 27 minutes 22 seconds apiece. A magnificent performance on a straight course, in weather that was just about at the top limit for accompanying boats, and in water temperature 15° C (59° F). This performance probably places him as the world's currently top-ranking amateur 8-miler. And at least assured of a place amongst the top half-dozen professionals. Further achievements of his are recorded in other chapters and appendices.

APPENDIX I

Successful Individual Channel Swims

	Date	Name	Nationality	Route	Time
1.	1875	*Matthew Webb	G.B.	E–F	21 h. 45 m.
2.	1911	*T. W. Burgess	G.B.	E–F	22 h. 35 m.
3.	1923	*H. Sullivan	U.S.A.	E–F	26 h. 50 m.
4.	1923	*E. Tiraboschi	Argentine	F–E	16 h. 33 m.
5.	1923	*C. Toth	U.S.A.	F–E	16 h. 54 m.
6.	1926	*Gertrude Ederle	U.S.A.	F–E	14 h. 34 m.
7.	1926	*Millie Corson	U.S.A.	F–E	15 h. 28 m.
8.	1926	*A. Weirkotter	Germany	F–E	12 h. 40 m.
9.	1926	G. Michel	France	F–E	11 h. 05 m.
10.	1926	N. L. Derham	G.B.	F–E	13 h. 55 m.
11.	1927	*E. H. Temme	G.B.	F–E	14 h. 29 m.
12.	1927	*Mercedes Gleitz	G.B.	F–E	15 h. 15 m.
13.	1927	Ivy Gill	G.B.	F–E	15 h. 09 m.
14.	1928	*Ivy Hawke	G.B.	F–E	19 h. 16 m.
15.	1928	*Hilda Sharp	G.B.	F–E	14 h. 58 m.
16.	1928	*I. Helmy	Egypt	F–E	23 h. 40 m.
17.	1930	*Peggy Duncan	South Africa	F–E	16 h. 15 m.
18.	1933	*Sunny Lowry	G.B.	F–E	15 h. 45 m.
19.	1934	E. H. Temme	G.B.	E–F	15 h. 54 m.
20.	1934	Emma Faber	Austria	F–E	14 h. 40 m.
21.	1935	*Haydn Taylor	G.B.	F–E	14 h. 48 m.
22.	1937	*Tom Blower	G.B.	F–E	13 h. 29 m.
23.	1938	Frau Wendell-Pharre	Germany	F–E	15 h. 33 m.
24.	1938	F. Wheatcroft	G.B.	F–E	13 h. 35 m.
25.	1939	Sally Bauer	Sweden	F–E	15 h. 23 m.
26.	1947	D. Carpio	Peru	F–E	14 h. 46 m.
27.	1948	H. A. Rheim	Egypt	F–E	17 h. 38 m.
28.	1948	T. Blower	G.B.	E–F	15 h. 31 m.
29.	1949	*P. Mickman	G.B.	F–E	23 h. 48 m.
30.	1949	F. Du Moulin	Belgium	F–E	21 h. 59 m.
31.	1949	H. A. Rheim	Egypt	E–F	15 h. 46 m.

	Date	Name	Nationality	Route	Time
32.	1949	M. H. Hamad	Egypt	F–E	15 h. 22 m.
33.	1949	J. Zirganos	Greece	F–E	18 h. 30 m.
34.	1950	Florence Chadwick	U.S.A.	F–E	13 h. 23 m.
35.	1951	A. L. Abou Heif	Egypt	F–E	15 h. 43 m.
36.	1951	W. E. Barnie	G.B.	E–F	19 h. 02 m.
37.	1951	*P. H. Rising	G.B.	F–E	15 h. 55 m.
38.	1951	*T. Blower	G.B.	E–F	18 h. 42 m.
39.	1951	*Florence Chadwick	U.S.A.	E–F	16 h. 19 m.
40.	1952	*Kathleen Mayoh	G.B.	F–E	16 h. 55 m.
41.	1952	*V. Birkett	G.B.	F–E	15 h. 36 m.
42.	1952	B. Soliman	Egypt	F–E	18 h. 12 m.
43.	1952	A. M. Abdu	Egypt	F–E	16 h. 30 m.
44.	1952	S. el Arabi	Egypt	E–F	17 h. 42 m.
45.	1952	*P. H. Rising	G.B.	E–F	18 h. 38 m.
46.	1952	*P. Mickman	G.B.	E–F	18 h. 44 m.
47.	1953	A. Heif	Egypt	E–F	13 h. 45 m.
48.	1953	D. P. Beltran	Mexico	F–E	15 h. 23 m.
49.	1953	*T. Bleik	Lebanon	F–E	16 h. 05 m.
50.	1953	*Florence Chadwick	U.S.A.	E–F	14 h. 42 m.
51.	1954	*M. Guler	Turkey	F–E	16 h. 50 m.
52.	1955	*Marilyn Bell	Canada	F–E	14 h. 36 m.
53.	1955	*Bill Pickering	G.B.	E–F	14 h. 06 m.
54.	1955	*F. C. Oldman	G.B.	F–E	14 h. 31 m.
55.	1955	*Florence Chadwick	U.S.A.	E–F	13 h. 55 m.
56.	1956	*Jacques Amyot	Canada	F–E	13 h. 03 m.
57.	1957	*Gerald Forsberg	G.B.	E–F	13 h. 33 m.
58.	1958	*Abilio Couto	Brazil	F–E	12 h. 45 m.
59.	1958	*Bert Thomas	U.S.A.	F–E	19 h. 31 m.
60.	1958	*Miss M. Tresseras	Spain	F–E	14 h. 14 m.
61.	1958	*Jose Vitos	Spain	F–E	15 h. 11 m.
62.	1958	*Miss June Gilbert	G.B.	F–E	16 h. 52 m.
63.	1958	*Paul Herron	U.S.A.	F–E	12 h. 00 m.
64.	1958	*Mihir Sen	India	E–F	14 h. 45 m.
65.	1959	*Denis Pearson	South Rhodesia	F–E	15 h. 36 m.
66.	1959	*Rod Rodriguez	Spain	F–E	12 h. 53 m.
67.	1959	*Niko Nestor	Yugoslavia	F–E	12 h. 06 m.
68.	1959	*M. Gonzalez	Mexico	F–E	14 h. 44 m.
69.	1959	*Bimal Chundra	India	F–E	13 h. 50 m.
70.	1959	*Osman Ghandour	Lebanon	F–E	12 h. 05 m.
71.	1959	*Paul Herron	U.S.A.	E–F	15 h. 00 m.
72.	1959	*Gordon Hill	G.B.	F–E	12 h. 48 m.
73.	1959	*Abilio Couto	Brazil	E–F	12 h. 49 m.
74.	1959	*Brojen Das	Pakistan	E–F	13 h. 26 m.
75.	1959	*Abilio Couto	Brazil	F–E	11 h. 33 m.
76.	1959	*Arati Saha	India	F–E	16 h. 20 m.

	Date	Name	Nationality	Route	Time
77.	1960	*Michael Jennings	G.B.	F–E	13 h. 31 m.
78.	1960	*Alfredo Camerero	Argentine	F–E	12 h. 23 m.
79.	1960	*A. Falkreddin	Lebanon	F–E	12 h. 56 m.
80.	1960	*S. Hasselburg	Sweden	F–E	14 h. 30 m.
81.	1960	*Brojen Das	Pakistan	F–E	14 h. 43 m.
82.	1960	*Mary Kok	Holland	F–E	12 h. 25 m.
83.	1960	*Helge Jensen	Canada	E–F	10 h. 23 m.
84.	1960	*Peter Fergus	G.B.	E–F	16 h. 30 m.
85.	1961	*Dorothy Perkins	G.B.	F–E	20 h. 26 m.
86.	1961	*Rosemary George	G.B.	E–F	21 h. 35 m.
87.	1961	*Margaret White	G.B.	F–E	15 h. 08 m.
88.	1961	*Montserrat Tresseras	Spain	E–F	16 h. 25 m.
89.	1961	*N. N. Ray	India	F–E	19 h. 00 m.
90.	1961	*Brojen Das	Pakistan	F–E	11 h. 48 m.
91.	1961	*Brojen Das	Pakistan	F–E	10 h. 35 m.
92.	1961	*Dogan-Sahin	Turkey	F–E	14 h. 21 m.

Notes

1. This tabulation applies to individual swims only. *Daily Mail* and *Butlin* race successes are recorded elsewhere.

2. The notes in the concluding paragraphs of Chapter 2 apply very forcibly. Although I have taken every possible care with the compilation, one or two errors and omissions may well have occurred. In this connection, it would help greatly if swimmers desiring to have their swims recognised beyond doubt would take the trouble to register with the Channel Swimming Association.

3. Swims marked * have been ratified by the C.S.A. The remarks in Chapter 2 about C.S.A. ratification are applicable.

4. The tabulation has been the result of much research and study. It would be appreciated if the author could be acknowledged in any public use of the matter.

Note. All the above are entitled to wear the badge of the British Long Distance Swimming Association.

APPENDIX 2

Morecambe Bay

Winners of the Men's Championships

		H.	M.	S.
1907	B. Law, Chadderton	3	45	18
1908	B. Law, Chadderton	3	25	6
1909	B. Law, Chadderton	3	42	29
1910	H. Tayler, Chadderton	2	5	52
1911	H. Taylor, Chadderton	2	19	8
1912	H. Taylor, Chadderton	2	34	10
1913	H. Taylor, Chadderton	2	13	52
1914	H. Taylor, Chadderton	2	2	55
1920	H. Taylor, Chadderton	2	47	0
1921	H. Taylor, Chadderton	3	0	58
1922	N. Wrigley, Burnley	3	4	0
1923	H. Taylor, Chadderton	2	46	52
1924	B. Law, Chadderton	2	38	30
1925	C. Daly, Manchester	2	50	0
1926	H. Taylor, Chadderton	2	45	0
1927	C. Daly, Manchester	2	47	0
1928	F. N. Catterall, Liverpool	2	36	45
1929	B. Law, Chadderton	2	44	26
1930	Ben Addy, Stalybridge	3	0	14
1931	C. Daly, Manchester	2	53	35
1932	B. Law, Chadderton	2	47	0
1933	J. Wallwork, Radcliffe	3	36	0
1934	Prizes divided			
1935	T. Blower, Nottingham	3	19	4
1936	T. Blower, Nottingham	3	17	0
1937	T. Blower, Nottingham	3	25	42
1938	T. Blower, Nottingham	2	15	52
1939	Alan Gorton, Failsworth	2	47	2

No swims in 1940–1–2–3–4–5.
No male entrant completed the Swim in 1946.

		H.	M.	S.
1947	Harry Hitchen, Ashton-under-Lyne	3	1	0
1948	Trevor Smith, Huddersfield	2	31	0
1949	Harry Hitchen, Ashton-under-Lyne	2	49	0
1950	Edward James May, Barrow-in-Furness	3	30	0
1951	Cdr. C. G. Forsberg, Otter S.C., London	3	2	8
1952	W. T. H. Bradley, Liverpool	2	18	27
1953	W. T. H. Bradley, Liverpool	2	36	20
1954	Bill Pickering, Bloxwich	2	43	2
1955	Barry Woodward, London	2	39	32
1956	Gordon J. Hill, Oxford	2	51	50
1957	Edward Hannam, Sheffield	2	44	25
1958	Arthur E. Ayres, Coventry	2	32	10
1959	Joe Smith, Rochdale	2	22	25
1960	Joe Smith, Rochdale	2	54	0
1961	Ray Holmes, Lancaster	3	10	37
1962	W. H. Pearce, Manchester	3	13	24

Winners of the Ladies' Championship

		H.	M.	S.
1912	Miss M. Wensley, Blackburn	2	20 (F.O.B.)	0
1913	Miss S. Entwistle, Blackburn	3	11	0
1914	Miss M. Wensley, Blackburn	2	21	0
1920	Miss L. Morton, Blackpool	2	59	0
1921	Miss H. Seymour, Chester	3	40	56
1922	Miss L. Morton, Blackpool	3	9	0
1923	Miss L. Morton, Blackpool	2	51	15
1924	Miss L. Todd, Preston	4	3	30
1926	Miss E. Hilton, Chadderton	3	48	0
1927	Miss E. Hilton, Chadderton	3	12	0
1928	Miss E. McCallum, Chadderton	2	53	0
1929	Miss M. Simpson, Mcbe	3	7	0
1930	Miss M. Simpson, Mcbe	3	26	16
1931	Miss E. A. England, Huddersfield	3	19	0
1932	Miss E. McCallum, Chadderton	3	36	54
1934	Miss E. McCallum, Chadderton	3	57	0
1935	Miss I. Balls, Bingley	4	5	0
1936	Miss F. Blackburn, Lyth'am	4	21	0
1937	Miss D. M. Simpson, Mcbe	4	30	55
1937	Miss E. K. Hodgson, Grange	4	30	55
1938	No lady finished Swim.			
1939	Miss J. Fisher, Grimsby	2	51	35
1946	Miss J. Fisher, Grimsby	4	11	54
1947	Miss J. Fisher, Grimsby	3	25	0

		H.	M.	S.
1948	Miss B. Fisher, Grimsby	2	37	0
1949	Flora Beaumont, Ashton-under-Lyne . .	2	56	0
1950	Kathleen Mayoh, Farnw'th	3	45	42
1951	June Anthony, Nottingham	3	16	34
1952	Shirley A. Dunbar, Nottingham	2	23	8
1953	Shirley A. Dunbar, Notts.	2	58	40
1954	June Anthony, Notts.	2	48	17
1955	Joyce Finch, Grimsby	2	52	19
1956	No ladies competed.			
1957	Mrs. C. Lumb, Huddersf'd . . . . . (F.O.B.—Finished Out of Bounds.)	3	45	6
1958	Ann Johnston, Grange	2	52	10
1959	Joyce A. Bricknell, Coventry	2	38	13
1960	Dorothy M. Perkins, Bfd.	3	33	30
1961	Ruth Oldham, Grange	3	23	17
1962	Hazel Holroyd, Elland	3	34	47

Morecambe Bay 20 Miles Championship

		Total time		
		H.	M.	S.
4 July 1959	Cmdr. C. G. Forsberg, Otter S.C., London	6	23	0
8 Aug. 1959	Ann Johnston, Grange	6	30	30
5 Sept. 1959	Kendall Mellor, Keighley & Otley S.C. .	6	19	0
10 Sept. 1960	Dorothy Perkins, Bradford . .	6	50	15
10 Sept. 1960	Cmdr. C. G. Forsberg, Otter S.C., London	6	2	45
10 Sept. 1960	Arthur E. Ayres, Coventry . .	6	40	27
12 Aug. 1961	Michael Jennings, Gravesend . .	6	45	50
12 Aug. 1961	Arthur Ayres, Coventry . . .	6	51	05
12 Aug. 1961	Derek Turner, Droylsden . . .	7	4	37
12 Aug. 1961	Cmdr. C. G. Forsberg, Otter S.C., London	7	14	50

APPENDIX 3

Windermere Swimmers

British Long Distance Swimming Association

Official List of Windermere Swimmers, Times and Records

L–W—Lakeside–Waterhead W–L—Waterhead–Lakeside BW—Both ways

(A) Championship record
(B) Ladies all comers record
(C) Ladies Championship record
(D) Gents breast-stroke record
(E) Ladies breast-stroke record
(F) Ladies two way record
(G) Gents back-stroke record
(H) Two way record
(I) Ladies back-stroke record
(J) All comers record

Year	*Name*	*Town*	*Time*	
1911	James Foster	Oldham	11.29	W–L
1933	John Humphreys	Preston	10.04	W–L
1934	Charles Daly	Denton	6.22	W–L
1950	Doris Fell	Barrow	10.20	W–L
	Edward May	Dartford	7.31	
	June Knight	Cardiff	8.28	W–L
1951	E. McCoy	Rotherham	7.30	L–W
	Mrs. W. Temme	Newport	7.38	W–L
	Kathleen Mayoh	Farnworth	10.02	W–L
	Philip Rising	Rotherham	8.00	W–L
	Jason Zirganos	Greece	8.45	
	Jason Zirganos	Greece	6.55	
	Jason Zirganos	Greece	6.49	
	Jason Zirganos	Greece	8.25	
	Charles Hague	Rotherham	8.21	L–W
	James Clancy	Lichfield	11.55	W–L
	Ken Wray	Southport	7.17	W–L
	Stanley Archer	Rotherham	9.27	L–W
	Edward May	Dartford	7.19	
1952	Philip Rising	Rotherham	17.38	BW
	Edward May	Barrow	18.10	BW
	Kathleen Mayoh	Farnworth	7.00	W–L

Year	*Name*	*Town*	*Time*	
	Kathleen Beverley	Stalybridge	7.25	W–L
	Brian Barton	Wakefield	9.43	W–L
	Bob Fletcher	Rotherham	6.31	W–L
1953	Molly Spencer	Heck'wike	8.30	W–L
	P. Aldam (I)	Rotherham	8.13	L–W
1955	H. Bracewell	Blackpool	9.50	L–W
	Fred C. Oldham	Huddersfield	5.53	W–L
	John K. Slater	Otley	5.20	W–L
	C. G. Forsberg	London	5.56	W–L
	Wm. Keeting	Sale	8.17	W–L
	Mrs. W. Temme	Newport	6.50	L–W
	E. Hannam	Sheffield	6.20	W–L
1956	Margaret Iredale	Huddersfield	10.08	L–W
	Barry Woodward	London	6.59	W–L
	W. (Billy) Thrall	Rotherham	6.20	L–W
	Joan Thrall	Rotherham	8.15	L–W
1957	John K. Slater	Todmorden	5.25	L–W
	George Foote	Keighley	6.32	L–W
	Fred C. Oldman	Huddersfield	6.54	L–W
	C. G. Forsberg	London	5.50	L–W
	John K. Mouat	Alderney	6.30	L–W
	June Gilbert	Bromley	7.10	L–W
	Roy Hunt	Pontypridd	8.02	L–W
	George Foote	Keighley	8.22	L–W
1958	John K. Slater	Todmorden	6.10	L–W
	Barry Watson	Bingley	7.12	L–W
	John Todd	Bradford	8.14	L–W
	William Fantom	Coventry	7.40	W–L
	C. G. Forsberg (H)	London	12.57	BW
	C. G. Forsberg (A)	London	5.19.5	L–W
	Jenny James	Pontypridd	5.39	L–W
	Arthur Ayres	Coventry	5.42	L–W
	J. Bricknell	Coventry	5.43	L–W
	Jean Adams	Southampton	5.58	L–W
	R. McCaughey	Greenock	6.02	L–W
	Wm. Fantom	Coventry	6.07	L–W
	George Foote	Otley	6.10	L–W
	John K. Slater	Todmorden	6.11	L–W
	A. Endersby (D)	Coventry	6.12	L–W
	June Gilbert	Bromley	6.25	L–W
	Kendall Mellor	Keighley	6.45	L–W
	Jack Kerwin	Bradford	6.49	L–W
	Edward Robinson	Otley	7.19	L–W
	Godfrey Beaton	Loughborough	7.38	L–W
	Wm. Wrenn	Luton	8.13	L–W

Year	*Name*	*Town*	*Time*	
	M. Lindsay	London	6.20	L–W
	Jack Graham	Rotherham	7.14	L–W
	Jean Adams	Southampton	15.45	BW
1959	Jean Adams (F)	Southampton	15.09	BW
	Keith Seymour	Bradford	10.08	W–L
	John Todd (G)	Bradford	7.29	L–W
	Dorothy Perkins	Bradford	7.47	L–W
	Arthur Ayres	Coventry	6.40	W–L
	Arthur Endersby	Coventry	7.38	W–L
	Hiram Baddeley	Northolt	11.06	L–W
	Susan Baddeley	Northolt	11.06	L–W
	H. Baddeley	Northolt	11.20	L–W
	D. Gill	Bradford	10.47	L–W
	J. Smith	Rochdale	5.32	L–W
	W. Thrall	Rotherham	5.55	L–W
	D. Payne	London	6.14	L–W
	A. Ayres	Coventry	6.22	L–W
	C. G. Forsberg	London	6.26	L–W
	P. Fergus	Coventry	7.16	L–W
	A. Endersby	Coventry	7.28	L–W
	A. Smith	Dundee	7.32	L–W
	K. Mellor	Keighley	7.47	L–W
	R. May	Plymouth	8.09	L–W
	J. Kerwin	Bradford	8.13	L–W
	G. L. Beaton	Loughborough	8.17	L–W
	J. Somerfield	Bloxwich	8.46	L–W
	B. Orritt	Blackpool	8.58	L–W
	G. T. Smith	Huddersfield	9.10	L–W
	Joyce Brickell	Coventry	6.39	L–W
	Jean Adams	Southampton	7.47	L–W
	Ann Johnston	Grange	8.11	L–W
	Madge McCarthy	Dewsbury	8.32	L–W
	Dorothy Perkins	Bradford	8.46	L–W
	Ruth Oldham	Grange	8.22	L–W
1960	H. Neukeicher		8.00	W–L
	Ruth Oldham	Grange	7.40	W–L
	Helge Jensen (J)	Canada	4.58	L–W
	Dorothy Perkins	Bradford	7.10	W–L
	Ruth Oldham	Grange o Sands	8.40	W–L
	Joe Smith	Rochdale	5.30	L–W
	Michael Jennings	Greenhithe	5.46	L–W
	C. G. Forsberg	Bath	5.51	L–W
	W. T. H. Bradley	Liverpool	6.03	L–W
	Derek Turner	Droylsden	6.07	L–W
	Peter Fergus	Coventry	6.08	L–W

Year	*Name*	*Town*	*Time*	
	Arthur Ayres	Coventry	6.22	L–W
	John Turnbull	Whitley Bay	6.23	L–W
	Keith Seymour	Bradford	6.46	L–W
	Dennis Sullivan	Dundee	7.08	L–W
	J. A. Daish	Kendal	7.19	L–W
	Brian Dove	Harrow	7.20	L–W
	Arthur Endersby	Coventry	7.52	L–W
	Jeffrey Taylor	Huddersfield	8.34	L–W
	Dorothy Perkins	Bradford	6.48	L–W
	Margaret White	Leigh on Sea	7.26	L–W
	Dorothy Perkins	Bradford	17.35	BW
	Philip Kaye	Huddersfield	7.42	L–W
1961	Gillian M. Blundell (E)	London	6.18	W–L
	A. J. Moorey	Portsmouth	5.28	L–W
	Susan Lynch (B) (C)	Stanmore	5.37	L–W
	Walter Bradley	Liverpool	6.03	L–W
	Derek Turner	Droylsden	6.11	L–W
	Bryan Finlay	Coventry	6.16	L–W
	Leon Walkden	London	6.30	L–W
	P. Kaye	Huddersfield	7.01	L–W
	Michael Davis	Southsea	7.04	L–W
	Dorothy Perkins	Bradford	7.27	L–W
	J. Taylor	Huddersfield	7.55	L–W
	A. Richards	London	11.12	L–W
	Michael Nanson	Dover	9.20	L–W
1962	Michael Jennings	Gravesend	5.49	L–W
	A. J. Moorey	Portsmouth	6.03	L–W
	Barry Watson	Bingley	6.12	L–W
	G. L. J. Beaton	Solihull	7.40	L–W
	Jeffrey Taylor	Huddersfield	8.01	L–W
	Hazel Holroyd	Elland	7.44	L–W

Note. All the above are entitled to wear the badge of the British Long Distance Swimming Association.

APPENDIX 4

Torbay Championships

Successful Swimmers

Year	*Name*	*Town*	*Time*
1958	C. G. Forsberg	London	4.08
	A. E. Ayres	Coventry	4.15
	M. J. Somerfield	Bloxwich	4.39
	E. Hannam	Sheffield	4.44
	Wm. Wrenn	Luton	4.51
	B. Rann	Portsmouth	4.56
	J. K. Slater	Menston	5.00
	B. Watson	Bingley	5.03
	P. W. Challon	Yeovil	5.07
	G. W. Foote	Keighley	5.10
	K. Mellor	Keighley	5.31
	A. Smith	Dundee	5.40
	E. Robinson	Otley	5.48
	Jean Adams	Southampton	5.11
	June Gilbert	Bromley	5.35
1959	(Torquay to Brixham only—shortened course due to rough seas.)		
	W. Thrall	Rotherham	2.06
	G. Wilson	Halifax	2.07
	B. Watson	Bingley	2.14
	J. Smith	Rochdale	2.16
	R. McCaughey	Gourock	Times not available
	A. E. Ayres	Coventry	
	M. J. Somerfield	Bloxwich	
	G. W. Foote	Keighley	
	K. Mellor	Keighley	
	G. T. Smith	Huddersfield	
	R. May	Plymouth	
	A. W. Endersby	Coventry	
	E. A. Hunt	Coventry	
	A. Smith	Dundee	
	G. Beaton	Loughborough	
	Joyce Bricknell	Coventry	
	Madge McCarthy	Dewsbury	
	Jean Adams	Southampton	

Year	*Name*	*Town*	*Time*
1960	M. Jennings	Greenhithe	3.49
	C. G. Forsberg	Bath	4.15
	G. Wilson	Halifax	4.17
	A. E. Ayres	Coventry	4.27
	P. J. B. Fergus	Coventry	4.29
	B. Dove	Harrow	5.03
	D. Sullivan	Dundee	5.04
	A. W. Endersby	Coventry	5.07
	Madge McCarthy	Dewsbury	6.40
1961	M. Jennings	Greenhithe	3.46
	A. J. Moorey	Portsmouth	3.59
	C. G. Forsberg	Bath	4.08
	A. E. Ayres	Coventry	4.26
	A. W. Endersby	Coventry	4.40
	P. J. B. Fergus	Coventry	5.50
	J. Taylor	Huddersfield	5.50
	Pauline Goddard	Rotherham	4.57
	Margaret White	Leigh-on-Sea	5.03
	Madge McCarthy	Dewsbury	5.43
	Marguerite M. Pike	Plymouth	5.50
1962	M. Jennings	Greenhithe	3.39
	A. J. Moorey	Portsmouth	4.15
	C. G. Forsberg	Otter S.C.	4.25
	K. Mellor	Keighley	4.34
	L. Walkden	Twickenham	4.39
	M. J. Mills	Plymouth	4.43
	B. Finlay	Coventry	4.46
	A. E. Ayres	Coventry	5.22
	M. Davis	Southsea	5.24
	Hazel Holroyd	Elland	5.16
	Dilys Beynon	Sutton Coldfield	5.48

APPENDIX 5

Success—the Dual Approach

THE WISH TO SUCCEED

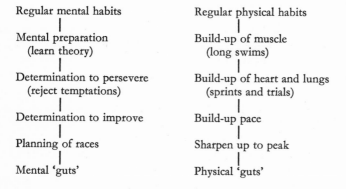

Regular mental habits	Regular physical habits
Mental preparation (learn theory)	Build-up of muscle (long swims)
Determination to persevere (reject temptations)	Build-up of heart and lungs (sprints and trials)
Determination to improve	Build-up pace
Planning of races	Sharpen up to peak
Mental 'guts'	Physical 'guts'

LAST MINUTE WRINKLES

Competitive swims at mental and physical peak

APPENDIX 6

British Long Distance Swimming Association Windermere Championship

Specimen of Rules and General Information Sheet

1. The Annual Windermere Championship will be held on Saturday, 25th August, 1962, and shall be open to all amateur swimmers who are members of this Association.

2. The course shall be approximately 10¼ miles, commencing at Lakeside, immediately opposite the first boating jetty, and finishing at Waterhead, between the last two boating jetties (opposite the Waterhead Hotel). In the event of a strong opposing wind, the course may be reversed, in which case similar arrangements will be in force.

3. The Association shall reserve the right to refuse any entry, in which case the entry fee will be returned.

4. A briefing meeting for competitors and officials will be held the evening before the Championship, in the Park Road Drill Hall at 8.0 p.m. All competitors and Pilot Life Savers and oarsmen must attend this meeting. Boat owners, trainers, etc., are cordially invited.

5. All competitors, oarsmen, trainers and officials etc., must be ready to leave Bowness Boating beach at 7.30 a.m. to be taken by boat to Lakeside or Waterhead.

6. Grease (if used) may be applied after landing. No grease or similar substance will be allowed in the boat during the race, and competitors must provide themselves with waste material and an old sheet or blanket, so that in the event of their leaving the water before the end of the race, no trace of grease (if used) will be left in the boat to the detriment of future passengers.

7. The competitor's number, as shown on the Championship pro-

gramme, will be displayed on the rowing boat which will be waiting. Boats will be numbered from the left. Suit cases, holdalls, etc., containing the competitor's clothing, food, thermos flasks, etc., must be placed in the rowing boat as soon as possible. At 8.45 a.m. opportunity will be given for photographs, Television, etc., and at 8.55 a.m. all competitors must report to the Championship referee, and be ready to enter the water. At 8.58 a.m. competitors will enter the water from the end of the boating jetty at the instruction of the Championship referee, and take up a position in line with the jetty. Competitor No. 1 will take up a position nearest to the end of the jetty, competitor No. 2 next to him, etc. Rowing-boats will take up a similar position in numerical order at least 100 yds. in front of the competitor. When the race is started, the boats should not wait until the competitors reach them, but should be moving up the Lake where the swimmer can gradually overhaul them, thus avoiding congestion and possible injury to swimmers at the start.

8. To start the races, a signal will be given simultaneously by whistle and flag.

9. The leading Pilot, in a rowing-boat, will take up a position in front of the leading competitor. This boat will be marked on the stern with the letter 'P'. Oarsmen in competitors' boats are advised to follow this boat, or as the competitors string out, to follow the competitor's boat in front of them. Reference to the map given in the Championship programme will be of assistance to trainers and oarsmen during the race.

10. During the race competitors must not receive support from any floating object. Food/drink may be taken, provided that this rule is complied with. Pacemaking by other swimmers is not permitted, and the competitor shall not use any aids to swimming other than goggles or mask. The boat accompanying the competitor shall display the competitor's number throughout the race.

11. Feeding can best be accomplished in the vicinity of Belle Isle, but care should be taken not to impede the progress of other competitors, as the course here is narrow and in parts shallow. Competitors wearing goggles will see the bottom of the Lake quite clearly in this area. The course is practically weed free, and the depth (with the exception of the Belle Isle area) is between 15 ft. and 247 ft. There are no currents in the Lake, but slight temperature variation may occur in parts, especially round Belle Isle. Average temperature in the Lake at this time of year is around 61·5° F., but has varied between 57° and 67° F.

12. To complete the course competitors must pass between the last two boating jetties, either at Lakeside or Ambleside (Waterhead).

13. Competitors who require a bath after the race are advised to make use of the bath where they have booked accommodation. Two Hotels at Waterhead have promised the use of their baths for urgent cases.

14. The Waterhead Hotel Garage will be available for those who wish to remove grease before going for a bath. Competitors must provide their own equipment for removing grease, i.e., an old kitchen knife and grease solvent.

15. If any competitor has to retire before the end of the race, the safest position from which he can enter the boat will be at the edge of the Lake where he can stand.

16. No intoxicating liquor may be given to a competitor or taken by a competitor immediately before or during the race.

17. A whistle, flag and inflated inner tube will be supplied to each rowing boat by the Chief Boat Steward. These three items must be returned to the Boat Steward by the person signing for them, otherwise the person concerned will be financially responsible for replacing them. In the event of an emergency, and/or medical assistance being required, long continuous blasts on the whistle must be given and the flag waved continuously.

18. Rowing-boats will be provided, but each competitor must bring one responsible person (who must be a strong swimmer) to accompany him during the race, and who, if necessary, can act as relief oarsman. If he is unable to do so he should inform the Hon. Championship Secretary immediately. Whilst every endeavour will be made by the Association to provide a qualified oarsman and life saver, no guarantee can be given. If an oarsman or life saver cannot be provided by either party, the competitor will be notified at least 7 days before the Championship and his entry fee returned. The rowing-boats are of the 4–6 seater type usually found on rivers and lakes, with pin rowlocks.

19. The Championship referee may, if he thinks fit, order from the water any swimmer who has contravened the rules, or whose condition is not satisfactory, or who has not completed the course within two hours after the winner of his/her Championship.

20. Postponement of the Championship will only be considered under the most adverse conditions. Presentation of the trophies and certificates will take place in premises to be announced in the Championship programme, at 8 p.m. the same evening.

21. A local guide book can be obtained from the Clerk to the Windermere U.D.C., Windermere, Westmorland.

22. The Association will not incur any legal liability for anything done or omitted to be done by them, and shall not be responsible for any personal injury or damage to, or loss of any property sustained by any person in connection with the race.

23. The above rules and information are subject to variation by the Emergency Committee of the Association, and any matter arising will be dealt with by that committee, whose decision shall be final.

JOHN O'HARA,
Windermere Championship
Hon. Secretary.

APPENDIX 7

Personal Qualifications

Through being the 'oldest inhabitant' of competitive distance swimming in Britain, I am pretty well known here. But overseas readers may wish to check my competency to write on the subject. An abbreviated list of achievements is therefore given below. Where times are not given it was a leisurely swim for pleasure only.

Sprint Swimming and Water Polo. Over 200 awards in this type of competition. From school, ship, and club standard to Inter-Service and County events. Plunging—up to fourth place in Nationals.

Long Distance Swimming

Notation. (a) Past champion.
(b) Past record holder.
(c) Current record holder.

A.S.A. (River Ouse) Championship. 5 miles downstream. 2 h. 10 m.
Bala Lake. 3 miles. Three occasions.
Brighton Pier-to-Pier. ¾ mile. Tidal.
Campbeltown Loch to Carradale Bay. 11 miles. 5 h. 58 m. (c)
Coniston Water. 5·25 miles.
English Channel. E–F. 20·8 miles. Tidal. 13 h. 33 m. (b)
Grange to Morecambe. 10 miles. Tidal. 10 occasions. Best time, 2 h. 27 m. (a)
Loch Lomond. 21·6 miles. 15 h. 33 m. (a) (c)
Loch Ness. Fort Augustus to Invermoriston. 5 miles. 2 h. 50 m. (c)
Lough Neagh. 19·4 miles. 13 h. 12 m. (c)
Malta to Gozo. 3 miles. Two occasions. Best 1 h. 24 m. 11 s. (c)
Morecambe to Grange. 10 miles. Tidal. Four occasions. Best time, 2 h. 37 m. (c)
Morecambe Inshore. 3½ miles. Tidal. Four occasions. Best time, 1 h. 06 m.
Morecambe Twenty-Mile Championship. Two occasions. Tidal. Best time, 6 h. 02 m. 32 s. (a) (c)

Morecambe Twenty-Five Mile Championship. Tidal. 7 h. 0 m. 42 s.
Mudros Bay, Greece.
Navy 'Polar Bear' Championship. 1 mile plus. 27 m. 30 s. (a). Open water. Straight swim.
Poole Harbour. 3 miles with tide. 59 m. 50 s.
Port Pirie (Australia). Swim through, 1·5 miles. 36 m.
Scottish Mainland to Arran. 3¼ miles. Tidal. 1 h. 43 m. (c)
Solent crossing. Ryde to Southsea. Tidal 4·5 miles. Four occasions. Best time, 2 h. 06 m.
Southsea Pier-to-Pier. 1¼ miles. Four occasions.
Torquay–Brixham–Torquay. 8 miles. Weakly tidal. Four occasions. Best, 4 h. 08 m. (a) (b)
Ullswater Lake. 7 miles.
Windermere Lake. 10·1 miles. Seven occasions. Best time, 5 h. 19 m. (a) (b)
Windermere Two-Way. 20·2 miles. 12 h. 57 m. (c)

General. In seven years, since returning to U.K., have swum 4,132 miles. Roughly the equivalent of distance from Britain to Brazil. Or Aden to Singapore. In training, have walked 12,600 miles during that period.

APPENDIX 8

Suggested Reading

By named authors. From these I have benefited:—

Across The Straits (all Channel successes and failures), edited and produced by *Dover Express*, Dover.

British Long Distance Swimming Association, Annual Reports, by Hon. General Sec. John Slater and by individual swim secretaries.

Channel Swimming Association, Annual Reports, by Hon. Sec. J. U. Wood.

'Clinical View of Channel Swimming' *The Times*, 5 August 1960. (This was a synopsis of a paper in *Clinical Science*, 19,257, which I have not read.)

'Grease and the Marathon Swimmer', by Dr. H. Baddeley, *Swimming Times*, March 1963.

Handbook of Channel Swimming Association.

It's Cold in the Channel, by Sam Rockett, 1956. Hutchinson.

Loch Ness Monster, by Tim Dinsdale, 1961. Routledge.

Shark Attack, by Professor V. M. Coppleson, 1959. Angus and Robertson.

Swim to Glory, by Ron McAllister 1959. McClelland & Stewart, Toronto (Marilyn Bell Story).

The Art of Swimming, by Captain Webb, 1875. Ward Lock.

'The Physiology of Channel Swimmers', by Doctors Pugh and Edholm. *Lancet*, 8 October, 1955.

By Myself:—

'Blast Snodgras!', *Blackwood's Magazine*, February 1958. (Description of preparing for Channel.)

'Channel Fever', N.A.A.F.I. *Review*, summer 1958. Subsequently in *English Digest* as 'How I Swam the Channel!'

Long distance section of Bill Juba's *Swimming*, 1961. Stanley Paul.

'Navigation in Channel Swimming', *Journal of Institute of Navigation*, Vol. xiii, No. 1, January 1960.
'Ordeal by Water', *Blackwood's Magazine*, October 1955 (description of Morecambe Cross Bay Swim).
Swimming Times. Monthly articles since 1957 (most of the durable material included in this book).
'This Is My Sport', N.A.A.F.I. *Review*, Autumn 1958.
'Weather Aspects of Channel Swimming', *Marine Observer*, July 1961.

APPENDIX 9

Useful Addresses

The last time I produced a list of addresses, it was the executive signal for everyone to 'up-anchor' and to start voyaging to new offices and residences. Some such list is however quite invaluable to overseas readers and I therefore once again take a calculated risk. But to lessen the risk as far as possible the list is now reduced to the absolute minimum. Here is a useful tip, though. If seeking information about a swim there are several possible useful sources—the Town Clerk, the Publicity Manager, the Entertainments Manager, the local newspaper, or the local swimming club. And two even more important tips; allow plenty of time for your enquiry to be passed on to the correct person and also enclose a stamped addressed envelope.

Admiralty Chart Agents. One in almost every port. In London—amongst others—J. D. Potter, 145 Minories, E.C.4.

Amateur Swimming Association. Hon. Sec., 64 Cannon Street, E.C.4.

British Long Distance Swimming Association. Hon. Sec., 29 St. Albans Avenue, Skircoat Lane, Halifax, Yorkshire.

Channel Swimming Association. Hon. Sec., 1 Marine Court, Marine Parade, Dover, Kent. (May change 1963 but will forward.)

Swimming Times, The. Editor, 4 Waddon Park Avenue, Croydon, Surrey.

Windermere. Bowness Boat Co., Bowness Bay, Windermere, for boats; B.L.D.S.A. for swim information.

Index

In this index names of individuals are confined to those that happened to occur in development of the text: very many others equally meritorious may be found in the lists of racing and individual successes.

INDEX